CASE STUDIES ON
Educational Administration

CASE STUDIES ON
Educational
Administration

THIRD EDITION

Theodore J. Kowalski
Kuntz Professor of Educational Administration
The University of Dayton

New York San Francisco Boston
London Toronto Sydney Tokyo Singapore Madrid
Mexico City Munich Paris Cape Town Hong Kong Montreal

Series Editor: Arnis E. Burvikovs
Senior Marketing Manager: Brad Parkins
Production Manager: Donna DeBenedictis
Project Coordinator, Text Design, and Electronic Page Makeup: Pre-Press Company, Inc.
Cover Design Manager: Linda Knowles
Manufacturing Buyer: Megan Cochran

Library of Congress Cataloging-in-Publication Data

Kowalski, Theodore J.
    Case studies on educational administration / Theodore J. Kowalski.—3rd ed.
        p. cm.
    Includes bibliographical references and index.
    ISBN 0-321-08143-9 (alk. paper)
    1. School management and organization—United States—Case studies.   I. Title.

LB2805 .K63 2001
371.2'00973—dc21   00-063422

Please visit our website at http://www.ablongman.com

ISBN 0-321-08143-9

    5 6 7 8 9 10—03

Contents

Preface

Effective practice in school administration is being redefined by three popular reform strategies—state deregulation, district decentralization, and school restructuring. These tactics bring into question long-standing role expectations for both district and school leaders. To what extent do these strategies move administrators away from a preoccupation with management? To what extent do they require administrators to provide leadership for changing the organizational cultures of districts and schools? How will the work lives of administrators change if teachers finally become true professionals? Such queries are central to current efforts to ensure that the next generation of school leaders will be adequately prepared for the realities of practice that await them.

Case Studies on Educational Administration (3rd ed.) is intended to help prospective administrators develop decision-making skills. Open-ended case studies are an excellent tool for achieving this objective for at least two reasons. First, they infuse contemporary issues into professional preparation; second, they provide a bridge between theory with practice. While addressing the cases presented in this book you are expected to frame problems, think critically, and reflect on your decisions—three activities central to effective practice in all professionals. Your work with cases helps you to hone three essential skills:

1. How to use information to identify and solve problems
2. How to develop and evaluate alternative solutions (contingencies)
3. How to continuously refine your professional knowledge base as a result of exposure to new knowledge, skills, and experiences

The cases in this book present a range of problems encountered by contemporary practitioners in local districts and individual schools. On page ix you will find a matrix that identifies the primary topics addressed in each case. None of the cases is taken to its conclusion so that you can assume the role of decision maker. This format allows you to frame the problem and to use your knowledge to determine a course of action.

My thanks go to many individuals who helped me to complete this edition. Among them are administrators who provided information necessary to develop the cases; students in my doctoral seminar who made countless suggestions about possible improvements to the book's format; colleagues at other universities who shared their experiences teaching with the cases; and my graduate assistants, Keith Roberts aned Tim Jahr.

I am especially grateful to the following individuals, who reviewed the manuscript and provided constructive criticisms and insightful recommendations: Judy A. Alston, Bowling Green State University; Jay A. Heath, University of South Dakota; Susan J. Rippberger, University of Texas at El Paso; Carl R. Steinhoff, University of Nevada, Las Vegas; Ward Weldon, University of Illinois at Chicago.

Theodore J. Kowalski

Matrix of Topics by Case Number

Topics	1	2	3	4	5	6	7	8	9	10	11	12	13	14	15	16	17	18	19	20	21	22	23	24
Administrator-Teacher Relationships		•																						
Assistant Principals		•	•	•	•	•																		
Assistant Superintendents/Central Office	•				•	•						•				•								
"Budgeting, Fiscal Issues"	•	•			•	•					•			•										
Business Manager						•					•													
Career Development				•				•																
Change Process	•	•	•	•		•	•																	
Communication Problems	•	•	•	•			•																	
Curriculum and Instruction	•	•	•			•	•																	
Decision-Making Procedures	•	•			•	•																		
Educational Outcomes	•									•														
Elementary Schools							•	•	•							•								
Employment Practices		•	•	•	•		•			•														
Employment Security / Stress		•	•	•	•		•																	
Ethical / Moral Issues	•	•	•	•			•	•																
Evaluation						•	•																	
High Schools		•	•	•	•				•	•														
Leadership Style / Theory		•	•	•	•																			
Legal Issues		•	•			•																		
Middle Schools																		•						•
Multicultural Issues							•	•		•		•												
Organizational Theory	•	•	•	•	•							•												
Philosophical Issues	•	•	•	•	•																			
Policy Development / Analysis	•	•	•			•																		
Political Behavior	•	•	•	•					•															
"Power, use by Administrators"	•	•	•	•				•	•															
Principalship	•	•	•	•	•	•																		
Public Relations (Community Relations)	•							•		•														
"Rural, Small-Town Schools"													•		•									
School Boards	•		•																					
School Reform	•																•		•					
Site-based Management												•					•							
Student Discipline (Student Services)							•				•						•							
Suburban Schools																						•		
Superintendency	•		•	•	•	•			•															
Teacher Professionalization			•				•			•						•								
Teacher Unions (Collective Bargaining)		•								•													•	
Urban / Larger City Schools	•	•	•	•	•		•					•												
Violence		•	•		•					•														
Women Administrators																								

CASE STUDIES ON
Educational
Administration

Introduction

In the varied topography of professional practice, there is a high hard ground overlooking the swamp. On the high ground, manageable problems lend themselves to solutions through the application of research-based theory and technique. In the swampy lowland, messy, confusing problems defy technical solution.

(Donald Schön, 1990, p. 3)

Since the late 1980s, there have been many calls for sweeping changes in the professional preparation of school administrators. Demands for reform have been fueled by recent efforts to address organizational and governance issues in elementary and secondary education. But meaningful change has been elusive for a variety of reasons. These include varying conditions across and within states, the absence of a standardized national curriculum, and differences of opinion about the effectiveness of public education and the nature of improvements needed.

Most students enrolled in university-based courses in school administration are either preparing to be practitioners or they already are practitioners. They are adult learners, many of them in the middle stages of their careers. They appropriately expect classroom learning experiences, even those involving abstract theories, to be relevant to the real world of elementary and secondary education. Consequently, professors of school administration are challenged to provide their students modern theories to guide practice and to link these theories to practical issues faced by school and district administrators. In addition, they are expected to prepare their students to be lifelong learners, especially by teaching them how to engage in the process of reflection.

Donald Schön (1983) aptly noted that practitioners in virtually all professions often become bewildered when the technical skills they acquired in academic preparation prove to be ineffective in relation to certain problems. Their surprise stems largely from a lack of understanding about contextual variables. That is, they fail to comprehend how human and material conditions surrounding a problem may attenuate the effectiveness of theoretical knowledge. In all professions, the most effective practitioners are those who possess both the requisite knowledge base and the artistry to adapt that knowledge to unique circumstances. In the case of school administration, the most outstanding principals are not those who consistently apply routine solutions, but rather those who adapt successfully when textbook solutions prove to be ineffectual.

Just in the past 10 to 15 years, changes in demographics, the economy, and the political structure have changed many communities. During this same period, advances in learning theory, technology, and planning procedures also have influenced practice in school administration. Consider how the Internet provides educators opportunities to access legal information and statistical data or how electronic mail provides two-way communication opportunities. These examples illustrate how environmental changes in schools and offices serve to modernize role expectations for organizational leaders. And in all professions, changing contextual variables are especially influential with respect to decision-making processes (Estler, 1988).

THE USE OF REFLECTION

If educational administration is to remain a true profession, its practitioners must possess (1) a theoretical base for practice, (2) technical skills required to perform managerial responsibilities, and (3) the ability to engage in reflective practice—the process by which the practitioner integrates knowledge, skills, and experience. Schön (1990) differentiated between "knowing-in-action" and "reflection-in-action." The former is embedded in the socially and institutionally structured context shared by members of a given profession. The latter represents a form of artistry that is especially critical when conditions are less than rational. If needs, motivations, and behaviors in schools were completely predictable, the application of professional knowledge would suffice. But in the real world of practice, artistry (a quality developed by refining professional knowledge on the basis of experience) often distinguishes effective administrators from others.

The degree holder in educational administration should be thoroughly practiced in theoretical reflection, philosophical inquiry, research, and history, as well as prepared in the areas of administrative and technical practice. The graduate experience should emphasize the theoretical dimensions of practice, the historical roots of school administration practice, and research. Training—that is, the process of transmitting management techniques—is an important part of professional preparation; but standing alone, it is insufficient. Traditional lecture and demonstration approaches may be suitable for teaching specific tasks, but other approaches are needed to educate students in areas such as information gathering, observation skills, and analytical skills (Clark, 1986).

Case Studies on Educational Administration (3rd ed.) relies on one proven method of associating academic study with the real world of school administration—the case study. Many of the educational reform reports issued over the past 20 years have cited the need for the infusion of reality into preparation programs for educators. In an interview regarding needed improvements in the preparation of professional educators, noted researcher Lee Shulman stated it this way:

> I'd like to see much greater use of cases, much like what is done in law and business education. That might reorient the teaching of teachers from the current model, which is either entirely field based, where you have little control over what goes on, or entirely classroom based, where everything is artificial. We have to create a middle ground, where problems of theory and practice can intersect in a realistic way. The genius of the case method, especially in business, is that you use realistic problems, but you can still deal with both the theoretical and the tactical aspects. (Brandt, 1988, p. 43)

Hence, one asset of the case study is that it provides a vehicle for honing the process of reflection.

DEFINING CASE STUDIES

A case is a description of an administrative situation, commonly involving a decision or problem (Erskine, Leenders, & Mauffette-Leenders, 1981). The terms *case study* and *case method* do not have the same meaning. A case study is the general description of a situation and may have several purposes: (1) as a method of research, (2) as a method of evaluation, (3) as a method of policy studies, and (4) as a teaching method. Thus, case study refers to the narrative description of the incident, not its intended purpose. Case method, on the other hand, has specific reference to using the case studies as a teaching paradigm. More specifically, the case method entails a technique whereby the major ingredients of a case study are presented to students for the purpose of studying behaviors or problem-solving techniques.

Several other related terms may cause confusion and, thus, deserve explanation. One of these is *case work.* This term is commonly used in psychology, sociology, social work, and medicine. It connotes the development, adjustment, remedial, or corrective procedures that appropriately follow diagnosis of the causes of maladjustment. Another term is *case history.* This has reference to tracing a person, group, or organization's past (Merriam, 1988).

Unfortunately, there is no universal definition of or style for a case study; some case studies may be only a few paragraphs, while others are hundreds of pages (Immegart, 1971). As Lincoln and Guba (1985) wrote "while the literature is replete with references to case studies and with examples of case study reports, there seems to be little agreement about what a case is" (p. 360). Variance in case length and style is often related to their intended purpose. Cases commonly fall into one of three categories: true cases (no alterations to names, dates, organizations), disguised cases, or fictitious cases (hypothetical examples to illustrate a principle, concept, or specific set of conditions) (Matejka & Cosse, 1981).

THE CASE METHOD AS AN INSTRUCTIONAL PARADIGM

The case method technique has gained acceptance in business administration, law, and medicine. The best-known successes belong to Harvard University. There the continued emphasis on the case method in the Harvard Business School is evidenced by publications such as *Teaching and the Case Method* (Christensen, 1987). In business courses, case studies use real incidents to sharpen student skills with regard to problem solving, formulating and weighing alternative decisions, and assessing leadership behaviors. The acclaim surrounding the effectiveness of the Harvard Business School approach has influenced the teaching methods at a number of other prominent business schools.

Essentially, case studies can serve two purposes when used in the classroom. First, they can be employed to teach students new information, concepts, and theories. For example, the professor may use a case study of a grievance in a high school to illustrate that conflict in organizations is inevitable. When cases are used in this manner, the student deals with new knowledge through the process of induction. That is, by reading a case that exemplifies the concept, the student will note associations between certain factors. When these associations are repeated (e.g., in other cases), the student is expected to master the concept through induction. Cases that are fact-driven and taken to their conclusion are often used in disciplines such as science where single correct answers are common (Herreid, 1997).

Second, cases can be a vehicle for applying acquired knowledge and skills in specific situations. When used for this purpose, cases are used to teach reasoning, critical thinking, problem-solving concepts (e.g., general problem solving), and problem-solving skills. The application alternative is especially effective for teaching and reinforcing reflection.

There are two universal aspects of the case method. One is the Socratic method and the other is the presentation of selected information included in the case study (e.g., facts about individuals, facts about school districts). The selected information is referred to as *situational knowledge.* Each person who reads a case is exposed to the same situational knowledge. Why, then, do students often interpret cases differently? The answer is that they process case information in different ways. This processing is called *abstraction.* Each reader essentially filters situational knowledge through his or her own values, beliefs, experiences, and acquired knowledge. Since our philosophies, experiences, and knowledge are not identical, and since we differ in our ability to process information, we usually frame problems differently and develop less than uniform conclusions.

In studying the ways in which teachers make decisions, Shavelson and Stern (1981) observed the following:

> ... people selectively perceive and interpret portions of available information with respect to their goals, and construct a simplified model of reality. Using certain heuristics, attributions and other psychological mechanisms, people then make judgments and decisions that carry them out on the basis of their psychological model of reality. (p. 461)

These outputs, referred to as *specific knowledge,* are critical to your experiences with the case method. They explain why individuals, even experienced practitioners, do not behave uniformly.

THE USE OF CASES IN EDUCATION

Within schools of education, case studies have been used most frequently as a diagnostic tool in counseling and as a research tool. Psychologists commonly employ case histories and case work in their practices. The growing acceptance of qualitative methodology in the social sciences has magnified the value of case studies in this arena. Ethnographic research is perhaps the best-known of the qualitative techniques, and the work of Yin (1984) and Merriam (1988) is particularly enlightening for individuals wanting to explore case-based research. Their writings describe this methodology in varying contexts, including policy analysis, public administration, community psychology and sociology, organization and management studies, and public service agencies. Both terms, *ethnography* and *case studies,* have become synonyms for qualitative research (Lancy, 1993). In the past few decades, case-based research has provided richer descriptions of the work environments of professional educators (Erickson, 1986).

However, beyond its use in psychology and research, the case study has not been a conspicuous component of graduate work in education. In school administration, two similar techniques have occasionally been used. They are simulations and "in-basket" programs. Even back in the mid-1950s, texts were published on case studies for educators (e.g., Hamburg, 1955; Sargent & Belisle, 1955), and some leaders in the University Council for Educational Administration (UCEA) have advocated the use of case studies and simulations for over three decades (e.g., Culbertson & Coffield, 1960; Griffiths, 1963). But the case study did not become an integral part of professional preparation. Recent research indicates the lecture method of teaching and classroom discussion remain the dominant instructional paradigms in school administration (McCarthy, 1999).

USING SIMULATION AND CASES

Professional schools rely on several methods to expose students to the real world of practice. The internship is one of the most common. This segment of the curriculum is typically structured as a capstone experience, and although valuable, it does not provide early and continuous experiences permitting the graduate student to reflect on both theory and practice. Thus, *simulation* is a more effective alternative to infuse reality into coursework.

Simulations provide vicarious experiences for students—an approximation of the practitioner's challenges, problems, opportunities, and so forth. It is a form of teaching that can be used at all stages of professional preparation. There are two general approaches: (1) providing complete data about a given situation before requiring the student to address the problem, and (2) providing basic information sufficient to permit the student to address the problem. The former is best characterized by in-basket techniques. In this process, the student receives detailed information about a position, problem, and so forth. Often this approach requires the student to spend a great deal of time studying the documents (e.g., budgets, memoranda), and it is considered most effective when specific problem-solving skills are being addressed.

The other approach focuses on using only essential information related to a given situation. This situational knowledge can be effectively transmitted through a case study. This option is usually employed when general problem-solving skills are the focus, and it is advantageous when time parameters do not permit students to review mounds of data. Simulations using what Cunningham (1971) called a *nonmaterial based approach* (i.e., using only basic situational information) were proven to be successful when used with educators at the University of Chicago as far back as the mid-1960s. In fact, Cunningham noted that he changed his own views about the necessity of detailed information after viewing the successes with simulation under these conditions. Hence, simulations and cases such as those presented here provide a powerful combination for integrating theory and practice, teaching critical thinking, developing problem-solving skills, and refining the process of reflection.

USING THEORY AS A GUIDE

There are many misconceptions about theory. Some students define theory as a dream representing the wishes of an individual or group. Others perceive it to be a supposition, speculation, or philosophy (Owens, 1998). In reality theories are used to synthesize, organize, and classify facts that emerge from observations and data collections in varying situations (e.g., research studies). Hoy and Miskel (1987) characterized theories in educational administration as interrelated concepts, assumptions, and generalizations that systematically describe and explain regularities in behavior.

Educational leaders have the same decision-making options available to all other types of administrators and managers. When confronted with circumstances demanding action, the individual may choose one of several behaviors:

1. Ignore the situation (no decision is made).
2. Act instinctively.
3. Get someone else to make the decision.

4. Duplicate a decision made by someone else under the same or similar circumstances.
5. Use the professional knowledge base to formulate a decision. (Kowalski, 1999)

Any of the first four alternatives may be effective in isolated situations, but eventually they cause problems. Use of a professional knowledge base distinguishes a professional practitioner from a trained technician. The professional gathers pertinent information and integrates that information with the knowledge base. Then he or she determines alternative decisions (contingencies), evaluates these alternatives, and selects the most prudent option given the prevailing conditions.

Among the numerous decision-making models used in administration, the best-known and most widely used is probably the *rational-analytical model*. This paradigm consists of four steps: (1) defining the problem, (2) diagnosing the problem, (3) searching for alternative solutions, and (4) evaluating alternative solutions (Romm & Mahler, 1986). The case method is an excellent format for applying this and similar decision-making models. Students can complete all four stages of the rational-analytical model by reading and reacting to cases. The advantage of the rational-analytical approach is that it permits you to apply general problem-solving skills to specific situations.

Each case in this book includes contextual variables that should affect the choices you make. The community, the school district, the challenge, and the individual personalities are examples. When you employ theoretical constructs and technical skills to analyze these conditions in relation to the challenge presented, you are using a scientific approach to decision making. Accordingly, you should become increasingly skillful in applying general problem-solving abilities to specific situations.

The evolution of literature on the topic of decision making exhibits the movement of graduate study in educational leadership from a narrow training focus on technical skills to one where behavioral studies now play a critical role. In concluding that accumulated information about decision processes was eradicating the comfort of simple solutions, Estler (1988) wrote the following:

> . . . we might replace recipes with skills in analysis of organizational dynamics and contexts. Though the ambiguities of educational decision making cannot be eliminated, they can be made more understandable and less threatening. By understanding a variety of approaches to decision making and the range of organizational conditions under which they may be applicable, the administrator can be better prepared to respond to, and even enjoy, organizational ambiguity and complexity. (p. 316)

More than any other element of graduate study in educational administration, it is the knowledge base relative to decision making that illuminates the value of infusing case studies into graduate education. Those who still contend that there are tried-and-true recipes for leadership behavior that work in all situations under all sorts of conditions are either misguided or uninformed.

THE CONTENT OF THE BOOK

This book contains 24 cases selected to exemplify the diversity of challenges in contemporary educational leadership. You should not look at any case as having a single dimension even though the title or primary focus of the material may lead you to that conclusion. The cases actually are quite intricate, with multiple foci—exactly the way problems exist in the real world of practice. For example, a case may involve conflict resolution, effective communication, power, participatory decision making, and leadership style.

The narrative format used in the cases is not uniform. Some cases are divided into sections with information about the community, school district, school, and the incident presented under subheadings. Other cases contain a great deal of dialogue. Information in the real world of practice is often neither predictable nor uniform. Variance in the way information is presented in the cases reflects the unevenness of communication that exists in districts and schools. Although the narratives vary, the format for material that follows each case does not. Following each case there are three components:

1. The Challenge
2. Key Issues/Questions
3. Suggested Readings

In a classroom setting, the instructor determines how these supplemental components will be utilized in conjunction with the case.

One of the goals of the case method is to help you become proficient at filtering information. The practitioner needs to learn to separate important and relevant facts from those that have little or no bearing on the problem(s). Remember, you must determine what information is most crucial to your decisions.

EFFECTIVELY PARTICIPATING IN THE CASE METHOD

Two extremely important factors already have been mentioned regarding the use of cases. First, information filtering permits you to isolate pertinent data needed for making a decision. Second, using accumulated information and knowledge in a systematic fashion (i.e., utilizing a decision-making model) produces more enlightened decisions. With regard to this latter point, you should constantly remind yourself of the differences between education and training. Educated persons rely on past experiences and knowledge to make behavioral choices; they interface contextual variables with knowledge before acting. Trained persons, by contrast, rely on predetermined responses; they use a manual or their memory to identify the appropriate action.

Beyond information filtering and the recognition of what constitutes an educated response, it is critical to note that the case method does not seek the "one right answer." Romm and Mahler (1986) noted that this is particularly true when the cases are used in conjunction with the rational-analytical model for making decisions:

> Basing the analysis of the case on the rational-analytical decision-making model, implicitly carries the message that there are no "right" or "wrong" solutions to the case. By applying the model to cases, students realize that a case always has many problems, and the definition of one of these problems as the "main" problem is often subjective and arbitrary. They also realize that once a problem has been defined, it can have different reasons and be solved in different ways, depending on whose interests are being served or being given priority. (p. 695)

Cases provide an open invitation to generalize (Biddle & Anderson, 1986), and consequently, you are apt to observe a range of behaviors as your peers frame problems and draw conclusions. You can learn by analyzing your own behavior, analyzing the behavior of others, and by having others analyze your behavior. Often when cases are discussed in group settings (e.g., the classroom), the opportunity for all three exists.

Remember that a person's behavior is never void of values and beliefs. This reality makes the case method even more challenging and exciting. Two graduate students sharing common educational experiences may make very different decisions when responding to the challenges presented in the cases. Why? As noted earlier, each of them develops specific knowledge through abstraction. Values and beliefs, as well as one's skill level in decision making, critical thinking, and problem solving influence the process of abstraction.

There is one additional dimension of the case method that is undervalued. You will work with these cases in a social context. The presence of others approximates the real world of practice. Superintendents and principals rarely make decisions in isolation. Their behavior is constantly influenced and evaluated by the social contexts of their work (e.g., district, school, community). Your experiences with cases permit you to grow in both the affective and cognitive domains.

FINAL WORDS OF ADVICE

Engaging in case studies requires several caveats regarding your personal behavior. First, the process is an active one. Case analysis in a classroom environment is a form of cooperative learning. You need to be an active participant to achieve maximum benefits. Second, you should not fear being candid or taking risks. The case method is an opportunity for you to learn how others will respond to your leadership style and decisions. Third, you should respect your classmates and try to understand their behavior. Your intention should be to identify how professional (constructs and skills) and personal (needs and motivations) variables influence administrative decisions.

The observations made of experiences with the case method provide a useful resource for practice. Thus, the development of a notebook in conjunction with classroom experiences is highly advised. Although no two situations are ever identical, the general principles that are addressed in the 24 cases are likely to recur throughout your career as an educational leader.

REFERENCES

Biddle, B., & Anderson, D. (1986). Theory, methods, knowledge, and research on teaching. In M. Wittrock (Ed.), *Handbook of research on teaching* (3rd ed., pp. 230-252). New York: Macmillan.

Brandt, R. (1988). An assessment of teaching: A conversation with Lee Shulman. *Educational Leadership, 46*(3), 42-47.

Christensen, C. (1987). *Teaching and the case method.* Boston: Harvard Business School Press.

Clark, V. (1986). The effectiveness of case studies in training principals: Using the deliberative orientation. *Peabody Journal of Education, 63*(1), 187-195.

Culbertson, J., & Coffield, W. (Eds.) (1960). *Simulation in administration training.* Columbus, OH: The University Council for Educational Administration.

Cunningham, L. (1971). A powerful but underdeveloped educational tool. In D. Bolton (Ed.), *The use of simulation in educational administration* (pp. 1-29). Columbus, OH: Charles E. Merrill.

Erickson, F. (1986). Qualitative methods in research on teaching. In M. Wittrock (Ed.), *Handbook of research on teaching* (3rd ed., pp. 119-161). New York: Macmillan.

Erskine, J., Leenders, M., & Mauffette-Leenders, L. (1981). *Teaching with cases.* London, Ontario: School of Business Administration, University of Western Ontario.

Estler, S. (1988). *Decision making.* In N. Boyan (Ed.), *Handbook of research on educational administration* (pp. 305-350). New York: Longman.

Griffiths, D. (1963). The case method of teaching educational administration. *Journal of Educational Administration, 2,* 81-82.

Hamburg, M. (1955). *Case studies in elementary school administration.* New York: Bureau of Publications, Teachers College, Columbia University.

Herreid, C. F. (1997). What is a case? *Journal of College Science Teaching, 27*(2), 92-94.

Hoy, C., & Miskel, C. (1987). *Education administration* (3rd ed.). New York: Random House.

Immegart, G. (1971). The use of cases. In D. Bolton (Ed.), *The use of simulation in educational administration* (pp. 30-64). Columbus, OH: Charles E. Merrill.

Kowalski, T. (1999). *The school superintendent: Theory, practice, and cases.* Upper Saddle River, NJ: Merrill, Prentice Hall.

Kowalski, T., & Reitzug, U. (1993). *Contemporary school administration: An introduction.* New York: Longman.

Lancy, D. (1993). *Qualitative research in education.* New York: Longman.

Lincoln, Y., & Guba, E. (1985). *Naturalistic inquiry.* Newbury Park, CA: Sage.

Matejka, J., & Cosse, T. (1981). *The business case method: An introduction.* Richmond, VA: Robert F. Dame.

McCarthy, M. (1999). The evolution of educational leadership preparation programs. In L. Murphy & K. Louis (Eds.), *Handbook of research on educational administration* (2nd ed.). San Francisco: Jossey-Bass.

Merriam, S. (1988). *Case research in education.* San Francisco: Jossey-Bass.

Owens, R. (1998). *Organizational behavior in education* (6th ed.). Boston: Allyn & Bacon.

Romm, T., & Mahler, S. (1986). A three-dimensional model for using case studies in the academic classroom. *Higher Education, 15*(6), 677-696.

Sargent, C., & Belisle, E. (1955). *Educational administration: Cases and concepts.* Boston: Houghton Mifflin.

Schön, D. (1990). *Educating the reflective practitioner.* San Francisco: Jossey-Bass.

Schön, D. (1983). *The reflective practitioner.* New York: Basic Books.

Shavelson, R., & Stern, P. (1981). Research on teachers' pedagogical thoughts, judgments, decisions, and behavior. *Review of Educational Research, 51*(4), 455-498.

Yin, R. (1984). *Case study research.* Beverly Hills, CA: Sage.

Case **1**

Fear of Outcome-Based Education

BACKGROUND INFORMATION

Efforts to restructure elementary and secondary education have reminded us of the conflicting values and beliefs held by the American public. Philosophical differences exist with regard to curricular content, as well as instructional methodology, and competing expectations often are expressed through the voices of groups that are both formal (e.g., national organizations) and informal (e.g., religious coalitions).

Although it is ideal to keep politics out of public education, this goal has rarely been achieved. In truth, education and school administration have always been subjected to tensions sparked by less than uniform purposes and expectations. Whenever individuals and groups in a democratic society have conflicting educational philosophies, politically driven behavior is inevitable. Yet, administrators are expected to manage this conflict sufficiently so that effective educational policy can be developed.

Two conditions are particularly noteworthy with respect to understanding the contemporary nexus between politics and policy. The first pertains to circumstances surrounding a problem or challenge. These contextual variables may include (1) characteristics of districts, schools, and communities; (2) the nature of values, needs, and wants being expressed; (3) conditions at any given time (e.g., economics, social relationships); and (4) the people who are involved. Rarely constant, these particulars make each administrative decision unique. The second condition involves a shifting balance between policy development and policy management. Through much of the twentieth century, superintendents and principals were expected to enforce policies and laws promulgated at the state level. Today, however, state deregulation is prompting or requiring local districts to forge their own school-improvement agendas. As a consequence, many administrators spend more time with policy development and analysis than they have in the past.

Compared to state-level policy development, local political activity often magnifies philosophical differences. In large measure this is because advocates and opponents know each other, and they usually can communicate directly with key decision makers (i.e., school board members and administrators). Conflict at the local level has a greater likelihood of becoming personal. Setting policy for a sex education program is an excellent example. Any administrative recommendation is likely to be opposed by some individuals and groups. This is because parents typically hold differing beliefs with respect to three fundamental questions: (1) Whose moral values should be emphasized? (2) How and when is sex information taught? (3) Who has the responsibility for sex education (family, church, or schools)?

Case 1 revolves around a controversial reform initiative—outcome-based education. In its most basic form, outcome-based education is a process of setting goals that students are expected to achieve and teaching and reteaching until everyone meets those goals (see Evans & King, 1994, in Suggested Readings for additional information about the goals of outcome-based education). Opposition has taken several forms. Some outcome-based plans have been criticized for having ambiguous and unmeasurable goals, while others have been judged to have goals so broad that they "water down" education. Then there were the plans condemned because they were seen as reducing local control, and yet others were attacked because they were viewed as an attempt to have schools control student attitudes and values. Fundamentalist groups who contend that outcome-based education is a ploy to control America's youth through political and moral indoctrination have focused on plans in this last group.

In Case 1, a superintendent attempts to implement outcome-based education in a suburban community. The negative reactions of parents become solidified when a local minister provides leadership to fight the proposed program. The minister distributes literature from national groups opposed to the program, and he and his followers attempt to dissuade individual board members from backing the superintendent's initiatives. These efforts take their toll, resulting in erosion of support for the superintendent.

KEY AREAS FOR REFLECTION

1. Political dimensions of educational administration
2. School reform and implications for local policy development
3. Public criticism and its effect on educational policy
4. Procedures for implementing policy decisions
5. Outcome-based education
6. Leadership style

THE CASE

The Community

Eagan Heights is a suburb of a major city in a mid-Atlantic state. With approximately 45,000 residents, the local government consists of a mayor and a nine-member town board. The community started to develop in the mid-1950s, and currently about 100 new homes are built each year. Even though the community initially grew in response to a need for relatively low-cost housing for workers at a local truck factory, homes built since the mid-1970s have been targeted more toward middle- and upper-middle-class families.

Housing patterns in Eagan Heights have resulted in a rather diverse community. Approximately 17 percent of the residents identify themselves as African Americans and another 4 percent as Hispanics; most of these residents have middle- or upper-middle-class incomes. About 15 percent of the families in the community reported annual incomes below $24,000, and virtually all of these were nonminority families.

The School District

Eagan Heights Community School District serves approximately 8,000 students. There are two high schools, two middle schools, and ten elementary schools. Nearly two-thirds of the schools are housed in facilities that have been either built or renovated in the past 15 years.

The district's boundaries are contiguous with the city limits of Eagan Heights. The five school board members are selected via nonpartisan, at-large elections; each serves a four-year term. Current members are as follows:

Annette Small, a social worker

Reggie Prescott, owner of a local restaurant

Sheila Evercott, a homemaker

Anthony Rodriquez, a podiatrist

Peter Meckava, production-line worker at the truck factory

Board members Small, Evercott, and Meckava are serving second terms, and Prescott and Rodriquez are serving first terms. Annette Small is president of the school board.

Located just 10 miles from a large urban district, Eagan Heights has been perceived by its residents to be a relatively safe and orderly school system. Prior to a state accreditation report three years ago, complaints about the quality of education were rare. The level of satisfaction changed, however, after the local newspaper printed a series of articles disclosing the content of the state report. Four weaknesses received considerable coverage: (1) technology not being integrated sufficiently into the curriculum, (2) less than rigorous high school graduation requirements, (3) a lack of program evaluation, and (4) below average student performance on statewide achievement tests. After reading the articles, many residents voiced concerns and demanded immediate action from the school board. Responding to public pressure, the board blamed long-term superintendent, Nicholas Luman, for the deficiencies. Three months after the articles were published, the superintendent was dismissed.

Rather than accept a teaching assignment, Mr. Luman opted to retire. After a lengthy national search, the board selected Dr. Ebert Jackson to be the new superintendent. He had been serving as superintendent of a 4,000-student district in New Jersey. An aggressive administrator in his mid-40s, Dr. Jackson had established a reputation as an expert in the application of outcome-based education.

Central-Office Administration

After becoming superintendent in Eagan Heights, Dr. Jackson replaced all three assistant superintendents in less than 12 months. The assistant superintendent for instruction, an applicant for the superintendent vacancy, was the first to leave; he opted to retire after the board did not select him for an interview. Dr. Jackson employed a trusted associate, Dr. Donna Price, in that position. She and Dr. Jackson had worked together in New Jersey for the previous four years.

The other two recently employed assistant superintendents are Walter Bridgeman, business services, and Tony Mori, administrative services. Dr. Jackson selected them after recommending that their predecessors not be reemployed. Mr. Bridgeman had been a controller for a small construction company, and Mr. Mori had been an elementary school principal in the school district.

While serving as a superintendent in New Jersey, Dr. Jackson was viewed as a bold, innovative leader who was not afraid to take risks. Administrators in Eagan Heights quickly learned of his reputation, and they were especially mindful of stories indicating that Dr. Jackson was not very tolerant of staff members who opposed his ideas.

Dr. Jackson had come to Eagan Heights confident that he could replicate the successes he had achieved in his previous position. During his first year, he appeared before numerous civic groups to outline his goals. He consistently told the community that improvement was needed and that the first step in that direction was to determine what students really accomplished in school. His message was never challenged.

Leadership Style

Superintendent Jackson held meetings with his administrative staff once every two weeks. The three assistant superintendents and the building principals were expected to be in attendance. These meetings were structured; they started and ended at specified times, and agendas were always distributed in advance. But this somewhat rigid framework did not mean that the superintendent dominated the sessions. A good portion of every meeting was devoted to open discussions of relevant issues. Dr. Jackson told his staff, "We can always read reports in advance of these meetings. Rather than consume our time listening to one person talk, these meetings offer an opportunity for open dialogue. If we can't level with each other, we can't function as a leadership team."

Dr. Jackson's contact with other administrators tended to be highly formal. He rarely engaged them in idle discussions. During administrative staff meetings and during his visits to schools, he often asked direct questions about operations or problems—and he expected direct answers. During their first year in Eagan Heights, Dr. Jackson and Dr. Price fulfilled a commitment to visit each district school at least three times.

Principals developed varying perceptions of their new leader. Those who had been comfortable with the previous superintendent, an administrator who rarely spent time outside of his office, tended not to like Dr. Jackson. By comparison, principals who liked Dr. Jackson and approved of his leadership style found his aggressive, no-nonsense demeanor refreshing.

Moving Toward Outcome-Based Education

Just several months after Dr. Jackson arrived in Eagan Heights, he presented his administrative staff with a schedule for implementing outcome-based education. He did so even though the initiative had not been discussed previously in administrative meetings. Dr. Jackson told the administrators, "The board is solidly behind my intention to implement outcome-based education. I hope all of you will be team players and do your part in making it work." According to the schedule, the first 16 months would be devoted to preparing curriculum, staff, and evaluation programs. Implementation would occur at the start of the subsequent school year.

After reviewing the schedule with the administrators, Dr. Jackson told them, "I expect each of you to be ambassadors for this program. I want you to help me sell it to the community. To do this, you must understand what we are trying to accomplish, and you should believe that we are moving in the right direction. Philosophical unity is extremely important."

During the following summer and school year, all administrators played a role in the planning process, as did a group of teachers appointed to the planning committee by Dr. Price. Although outcome-based education initiative was identical to what Dr. Jackson had implemented in his previous position, some minor modifications were made to accommodate unique features of the Eagan Heights schools.

After the planning phase was completed, informational meetings were held at each school to explain implementation. These meetings were open to the public. Dr. Price, who was coordinating the project, outlined the philosophy, procedures, and goals of the program. Central to her presentation were the following objectives, which were stated as expectations for students (she referred to them as "exit outcomes"):

1. Ability to engage in independent learning
2. Appreciation of cultural diversity and individual differences
3. Ability to think critically
4. Ability to identify and solve problems
5. Ability to work with others
6. Positive self-images and positive attitudes toward school

The informational meetings were not very well attended, especially at the secondary schools. In most instances, more teachers were in the audience than either parents or students. Teachers almost always dominated the discussions at these sessions, often asking questions about how the exit outcomes would be measured. Dr. Price usually responded vaguely by suggesting that methods and criteria for evaluation would evolve as teachers and administrators had the opportunity to weigh alternatives.

Although Dr. Jackson attended all but three of these meetings, he typically sat in the back of the room while Dr. Price made presentations and answered questions. The principals reacted in various ways. Some were openly supportive; others said they looked forward to the new challenges; but most were passive, showing no indication of either support or enthusiasm. Despite observing these differences, Dr. Jackson believed that all of the administrative staff would be cooperative.

Community Opposition

About four weeks after the informational meetings, Dr. Jackson received the first indication of overt opposition. A local minister, Reverend Arnold Morgan, wrote a letter to Mrs. Evercott, a member of the school board and his church. In it, he voiced concerns about outcome-based education and urged her to withhold her support until the community had an opportunity to debate the concept. Mrs. Evercott showed the letter to Dr. Jackson and asked him if he knew what might be bothering the minister. The superintendent said he had no knowledge of Reverend Morgan's concern, but explained that the intentions of outcome-based education had often been misinterpreted. "Some conservative religious groups have been suspicious of outcome-based education. They think it is all about teaching values," he told her. "But our program is focused on instructional outcomes. I think Reverend Morgan would be less inclined to be concerned if he took the time to examine our plan."

Mrs. Evercott telephoned her minister and suggested that he make an appointment with the superintendent to discuss his letter. She asked him not to jump to conclusions until he had an opportunity to talk to Dr. Jackson about the specifics of the program he was proposing. Reverend Morgan made no commitment to heed her advice.

Rather than meeting with the superintendent, Reverend Morgan adopted a more confrontational approach. He and 12 supporters appeared at a regularly scheduled school board meeting seeking permission to read a prepared statement. Mrs. Small, the board president, denied the request because the superintendent had not been notified that such a request would be made. (All persons wanting to speak at board meetings, except in emergency situations, are required by school board policy to present a request in writing to the superintendent at least three calendar days prior to the meeting.)

Dr. Jackson intervened, "Madam president, I respectfully request that you grant an exception and allow Reverend Morgan to speak. Mrs. Evercott showed me a letter he wrote to her several weeks ago about our plans to move to outcome-based education. It is obvious to me that he feels very strongly about the matter, and I think it would be to everyone's benefit if he shared his apprehensions."

Mrs. Small asked the other board members if there was an objection. Hearing none, she nodded approval and said, "Reverend Morgan, you may proceed with your statement."

As Dr. Jackson expected, Reverend Morgan's opposition centered on the issue of values. He argued that teaching values was a responsibility of the family and church. He concluded by expressing hope that each school board member would look at Dr. Jackson's program carefully.

Mrs. Evercott, the first school board member to respond, said, "After I read your letter several weeks ago, I suggested that you sit down with Dr. Jackson and discuss what we are attempting in this school district. Unfortunately, that discussion did not occur. I still think it is a good idea. If you talk to Dr. Jackson, you will discover the real goals of this program. This effort is not about values. It focuses on educational outcomes, and we need to improve performance in this district."

"I'm afraid, Mrs. Evercott," the minister responded, "that Dr. Jackson does not have an open mind about outcome-based education. He came to Eagan Heights with the intention of pushing his ideas on us. I know you want to be a good school board member, and I know you want to support your superintendent, but it is the public and their representatives who must examine this program. This outcome-based education is being promoted all over the country, and I already know that one of the intentions is to select the values we teach our young boys and girls. I'm here to warn board members. Open your eyes before it is too late."

Then Reverend Morgan's supporters distributed material obtained from a national group opposing outcome-based education. The contents included claims that outcome-based education was a devious ploy to control the minds of young children by teaching them the values and beliefs of secular humanism.

Within days following his appearance at the school board meeting, Reverend Morgan took his campaign against outcome-based education to the general public. He wrote letters to the local newspapers, made appearances on talk-radio programs, and enlisted six other local ministers as his allies. By the time the school year ended in late May, Dr. Jackson and the board realized that Reverend Morgan had been able to garner significant support for his crusade against outcome-based education.

Dr. Jackson and Mrs. Small tried to counteract negative statements by making themselves available to the media and community groups. At first these encounters were congenial, but Reverend Morgan and his followers eventually made them confrontational. Opponents to outcome-based education picketed the district's administrative offices and informational meetings, and the superintendent and board president were often interrupted as they tried to speak.

By mid-June, the first defection on the board occurred. Mrs. Evercott, the board member closest to Reverend Morgan, said she would not support implementation as scheduled. She announced her decision at a board meeting without prior notice to either the superintendent or the board president. Reverend Morgan and his supporters cheered her statement. A week later, Peter Meckava became the second defection; he too argued that outcome-based education should be delayed pending further study and discussion.

For the first time since arriving in Eagan Heights, Dr. Jackson doubted whether he could succeed in this environment. After Mr. Meckava's change of heart, he asked Annette Small, the board president, to meet him for lunch the next day. He candidly expressed his disappointment and voiced concern that both he and the district could be damaged by the board's reversal. Although Mrs. Small remained totally committed to implementing outcome-based education as initially proposed, she admitted that Reverend Morgan and his followers were gaining political power daily.

"Reggie Prescott is the next target," she told Dr. Jackson. "He told me that he is getting calls and letters from patrons asking him to change his position. Since he has to consider his business, I think there is a good chance that he will also ask for implementation to be delayed."

Dr. Jackson also turned to his trusted associate, Dr. Price, for advice. She continued to favor implementation at the start of the coming school year as planned.

"Look, if Prescott changes, we won't be able to move forward anyway," she told the superintendent. "So why back down at this point? I think we have to take these people to task for putting out misinformation. If we say we are going to delay for a semester or a year to do further study, you can bet that we will never be able to move to the outcome-based program. And besides, do we really want to stay here if people are unwilling to improve their schools?"

THE CHALLENGE

Place yourself in Dr. Jackson's position. Would you follow Dr. Price's suggestion?

KEY ISSUES/QUESTIONS

1. Why do programs such as outcome-based education spawn political activity?
2. Was it appropriate for Dr. Jackson and the school board to decide so quickly that outcome-based education was the solution for improving school performance? Why or why not?
3. Assess Dr. Jackson's relationship with his administrative staff. What are some possible reasons why he adopts this leadership style?
4. If you were the superintendent, would you have made an effort to meet with Reverend Morgan or would you have waited for him to contact you?
5. Dr. Jackson and Mrs. Small decided to make themselves available to the media and community groups to answer questions. Was this a good idea? Why or why not?
6. Analyze the behavior of board members Evercott and Meckava. What caused them to change their minds?
7. How do you evaluate the behavior of the principals? To what extent would their behavior influence your decision to follow Dr. Price's suggestion?

8. What are the advantages and disadvantages of deciding to delay implementation of the program for another year?
9. Is it common for individuals who oppose public policy to form pressure groups? What evidence do you have to support your response?
10. What contextual variables contribute to the difficulties experienced by the superintendent?
11. How might you determine the extent to which community opposition stems from general resistance to change as opposed to the specific program in this case?
12. Assess the behavior of the principals at the meetings held in each school to inform the parents about the outcome-based program.
13. Describe the leadership strategy that was employed by Dr. Jackson and Dr. Price.
14. To what extent do you think that Dr. Jackson has created an open climate in the school district (i.e., a climate that encourages interaction with the community)?

SUGGESTED READINGS

Arocha, Z. (1993). The religious right's march into public school governance. *The School Administrator, 50*(9), 8-15.

Berreth, D., & Scherer, M. (1993). On transmitting values: A conversation with Amitai Etzioni. *Educational Leadership, 51*(3), 12-15.

Boeckx, J. K. (1994). Developing community support for outcome-based education. *The School Administrator, 51*(8), 24-25.

Cohen, A. (1993). A new educational paradigm. *Phi Delta Kappan, 74*(10), 791-795.

Davis, E. D. (1984). Should the public schools teach values? *Phi Delta Kappa, 65*(5), 358-360.

Doyle, M. (1993). Public education: A fertile field for religious educators. *Momentum, 24*(1), 14-16.

Education Commission of the States. (1993). *How to deal with community criticism of school change.* Denver, CO: Author.

Eisner, E. (1993). Why standards may not improve schools. *Educational Leadership, 50*(5), 22-23.

Evans K., & King, J. (1994). Research on OBE: What we know and don't know. *Educational Leadership, 51*(6), 12-17.

Glatthorn, A. (1993). Outcome-based education: Reform and the curriculum process. *Journal of Curriculum and Supervision, 8*(4), 354-362.

Graves, B. (1992). The pressure group cooker. *School Administrator, 49*(4), 8-13.

Haas, J. (1992). Issues in outcome-based education. *NASSP Bulletin, 76*(551), 97-100.

Harmin, M. (1988). Value clarity, high morality: Let's go for both. *Educational Leadership, 45*(8), 24-27.

Huffman, H. (1993). Character education without turmoil. *Educational Leadership, 51*(3), 24-27.

Jones, J. L. (1993). Targets of the right. *American School Board Journal, 180*(4), 22-29.

King, J. A., & Evans, K. M. (1991). Can we achieve outcome-based education? *Educational Leadership, 49*(2), 73-75.

Kowalski, T. J., & Reitzug, U. C. (1993). *Contemporary school administration: An introduction.* New York: Longman (see chapters 8, 13).

Lickona, T. (1993). The return of character education. *Educational Leadership, 51*(3), 8-11.

Lutz, S. W. (1997). Whose standards? Conservative citizen groups and standards-based reform. *Educational Horizons, 75*(3), 133-142.

McKernan, J. (1993). Some limitations of outcome-based education. *Journal of Curriculum and Supervision, 8*(4), 343-353.

Nyland, L. (1991). One district's journey to success with outcome-based education. *The School Administrator, 48*(9), 29, 31-32, 34-35.

O'Neil, J. (1993). Making sense of outcome-based education. *Instructor, 102*(5), 46-47.

Outcome-based education: The religious right's latest bogeyman. (1993). *Church and State, 46*(5), 8-9.

Paul, R. (1988). Ethics without indoctrination. *Educational Leadership, 45*(8), 10-12.

Reed, R., & Simonds, R. (1993). The agenda of the religious right. *The School Administrator, 50*(9), 16-23.

Spady, W., & Marshall, K. (1991). Beyond traditional outcome-based education. *Educational Leadership, 49*(2), 67-72.

Ternasky, P. (1992). Moral realism revisited: On achievable morality. *Educational Theory, 42*(2), 201-216.

Towers, J. (1992a). Outcome-based education: Another educational bandwagon? *Educational Forum, 56*(3), 291-305.

Towers, J. (1992b). Some concerns about outcome-based education. *Journal of Research and Development in Education, 25*(2), 89-95.

Townsend, R. (1993). Coping with controversy. *The School Administrator, 50*(9), 24-27.

Wadsworth, D. (1997). Building a strategy for successful public engagement. *Phi Delta Kappan, 78*(10), 749-752.

Case **2**

Protecting the Organization: Legitimate Power or Compromise?

BACKGROUND INFORMATION

Historically, theories and practices used in business administration have influenced practice in educational administration. During the quarter-century following the Industrial Revolution, school boards and administrators were especially prone to emulate the behaviors of successful managers who led their corporations to ever-increasing profits. Over the years, however, scholars recognized that there were weighty differences between profit-seeking industries and public service organizations. This awareness helped to shape today's academic preparation of school administrators. However, many outside the profession use business values to evaluate schools; for them, public schools are ineffective largely because they are judged to be inefficient.

This case entails different perspectives about the degree to which organizational and individual needs should be balanced. Processes that contribute to inefficiency and diminish the legitimate authority of administrators disturb traditional managers who believe that organizational integrity must be protected above all else. By contrast, those who see organizations as sociopolitical entities are more willing to seek compromises that meld organizational and personal (or group) interests. Central to this case is the question of whether the school district's interests are best served by political compromises or by protecting the legitimate authority of administrators and the school board.

The problem faced by the young administrator in this case pertains to differences between private, industrial, profit-seeking organizations and public, professionally dominated organizations (such as schools). How should teachers and other employees be treated? To what degree should administrators share their authority to make decisions? Does shared decision making diminish the effectiveness of an administrator? Questions such as these are inevitable when the principles of industrial management are imposed on public schools.

In this case, the personnel director for the local public schools seeks counsel from his neighbor who is the personnel director for a local industry. The advice he receives conflicts with direction provided by the district superintendent.

KEY AREAS FOR REFLECTION

1. Differences between private and public organizations
2. The exercise of legitimate power by administrators
3. Referent and expert power and their ability to influence individual behavior
4. Conflict resolution in professionally dominated organizations
5. The use of compromise and the interests of a school system

THE CASE

The Shoreline School District is located on the banks of one of the great lakes in an industrial section of an upper-midwest state. It is a large school system enrolling 19,400 pupils; but enrollment declines have been rather substantial in the past two decades. For the last ten years, the reduction in students has averaged about 1 percent per year.

Despite steady enrollment declines the school board and administrative team have attempted to maintain a positive posture with respect to population trends. Rather than continuously reducing staff and budgets, school officials treated the loss of students as an opportunity to improve and expand programming. Supported by the teachers' union, the superintendent and school board waged a public relations campaign to increase tax revenues rather than reduce staff. Both tax referenda they initiated over the past 12 years were successful.

Tim Anderson, a former middle school science teacher and principal, accepted the position of personnel director in the Shoreline district just 11 months ago. He had just finished his Ph.D. in school administration when he accepted the job. At age 33, Tim was substantially younger than any other administrator in the central office and younger than most of the building principals.

Shoreline's superintendent, Dr. Alex Pryor, made a special effort to involve Tim in the community. For example, he sponsored Tim for membership in the Rotary Club, and he made sure that his new staff member was invited to speak before a variety of civic groups. Dr. Pryor believed that Tim's youth and enthusiasm would symbolically convey a progressive attitude about the school district's future.

Tim's wife, Margie, and their two children readily adapted to their new home in Shoreline. Located in one of the city's more affluent neighborhoods, their house was just a few blocks from the beach and city marina. Most of their neighbors were middle-aged professionals who had resided in Shoreline for some time.

However, Tim's next-door neighbor, Bill Stanton, was his age and was also a relative newcomer to the community. He and his family had moved to Shoreline just about one year before Tim. Bill was the personnel director of Shoreline Metal Products, one of the city's major industries. The two neighbors shared many common interests including their occupations.

Despite having the same job title, Bill and Tim had very different backgrounds. Bill graduated from a small, liberal arts college in Pennsylvania with a major in business and subsequently received a law degree from a Washington, D.C., university. He developed an interest in personnel administration as a result of handling labor issues in a large law firm for six years. One of his clients was Shoreline Metal Products, a company that had a long history of union-related problems. Tim, on the other hand, earned three degrees at a large state university. He was a classroom teacher for six years and principal for two years. Prior to his current position, he had been a full-time doctoral student for two years.

One sunny October day while the two friends were out on the lake sailing, Tim mentioned that the school district faced the possibility of having to eliminate as many as 25 teaching positions. Over the last five years, resignations and retirements allowed the teaching force to be trimmed; but now, large-scale reductions seemed necessary unless the voters would approve another tax increase. The most recent tax referendum was six years ago, and it narrowly passed.

"The superintendent," he told Bill, "favors another referendum. But he doesn't think the school board will support it."

Bill commented, "So what's the problem? It looks like you have to bite the bullet and eliminate the necessary number of jobs. You have a union contract. Surely it addresses how this will be done."

"Right," answered Tim. "However, the master contract calls for us to form a joint committee between representatives of the teachers' union and the administration to determine if reductions are necessary and how they should be carried out."

Bill looked surprised. "You have to be pulling my leg! Who in their right mind would agree to those provisions? Establishing a committee and letting them decide how many and which reductions are necessary takes away management's authority to make personnel decisions. How do you know, for example, that the union won't make these decisions solely on the basis of seniority or loyalty to the union? They may select some of your best teachers for dismissal simply because they don't belong to the union."

"Bill, I wasn't here when this provision was put in the contract, and we have never had to eliminate a large number of positions before. In the past, this joint committee agreed to eliminate a few jobs each year; but no one was terminated because the reductions were covered by resignations and retirements. So I don't know how the union leaders will react if we tell them that as many as 25 positions have to be eliminated," Tim replied. "This language has been in our contract for seven years."

"Well, I think you ought to do something about it—and I mean right away," Bill advised him. "If reductions are not handled properly, you could encounter serious political and possibly legal problems. People who supported previous tax increases might rebel if some of the district's best teachers lose their jobs just because they lack seniority. Or you could end up with a financial crisis if the union refuses to agree to sufficient reductions."

For the next several days, Tim could not quit thinking about Bill's comments. He trusted his friend and respected his knowledge of labor relations. The following week while he was meeting with the superintendent, Tim brought up the reduction-in-force provision in the master contract.

"Dr. Pryor, I've been thinking about our last administrative meeting. We discussed the possibility of having to eliminate about 25 teaching positions before next school year. If that becomes necessary, the language in our master contract would be very problematic. First, the reduction committee members, half of whom are union leaders, must agree that this many reductions are necessary. Second, the committee determines which jobs get eliminated. The number of jobs to be cut is a financial matter and actual reduction decisions should be based on performance and specific staffing needs. There is a possibility that both of these decisions will be made politically. The union representatives will never agree to cutting 25 positions, and they are likely to protect their most senior members."

Dr. Pryor walked over to a bookcase and picked out his copy of the contract. He turned to the page containing the reduction provision and read it silently. When he finished, he looked up at Tim and said, "What's the problem? This is the same language that we have had for the past seven years. What bothers you?"

Tim responded, "As I said, I'm troubled by the fact that this committee's decisions will be purely political. Can we really expect the union representatives to be objective?"

Superintendent Pryor's reading glasses were on the tip of his nose, and his eyes focused above the rims at Tim as he spoke. "We had to reduce several teaching positions in each of the last five years, and we managed to do it without serious conflict. We always found a way to compromise—to work it out. If we have good data indicating our need to reduce staff, the teachers have worked with us."

"But Dr. Pryor, one of the reasons we are faced with up to 25 reductions now is that we didn't make sufficient reductions previously," Tim noted.

"Tim, stop worrying. We've faced big problems before, and we always find a way to work things out. Besides, we have an obligation to live up to the negotiated agreement with the teachers. So even if we wanted to change things, we couldn't do that until we negotiate a new contract."

Tim left the superintendent's office feeling a little bit better about the matter. He considered the possibility that his friend, Bill, may not have a good grasp of employee relations in the public sector. Maybe the political dimensions of making decisions in the school district were quite different than those that existed in a steel company.

That evening Tim saw Bill barbecuing in his backyard and walked over to talk with him. "Bill, the other day you commented about the school system's reduction-in-force policy. You were pretty critical. Your comments led me to give this matter a great deal of thought. Could you be more specific about why you think our policy will not work?"

"Sure," Bill answered. "For one thing, you can't make any decisions about reductions unless the union agrees. That's simply bad management. What if they decide that you don't need to release any teachers—or maybe just two or three teachers? Can you afford to do that? Are the union bosses willing to share the blame if you go bankrupt because you didn't save enough in salaries? It's as simple as that."

Tim explained that the school administrators have been able to compromise with the union in the past. "Alex Pryor assured me that the union representatives on this committee have been objective and that they were willing to look at facts and figures. He thinks that they will be objective if we provide evidence that 25 positions must be eliminated. He's convinced that the provision in the master contract has worked in the past."

Bill immediately responded, "Last year, you eliminated just three jobs; I remember reading about it in the paper. All three were covered by resignations. This decision didn't threaten the union. Now, you may have to cut as many as 25 jobs, and this reduction probably will affect loyal union members. Tim, unions look out for their own. Your job is to protect the organization. Sure, you might be able to cut some political deals, but will these deals be in the best interests of students and taxpayers? Have you considered that you're facing this problem now because this committee failed to make sufficient reductions in the past?"

Tim still wasn't convinced that Bill was correct. He asked further, "Don't you think workers ought to have some say in what happens to them? Since they are the ones who stand to lose their jobs, shouldn't they be allowed to play a role in these decisions?"

"Do you think any of the teachers appointed to this committee will be released? Of course not!" Bill exclaimed. "And what do you expect, Tim? You think they are going to say it's fine for you to take away jobs from their union brothers and sisters? Of course not. I think you have a no-win situation here. And just for a moment, think about your personal role in all of this. You're the one who has to work with this committee. You're the one who has to implement the compromises. If they turn out to be bad decisions, and that's likely to be the case, who's going to get criticized for not protecting the school district's interests? Dr. Pryor or you? If I were you, I'd make sure that the superintendent gets involved directly."

At the administrative team meeting three days later, fiscal and demographic reports provided additional evidence that everyone's worst fears were real. Reductions would be necessary to remain fiscally solvent, and the number of necessary reductions would be approximately 25 as earlier projected. Dr. Pryor instructed Tim to take immediate steps to activate the reduction committee as stipulated in the collective-bargaining agreement.

Tim's self-confidence had been eroded by the contrasting positions of Bill and Dr. Pryor. He respected both of them, but he decided to follow his neighbor's advice about asking the superintendent to become directly involved. That afternoon he called the president of the teachers' union, and notified her of the need to activate the committee. He explained that more than a few reductions were necessary. She reacted with surprise.

"We cooperated in the past, because major reductions were avoided. I must warn you that there will be little or no support for major budget cuts."

Tim replied, "All I can tell you is that enrollment reports and financial data indicate that we have to make substantial reductions. We are prepared to make our case to the committee. All I ask is that you remain open-minded."

The union president then asked, "Can you give me any idea about how many positions we will be talking about?"

Tim answered, "Our data suggest that it may need to be as many as 25."

The union president concluded the telephone conversation by predicting that the committee would never agree to such large-scale reductions.

Immediately after this conversation, Tim called Bill at his office and told him what had just occurred. Bill responded confidently, "Didn't I tell you this would happen? Forget about the past. Unions are unpredictable. They respond solely on the basis of political considerations that benefit their well-being."

"What do you think I should do?" Tim asked.

Bill answered, "You have to convince your boss to get directly involved. You are probably going to end up in court over this one. I'd play tough. Tell the union that you'll go public unless they agree to a sufficient number of reductions and unless they agree to make the reductions on the basis of performance and need."

Tim hung up the phone and went immediately to see the superintendent. He told him about his discussion with the union president, and urged Dr. Pryor to attend the committee meetings. He also outlined a strategy of taking the matter to the public if the union members were uncooperative. The disappointment on Dr. Pryor's face was obvious.

"Tim, maybe your inexperience is clouding your thinking. You have to understand that unions always say they can't agree to things. But somehow we always manage to work it out. This school district isn't a steel company. Teachers are taxpayers. They have friends and relatives on the school board. They can influence elections. We have learned to work with the union. You need to do that too." With that sobering comment, the superintendent ended the brief discussion.

THE CHALLENGE

Place yourself in Tim's position. What would you do at this point?

KEY ISSUES/QUESTIONS

1. Why do you think Dr. Pryor and Bill have such different opinions about the reduction-in-force provision in the master contract?
2. In what ways are the climates of private and public organizations different?
3. Do you believe that Bill's assessment of unions is correct? Why or why not?
4. Is Bill exerting power over Tim? If so, what is the source of this power?
5. Was it ethical for Tim to discuss this issue with Bill? Why or why not?

6. Should Dr. Pryor become directly involved with the reduction-in-force committee? What are the advantages and disadvantages for Tim if he does so?
7. Is Bill's assessment correct that school administrators should not rely on past successes to direct their future actions in working with unions? Why or why not?
8. Assess Dr. Pryor's behavior in this case. Do you think he is providing sufficient leadership?
9. Are there community variables that should be weighed in this case? If so, what are they?
10. Do you believe that Dr. Pryor contributed to the current problem by delaying inevitable reductions?
11. If you were going to advise Tim, what information would you want that was not presented in the case?
12. Are most policy decisions in public education political? Provide a rationale for your response.

SUGGESTED READINGS

Allen, R., & Nixon, B. (1988). Developing a new approach to leadership. *Management Education and Development, 19*(3), 174-186.

Burke, R. (1983). Don't be a slave to seniority when developing RIF procedures. *American School Board Journal, 170*(7), 20-21.

Chandler, T. (1984). Can theory Z be applied to the public schools? *Education, 104*(4), 343-345.

Chesler, N. (1991). Personnel cuts: Tough but effective. *The School Administrator, 48*(8), 28.

Collins, P., & Nelson, D. (1983). Reducing the teacher workforce: A management perspective. *Journal of Law and Education, 12*(2), 249-272.

Conway, J. (1984). The myth, mystery and mastery of participative decision making in education. *Educational Administration Quarterly, 20*(3), 11-40.

Duke, D. L. (1998). The normative context of organizational leadership. *Educational Administration Quarterly, 34*(2), 165-195.

Dunnerstick, R. (1987). If RIFs are in the cards for your schools, deal with them deftly. *American School Board Journal, 174*(1), 34.

Feuerstein, A., & Opfer, V. D. (1998). School board chairmen and school superintendents: An analysis of perceptions concerning special interest groups and educational governance. *Journal of School Leadership, 9* (4), 373-398.

Kowalski, T., & Reitzug, U. (1993). *Contemporary school administration: An introduction*. New York: Longman (see chapters 7, 10, 16).

Lieberman, A. (1988). Teachers and principals: Turf, tension, and new tasks. *Phi Delta Kappan, 69*(9), 948-953.

Lieberman, M. (1986). *Beyond public education*. New York: Praeger (see chapter 2).

Lifton, F. (1992). The legal tangle of shared governance. *The School Administrator, 49*(1), 16-19.

Nelson, R. (1991). Can corporate management work in schools? *Principal, 71*(2), 32-33.

Rosen, M. (1993). Sharing power: A blueprint for collaboration. *Principal, 72*(3), 37-39.

Shedd, J., & Bacharach, S. (1991). *Tangled hierarchies: Teachers as professionals and the management of schools*. San Francisco: Jossey-Bass.

Smit, G. (1984). The effect of collective bargaining on governance in education. *Goverment Union Review, 5*(1), 28-34.

Wishnick, Y., & Wishnick, T. (1993). Collective bargaining and educational reform: Establishing a labor-management partnership. *Journal of Collective Negotiations in the Public Sector, 22*(1), 1-11.

Wood, C. (1982). Financial exigencies and the dismissal of public school teachers: A legal perspective. *Government Union Review, 3*(4), 49-66.

Case **3**

A Bully's Threat

BACKGROUND INFORMATION

Not all administrators recognize that there is a difference between *safety* and *security*. The former addresses issues such as accident prevention, air quality, and fire or storm damage. Security, on the other hand, is concerned with preventing and responding to criminal acts and severe misbehavior (Trump, 1998). Criminal acts committed in schools provide clear evidence that educational environments are not immune from the ills of society. The potential for violence generates three critical questions for school administrators: How can behaviors that threaten the security of a school be prevented? What measures should be taken when threats of violence are made? What measures should be taken when violence occurs?

Experts who have examined crime-related crises have concluded that many schools remain especially vulnerable for the following reasons:

- Administrators are often unprepared to deal with violence. This is because they seldom have had training to manage violent crimes and because they have either no experience or only very limited experience with such situations.
- School or district crisis plans are often not developed because of administrators' fears that the intent of these preventative documents will be misinterpreted. That is, parents, students, and others are likely to judge that the plans are an admission that serious security problems already exist (Moriarity, Maeyama, & Fitzgerald, 1993).

- Even when crisis plans have been developed, chaos often occurs because the plans have not been carefully coordinated with relevant community agencies (e.g., police, fire departments) (Seifert, 2000).
- The content of crisis plans may have been influenced by political conditions within the community, district, or individual school that dissuade administrators from adopting best practices (Trump, 1998). For example, punishment for violent behavior may be influenced by a school district's goal of reducing expulsions.

This case occurs in a multicultural urban high school. A student who has a reputation as a bully threatens the life of another student. The principal must decide how to deal with the situation. He involves three staff members in the decision-making process. As you read the case, pay special attention to identifying factors that have contributed to the problem.

KEY AREAS FOR REFLECTION

1. Multicultural school environments
2. Political influences on crisis management
3. Racial tensions in schools
4. Dealing with threats of violent behavior
5. Leadership style

THE CASE

The Community

Like most urban areas in the United States, Central City has experienced considerable change in the past 30 years. The total population has declined from 325,000 in 1960 to its current level of 258,000. The property tax base has been eroded by the flight of many businesses to the suburbs. The current mayor, who is now serving a second four-year term, has been more successful than his predecessors in curbing population decline. Two of the programs he has sponsored, inner-city renewal and a vigorous campaign to attract new businesses, have helped to stabilize the population.

Statistics for crime and violence in Central City, however, have not declined. Nor have poverty statistics. Nearly 40 percent of the school-age children in the city live in families with annual incomes below the poverty line. Many of them are also being reared in dysfunctional families, and it is estimated that as many as 15 percent of school-age children have been victims of physical or emotional abuse.

The following demographic profile developed from the most recent census reveals the city's racial diversity:

- 48 percent identified themselves as African American
- 18 percent identified themselves as Hispanic
- 5 percent identified themselves as Asian American

- 28 percent identified themselves as white (non-Hispanic)
- 1 percent identified themselves as "other"

White residents are heavily concentrated in two sections of Center City: Memorial Park (where virtually all of the Asian-American families also reside) and Kensington.

The School District

The Central City School District remains the largest district in the state; however, its enrollment has declined about 25 percent in the past three decades. Two high schools, two middle schools, and six elementary schools have been closed during that period. Most of the remaining buildings that continue to be used as schools are more than 50 years old, many needing extensive renovation or replacement.

The district is governed by a school board whose seven members are elected. Five of them are elected from specified districts and two are elected at-large. The following data profile the present board:

Member	Board Position	District	Occupation	Race
Venus Bronson	President	3	Lawyer	African American
Walter Sullivan	Vice-President	At-large	Plumber	White
Emily Drovak	Secretary	5	Housewife	White
Alexander Adams	Member	1	Minister	African American
James Chin	Member	4	Engineer	Asian American
Rose Ann Hildago	Member	2	Social Worker	Hispanic
Maynard Truax	Member	At-large	Dentist	African American

Districts 1, 2, and 3 are in the central part of the city. All three districts have high concentrations of African-American residents, with District 2 being almost evenly divided between African-American and Hispanic populations. District 4, known as the Memorial Park area, is located at the southern edge of the city. Nearly all of the district's residents are either white or Asian American. District 5, known as Kensington, is located in the northern edge of the city; the population here is about 60 percent white with the remainder being predominately African American.

Dr. Ruth Perkett is the district's first female and first African-American superintendent. A veteran administrator in Central City, she has held her current position for two years. Prior to becoming superintendent, she served as an elementary school principal, director of federal programs, and associate superintendent for elementary education. She has a close working relationship with the current mayor.

The School

Forty years ago, Memorial Park High School was recognized as one of the finest academic schools in the state. It still maintains the reputation of being the most academic-oriented high school in the Center City district. Memorial Park serves approximately 1,350 students in four grades, a little over a third of whom do not reside in the Memorial Park area; they are bussed from other parts of Central City as part of a desegregation plan.

Joseph Milhoviak has been the principal at Memorial Park for 14 years. He grew up in the neighborhood surrounding the school. After graduating from Memorial Park, he went to college, received his license to teach science and physical education, and returned to Memorial Park as a teacher and coach. He has worked at the school for the past 28 years.

Prior to the implementation of the district's desegregation plan 12 years ago, Memorial Park had just a handful of African-American and Hispanic students. The present student profile shows that conditions have changed:

- African American—40 percent
- Hispanic—10 percent
- Asian American—16 percent
- White—34 percent

The faculty, however, is less diverse. Despite assigning only African-American or Hispanic educators to the school in the past five years, approximately two-thirds of the teachers and administrators, including principal Milhoviak, are white.

Principal Milhoviak lives in the Memorial Park area and is highly involved in the neighborhood's activities. Several years ago, the Memorial Park Neighborhood Association urged him to become a candidate for the office of Center City mayor; he declined. Joseph Milhoviak is known as a tough principal—a disciplinarian who is not afraid to deal with problem students. While his "get-tough" approach is applauded by Memorial Park residents, Superintendent Perkett has been less complimentary. She has been openly critical of the fact that three-fourths of the Memorial Park High School students who either get expelled or drop out are minorities. She believes that the principal's inflexibility toward students who are bussed to the school from other sections of the city contributes to this statistic. She has urged him to implement programs such as in-school suspension and group counseling to better serve students with behavior problems. To date, he has not done so.

The Incident

Brian Isaacs entered the principal's office between the third and fourth periods and told the receptionist, "I need to see Mr. Milhoviak right now. It's an emergency!"

"What's wrong," she inquired.

He answered, "I'm not going to talk about the problem with anyone except the principal."

The receptionist interrupted Mr. Milhoviak's meeting with a parent to inform him that a student was reporting an emergency. She revealed the student's identity to the principal and informed him that Brian refused to talk to anyone but him. The principal knew the student and members of his family. Brian, a sophomore, was an above-average student who had never been in trouble. Mr. Milhoviak quickly concluded the meeting with the parent and asked the receptionist to send Brian into his office.

As the student entered, the principal saw that Brian was visibly shaken. "What's the problem?" the principal asked.

The student immediately answered, "Carl Turner, a senior, told me that he is going to blow my brains out. And Mr. Milhoviak, he is crazy. I think he might just do it," the nervous student said. "This whole thing really has nothing to do with me. Carl had a couple dates with my sister, Angie, and now she doesn't want to see him anymore. He's blaming my family and me for her decision. He says he is in love with Angie, and we're all prejudiced. He thinks my parents have ordered Angie not to see him anymore just because he is black."

Mr. Milhoviak was familiar with Carl Turner. He had been a football player until he was dismissed from the team earlier in the year. Carl's family lives outside of the Memorial Park neighborhood. In addition to his dismissal from the football team, he had been suspended twice in the past two years for fighting. Many students at the high school refer to Carl as a bully.

The principal also knew Brian's sister, Angie. She too was a senior. Somewhat introverted, she had not been highly involved in school activities. She was, however, a good student—a member of the National Honor Society. Mr. Milhoviak was surprised that she would be dating someone with Carl's reputation.

"What exactly did Carl say to you, Brian?" the principal asked.

"He told me that he loved Angie and he wasn't going to let my family stand between them. He said he owned a gun and wasn't afraid to use it. He said unless we stopped pressuring Angie, he would get me and my parents."

The principal immediately asked another question, "And what does Angie have to say about all of this?"

"I don't know. I didn't know that she ever went out with him. I don't think my parents knew either."

"Brian, I am going to alert the security officer about this threat. He'll keep an eye out for Carl. If he threatens you again, even if he calls you at home, you let me know immediately. In the mean time, I'll decide how I'm going to handle this. Whatever you do, don't agitate him," the principal advised the student.

Brian's fear was not eliminated by the principal's words. He told Mr. Milhoviak, "Carl said he was tired of being treated like dirt. I really think he's crazy enough to shoot someone."

After a few more minutes, the principal convinced Brian to return to class. As soon as the student left his office, the principal asked that Angie Isaacs be brought to see him. When she arrived, the principal immediately told her about the threat reported by her brother. She appeared surprised.

"I went out with Carl twice, and no one in my family knew about it. He had asked for a date at least six times before I said 'yes.' We went to a movie on our first date. I met him at the theatre. We went to a concert on the second date. My parents thought I was with my girlfriends both times. After the last date, I decided that I didn't want to go out with him again. So I told him that two days ago. He got very angry," she told the principal.

"Did he ever threaten you?" the principal asked.

"No. But he scares me. He's a very angry person, and he gets mad easily."

Mr. Milhoviak told Angie to return to class and to avoid contact with Carl. He also advised her to tell her parents about the situation when she got home from school that day. After she left his office, he tried to call her parents but was unsuccessful. No one answered the phone at their residence and the school records did not contain a work telephone number.

Next, the principal asked the school security officer, Carl Turner's counselor, and the assistant principal who handled much of the discipline in the school to meet with him. He informed them of the threat against Brian and told them about his conversations with Brian and Angie. The four agreed that their first course of action was to bring Carl to the office so he could present his side of the story. A few moments later, they were told that Carl had never arrived at his fourth period English class.

Carl's counselor, Mrs. Bruner, suggested that Mr. Milhoviak call the police and report the incident. Although she did not think Carl was likely to shoot someone, she thought that he might physically attack Brian or Angie with his fists. The assistant principal and security guard, however, wanted to wait until they located Carl.

The assistant principal commented, "What if we call the police and then find out Brian is not telling the truth? So many things that happen in this school end up being cast as racial problems. If Brian is not telling the truth, or if he is exaggerating, we may be accused of jumping to conclusions. You know that Dr. Perkett is always raising questions about suspensions and expulsions here. I say we try to find Carl before we do anything else. If we can't locate him by the end of the school day, let's get back together and reconsider our options."

The school's security guard, who is an African American and a retired deputy sheriff, recommended that they continue trying to find Brian's parents. First, he thought that they could be in danger, and second, the school officials needed to know if they would file a complaint with the police. He also noted that he would make sure that Brian was safe for the remainder of the school day.

Each school in the Center City district was required to have a crisis plan. The one for Memorial Park provided suggestions for handling threatened violence, but it did not require a specific course of action. Among the suggested actions were:

- Notifying the police if the incident was considered sufficiently serious
- Notifying the parents of all students involved
- Notifying the teachers of all students involved
- Suspending the student from school pending a full investigation if the incident was considered sufficiently serious

The principal decided to delay calling the police. The group agreed to reconvene immediately after the last class period.

Mr. Milhoviak repeatedly tried to call Carl Turner's mother and the parents of Brian and Angie Isaacs. He was unable to reach any of them. At 3:00 P.M., the end of the regular school day, the four school officials reconvened in the principal's office. Carl had not been located, the police had not been notified, the parents had not been notified, and no further threats had been made. Joseph Milhoviak knew that they could wait no longer. They had to decide how they were going to deal with this matter.

THE CHALLENGE

Assume you are the principal. How would you manage this situation?

KEY ISSUES/QUESTIONS

1. To what extent are the racial, social, and economic characteristics of the school district relevant to the problem presented in the case?
2. The assistant principal alludes to the superintendent's concerns over discipline policies at Memorial Park High School. How might the superintendent's concerns affect the principal's deliberations in this matter?
3. Evaluate the security guard's advice, i.e., to tell the parents and let them file a complaint with the police if they wish to do so.
4. Evaluate the school counselor's advice, i.e., contact the police about the incident.
5. To what extent is it probable that students will become violent over issues such as dating?
6. Is Carl Turner's record of fighting relevant to this case? Why or why not?
7. Although the school crises plan offers suggestions, it does not require a specific action. What judgments can you make about the adequacy of the plan?
8. Evaluate the principal's decision to wait until the end of the school day before doing anything other than having the security guard watch Brian.
9. List contingency approaches to dealing with this situation. Evaluate each of them.
10. To what extent might political considerations affect a decision in this matter?
11. In your state, does a principal have a legal responsibility to report students to law officials when they threaten bodily harm to others?
12. To what extent is the principal's reputation as a disciplinarian and his popularity in Memorial Park relevant to this case?
13. Is Carl's unexcused absence from school relevant to what should be done? Why or why not?

SUGGESTED READINGS

Baker, J. A. (1998). Are we missing the forest for the trees? Considering the social context of school violence. *Journal of School Psychology, 36*(1), 29–44.

Bock, S. J., Savner, J. L., & Tapscott, K. E. (1998). Suspension and expulsion: Effective management of students. *Intervention in School and Clinic, 34*(1), 50–52.

Clark, C. (1998). The violence that creates school dropouts. *Multicultural Education, 6*(1), 19–22.

Constenbader, V., & Markson, S. (1998). School suspension: A study with secondary school students. *Journal of School Psychology, 36*(1), 59–82.

Edmonson, H. M., & Bullock, L. M. (1998). Youth with aggressive and violent behaviors: Pieces of a puzzle. *Preventing School Failure, 42*(3), 135–141.

Haynes, R. M., & Chalker, D. M. (1999). A nation of violence. *American School Board Journal, 186*(3), 22–25.

Johns, B. H. (1998). What the new Individuals with Disabilities Act (IDEA) means for students who exhibit aggressive or violent behavior. *Preventing School Failure, 42*(3), 102–105.

Jones, R. (1997). Absolute zero. *American School Board Journal, 184*(10), 29–31.

Kenney, D. J., & Watson, T. S. (1996). Reducing fear in the schools: Managing conflict through student problem solving. *Education and Urban Society, 28*(4), 436–455.

Levin, J. (1998). Violence goes to school. *Mid-Western Educational Researcher, 11*(1), 2–7.

Moriarity, A., Maeyama, R. G., & Fitzgerald, P. J. (1993). A clear plan for school crisis management. *NASSP Bulletin, 77*(552), 17–22.

Myles, B. S., & Simpson, R. L. (1998). Aggression and violence by school-age children and youth: Understanding the aggression cycle and prevention/intervention strategies. *Intervention in School and Clinic, 33*(5), 259–264.

Page, R. M., & Hammermeister, J. (1997). Weapon-carrying youth and violence. *Adolescence, 32*(127), 505–513.

Rasicot, J. (1999). The threat of harm. *American School Board Journal, 186*(3), 14–18.

Seifert, E. H. (2000). Responding to crisis. In T. J. Kowalski (Ed.), *Public relations in schools* (2nd ed.) (pp. 294–314). Upper Saddle River, NJ: Merrill, Prentice Hall.

Sheley, J. F., & Wright, J. D. (1998). *High school youths, weapons, and violence: A national study* (ERIC Document Reproduction Service No. ED426 468)

Stephens, R. D. (1998). Ten steps to safer schools. *American School Board Journal, 185*(3), 30–33.

Trump, K. S. (1998). *Practical school safety: Basic guidelines for safe and secure schools.* Thousand Oaks, CA: Corwin Press.

Valois, R. F., & McKewon, R. E. (1998). Frequency and correlates of fighting and carrying weapons among public school adolescents. *American Journal of Health Behavior, 22*(1), 8–17.

Case **4**

Lounge Talk

BACKGROUND INFORMATION

Role conflict is a condition created by incompatible job expectations. For example, some teachers, students, and parents expect principals to be caring and loving individuals; others expect principals to be effective managers; and still others expect principals to be dynamic political leaders. The issue of role conflict has received increased attention in recent years as a result of efforts to reconstruct organization and governance in schools and districts.

Studies of role conflict and leadership styles have contributed to theory building in the areas of *transformational* and *charismatic* leadership. As Yukl noted (1989), these two terms

> ... refer to the process of influencing major changes in the attitudes and assumptions of organization members and building commitment for the organization's mission and objectives. Transformational leadership is usually defined more broadly than charismatic leadership, but there is considerable overlap between the two conceptions. (p. 204)

The seminal work of Burns (1978) distinguished between transactional and transformational leadership. The two were described as opposite behaviors. In summarizing these polar positions, Kowalski and Reitzug (1993) wrote, "Transactional leadership involves an exchange between leader and follower for purposes of achieving individual objectives. For example, a principal may agree to let a teacher attend a national reading conference in exchange for the teacher's work on a textbook-adoption committee" (p. 233). Transactional leaders concentrate on the self-interests of subordinates in an attempt to motivate them to do desired things. Bennis and Nanus (1985) concluded that this type of interaction between leader and follower is used to accomplish much of the work in organizations. By contrast, transformational leadership has been described as

> . . . the pursuit of higher-level goals that are common to both leader and followers. There are two components to transformational leadership: (1) It elevates the motives of individuals toward a common goal. (2) It focuses on higher-order, intrinsic, and moral motives. (Kowalski & Reitzug, 1993, p. 233)

Transformational leadership is concerned with vision and culture. Change in schools, for example, is attempted by appealing to the professional commitment of teachers.

In this case, four high school teachers share their perceptions of the school's new principal who is unlike her predecessor in many ways. Differences between the current and former principal range from gender and experience to leadership style. As you read this case, try to determine factors that may have influenced the perceptions of the four teachers. Also consider how school climate, including culture, may have contributed to support or criticisms of the new principal.

KEY AREAS FOR REFLECTION

1. Principal succession
2. Role conflict
3. Teacher expectations of principal behavior
4. The effects of culture on expectations of leader behavior
5. Transformational and transactional leadership styles
6. The importance of moral, professional, and ethical issues in transformational leadership

THE CASE

As Peter Weller entered the teachers' lounge, the room fell silent. Three other teachers, Debra Lowler, Linda Mays, and Jake Brumwell, were in the room. They were seated together at one of the small round tables scattered randomly in the room. Peter nodded and joined them. The silence, however, continued. Finally Peter asked, "Okay, what's going on here? You people look like you got caught doing something terribly wrong."

Over the course of the year, the four teachers had gotten to know each other quite well, because they had a common preparation period. It had become customary for them to convene for coffee about 15 minutes before their next class.

"Peter," Linda answered, "We were just discussing your favorite principal. Maybe she has a bug in this room and sent you in here to defend her! Just a joke, Peter, so don't get hostile."

Peter smiled and brought the coffeepot to the table where his colleagues were seated.

"Anyone want a refill?" he asked before he sat down. "Don't you people have better things to discuss? Now I realize that you excel at criticizing principals. But come on now, let's ease up on Dr. Werner."

Dr. Colleen Werner had been appointed principal of Drewerton South High School less than a year ago. She is only the second principal in the school's 14-year history. Enrolling about 1,050 students, Drewerton South serves primarily a middle-class suburban population.

George Calbo, Dr. Werner's predecessor, retired a year ago. A tall man, approximately 6'5", he was named as the first principal of Drewerton South after having been a teacher and highly successful basketball coach at the district's other high school. He was well-liked by most of the teachers, because he was a people person who often sided with his faculty during conflict situations.

The selection of Dr. Werner as the second principal for Drewerton South surprised many of the teachers and community members. She was much younger (32 years old) than her predecessor, and she was the first female secondary school principal to be employed in the district. The differences between Dr. Werner and her predecessor became even more obvious with time. For example, Mr. Calbo spent much of his time with management tasks and Dr. Werner's primary area of interest was instructional leadership. Mr. Calbo rarely planned his workdays, rarely missed an athletic event, and rarely missed going to the faculty lounge two or three times a day for coffee. Dr. Werner, by comparison, carefully planned her daily activities, attended only about one-third of the athletic events, and almost never visited the faculty lounge.

Peter Weller liked Dr. Werner and often defended her. He thought that she was a highly competent, professional, and dedicated leader. While he did not dislike the former principal, he thought that Mr. Calbo lacked vision and was unwilling to take risks to improve the school.

"Well, what are you crucifying her for today?" Peter asked the other teachers.

"Come on Peter," Jake answered. "You know we have to talk about somebody, and it might as well be Colleen."

"Unfortunately, you talk about her almost every day. She's become an obsession for you three," Peter noted.

Debra Lowler, usually the quietest person in the group, spoke next. "I'll tell you what bothers me. It's her repeated comments about how we should be professionals, about why we should always do things for the students, and about how we should be willing to volunteer for this and that. We never got any of that from George. He knows what it is like to be a teacher. He had his feet on the ground."

"Yes," Linda chimed in, "George fought for teachers' rights. He made sure we got paid for doing extra things. He didn't expect us to do more work without additional pay. And more important, he didn't let the superintendent and school board walk all over us."

"Don't you think that Colleen cares about teachers?" Peter asked. "She was a teacher. She knows what our lives are like. Is it possible that she wants to make sure that everyone, including students, receives fair treatment? Just because she doesn't go around praising you every minute of the day doesn't mean she's indifferent about teachers."

Jake Brumwell, who teaches mathematics and coaches track, is a close personal friend of Mr. Calbo. He responded to Peter's comments.

"Peter, this principal still has a lot to learn. She especially has a lot to learn about dealing with teachers. Just last week, for example, she called me into her office and asked if I would be willing to take a group of students camping for a weekend in June. These are basically problem students involved in her drop-out prevention program. She told me that two other teachers had agreed to participate, but she thinks I should go too. When I asked her how much we would get paid for doing this, she looked at me like I was crazy. She thinks doing these assignments are part of our job as teachers. I told her I was too busy and couldn't go. But I don't like her putting me in a position where I look like an uncaring teacher."

Peter then asked, "Did you know, Jake, that I'm one of those who volunteered to supervise this trip?" Not waiting for an answer, he asked another question. "Did you know that Colleen, herself, was going to go? So, it wasn't like she was asking you to do something that she wasn't doing."

Debra came to Jake's defense. "Sure, she's going. But she's on a 12-month contract. We're not."

"But she's not paid for working on weekends, is she?" Peter shot back.

Linda entered the conversation again. "Look, it's more than just asking us to give up our time. Colleen's whole approach toward administration is different—she doesn't do things the way George Calbo did them. He saw to it that teachers got paid for extra assignments. It seems that Colleen only cares about the students—and she cares most about the students with serious problems. If you ask me, she's got this thing about trying to save lost causes. Hey, let's face it—we all care about kids, but how about our principal looking out for us too."

"Yeah, maybe she should pay as much attention to our welfare as she does the welfare of these problem students. She would be a much better principal if she did," Jake noted. "Personally, I think she would be a more effective principal if she paid more attention to our best students. They are the ones who ought to be receiving special trips and pats on the head from the principal. What kind of messages are sent to our students and taxpayers when the worst students get all the attention?"

Peter was getting frustrated. "You three realize, don't you, that I'm not the only one in the school who supports Colleen?" he asked rhetorically. "Why don't you give her credit for the things she's accomplished in just a short time she's been here? What about the way she helped Deloris Hutchins?"

Ms. Hutchins was a home economics teacher at the school. Prior to Dr. Werner working with her, she was recognized as one of the worst teachers in the district.

"Dr. Werner made Deloris her pet project. She worked with her to improve her planning skills and classroom management. George Calbo never tried to help her become a better teacher; he just covered up her poor performance. Deloris Hutchins is a better teacher now, and she openly attributes her improved performance to Dr. Werner. Now you tell me, who is the better principal—the one who made excuses for poor teaching or the one who did something about it? I'll tell you how Deloris answers that question. She thinks Dr. Werner is the best administrator she has ever known. To casually charge that Colleen doesn't care about teachers is irresponsible."

Jake responded, "See, that's what I was trying to say a minute ago. No matter whether it's teachers or students, she only cares about those who are doing poorly. Shouldn't those of us who are doing a good job day after day get some attention from the principal? No, instead of praise and recognition, we get to give up a weekend to supervise a bunch of rowdies out in the woods! And if we say no, we're labeled uncaring teachers and insensitive human beings. I don't like the way this administrator operates; and I'll say it again, she's not cut out to be principal of this school."

Peter recognized that he was not going to gain any converts today. There had been a dozen or so previous conversations like this one, and each had ended without anyone changing his or her views. Yet, the four teachers always felt better after sharing their feelings about Dr. Werner. Fortunately, the 15-minute debates did not negatively affect personal relationships among the four teachers.

"Well, colleagues," Peter said as he stood up, "time to get back to work. But before I go, I just wanted to say again that you are wrong about Colleen. Why are you so unwilling to give her a fair chance? She's a bright, energetic leader. She's not perfect, but the perfect principal probably doesn't exist."

"Oh Peter," Linda said, "wipe that smile off your face. Don't you recognize when you have lost another argument? I will say this, I think Colleen has good intentions."

Jake added sarcastically, "Yeah, I'll give her a 'B' for effort and a 'D' for achievement!"

The group always had a way of ending their discussions with a little humor. Maybe it was their way of checking to see if anyone's feelings got hurt. The four teachers laughed as they scattered down different hallways to their next classes.

THE CHALLENGE

Utilize your knowledge of leadership and organizational behavior to analyze the discussion that took place. Specifically, provide an explanation of why teachers in this school react to Dr. Werner so differently.

KEY ISSUES/QUESTIONS

1. Is it common for teachers to disagree on the type of leadership style that should be used by the principal? What evidence do you have to support your response?
2. In the case, a charge is made that Dr. Werner spends an inordinate amount of her time trying to assist students and teachers experiencing problems. Assuming this observation is accurate, are you troubled by the principal's behavior? Why or why not?

3. Compare and contrast the leadership styles of Mr. Calbo and Dr. Werner. Which do you prefer?
4. Do you think that Dr. Werner should try to improve her relationship with teachers by visiting the faculty lounge more often? Why or why not?
5. Some principals try to maintain a positive relationship with teachers by interacting with them socially outside of school. Is this a good idea? Why or why not?
6. Assume you are asked to judge whether Dr. Werner is a competent principal. Beyond what you learned reading the case, what information, if any, would you want before making this decision?
7. What variables commonly contribute to perceptions of administrative performance?
8. Organizational cultures have "heroes." Is George Calbo, the previous principal, a hero in this school's culture? Why or why not?
9. Assume that you are seeking a position as assistant principal. Would you like to work for Dr. Werner? Why or why not?
10. Are the teachers behaving ethically when they talk about Dr. Werner in the lounge?
11. As described in this case, would you consider Dr. Werner's behavior to be closer to a transactional or a transformational leadership style?
12. If you were Peter, would you tell Dr. Werner that many appear not to support her leadership style? Why or why not?
13. Do you believe that age and gender contribute to perceptions of Dr. Werner's effectiveness as a principal? Defend your response.

SUGGESTED READINGS

Bass, B., & Avolio, B. (1989). Potential biases in leadership measures: How prototypes, leniency, and general satisfaction relate to ratings and rankings of transformational and transactional leadership constructs. *Educational and Psychological Measurement, 49*(3), 509-527.

Bennis, W., & Nanus, B. (1985). *Leaders: The strategies for taking charge.* New York: Harper & Row.

Blase, J. (1986). Leadership behavior of school principals in relation to teacher stress, satisfaction, and performance. *Journal of Humanistic Education and Development, 24*(4), 159-171.

Burns, J. (1978). *Leadership.* New York: Harper & Row.

Cunningham, W., & Gresso, D. (1993). *Cultural leadership: The culture of excellence in education* (pp. 41-50). Boston: Allyn & Bacon.

Erickson, H. (1985). Conflict and the female principal. *Phi Delta Kappan, 67,* 288-291.

Foster, W. (1988). The administrator as transformative intellectual. *Peabody Journal of Education, 66*(3), 5-18.

Hallinger, P. (1992). The evolving role of the American principals: From managerial to instructional to transformational leaders. *Journal of Educational Administration, 3*(3), 35-48.

Hart, A. (1991). Leader succession and socialization: A synthesis. *Review of Educational Research, 61,* 451-474.

Hart, A. (1993). *Principal succession: Establishing leadership in schools.* Albany, NY: State University of New York Press.

Kowalski, T., & Reitzug, U. (1993). *Contemporary school administration: An introduction.* New York: Longman (see chapter 10).

Krug, S. (1993). Leadership craft and the crafting of school leaders. *Phi Delta Kappan, 75*(3), 240-244.

Leithwood, K. (1992). The move toward transformational leadership. *Educational Leadership, 49*(5), 8-12.

Meadows, B. (1992). Nurturing cooperation and responsibility in a school environment. *Phi Delta Kappan, 73*(6), 480-481.

Ogawa, R. (1991). Enchantment, disenchantment, and accommodation: How a faculty made sense of the succession of its principal. *Educational Administration Quarterly, 27*(1), 30-60.

Roesner, C. (1987). Principals' leadership behavior—Do you see yourself as your subordinates see you? *NASSP Bulletin, 71*(502), 68-71.

Rossmiller, R. (1992). The secondary school principal and teachers' quality of work life. *Educational Management and Administration, 20*(3), 132-146.

Valentine, J., & Bowman, M. (1991). Effective principal, effective school: Does research support the assumption? *NASSP Bulletin, 75*(539), 1-7.

Wells, D. (1985). The perfect principal: A teacher's fantasy. *Principal, 65*(1), 27.

Yukl, G. (1989). *Leadership in organizations* (2nd ed.). Englewood Cliffs, NJ: Prentice-Hall (see chapter 10).

Case **5**

An Assistant Principal Who Does Not Fit the Image

BACKGROUND INFORMATION

Behavior in organizations, including schools, may be shaped by multiple variables that include personal characteristics (e.g., personality, needs, values, and beliefs), role expectations, and environmental conditions (e.g., social relationships, resources, institutional culture). For most people, rules, regulations, rewards, and punishments are sufficient to ensure conformity to prescribed roles and norms. But clearly there are those who do not conform, and their behavior presents a difficult challenge for administrators.

Role conflict—essentially opposing or competing perspectives related to job performance—can be caused by many different forces in an organization (Owens, 1998). For example, discord could be rooted in different perspectives of two individuals, such as a principal and an assistant superintendent; different perspectives of an individual and a group, such as a principal and the faculty; or even different perspectives within a single individual, such as a principal's desire to be liked conflicting with his or her desire to be an effective manager. Role conflict also can be created by uncertainty. As an example, a principal may receive two very different messages about taking risks to improve school performance. Although the board and superintendent may verbally encourage innovative, risk-taking behaviors, their policies and formal evaluation systems express an opposite set of values. The principal is left wondering which of the two conflicting messages is correct. Unfortunately, with a double bind there is no correct way to respond to the messages.

One major reason why role conflict is so prevalent in schools is that administrators are expected to wear so many different hats. Their job descriptions commonly include activities related to planning, evaluating, managing, mediating, organizing, facilitating, and leading, as well as serving as the formal representatives of their organizations (Kowalski, 1999). Disagreements may exist over the importance or nature of any of these distinctive roles.

This case is about role conflict being experienced by an assistant principal. He is recommended for reassignment essentially because he does not meet the superintendent's expectations with regard to personal appearance. The setting is an affluent suburban community.

KEY AREAS FOR REFLECTION

1. Relationship between organizational role and individual personality
2. Behavioral transitions between teaching and administration
3. Socialization and its effect on administrative behavior
4. Community environment and its effect on role expectations
5. Criteria for performance evaluation success
6. Communication processes and organizational conflict

THE CASE

The Community

Thomas Creek is located approximately 12 miles from a major city in the western part of New York State. With quiet, tree-lined streets and attractive homes, it is appropriately described as an upper-middle-class suburb. Nearly two-thirds of the adult residents are college graduates, with about 15 percent being self-employed professionals (e.g., lawyers, physicians, architects).

Two out of three Thomas Creek families have annual incomes over $150,000, and the community is racially and ethnically diverse. The following population profile was developed from official census data:

- Caucasian – 75 percent
- Asian American – 14 percent
- African American – 7 percent
- Hispanic – 2 percent
- Other – 2 percent

The population of the community is stable because very little land remains available for residential development. When houses go on the market, they usually sell within two or three weeks.

The School System

A brochure prepared by the local Chamber of Commerce describes Thomas Creek as "a community where cultural diversity and public education have been made assets." The school district is widely recognized as one of the best in the state. The high school recently received several citations from state and national groups for having excellent educational programs, and the Scholastic Aptitude Test scores for high school students have been among the top 5 percent in the state. The district includes three elementary schools (grades K–5), a middle school (grades 6–8), and a high school (grades 9–12). The overall enrollment is 2,500 students. The number of students in the system declined steadily from 1976, when the total enrollment peaked at 3,150. In the past decade, however, enrollments have remained relatively stable.

There are two nonpublic elementary schools located within the district's boundaries: (1) St. Jerome Catholic School (grades K–6) and (2) Thomas Creek Academy (grades K–5). Virtually all students from St. Jerome enter the public schools after sixth grade, while only about 40 percent of those attending Thomas Creek Academy do so.

Salaries in the school district are among the highest in the nation. Teachers at the top of the salary schedule are paid approximately $78,000. The superintendent's salary is over $160,000. The five members on the school board are elected to three-year terms. The central office professional staff includes the superintendent, an associate superintendent, a business manager, and a director of special services. Central administration is housed in a relatively new office building that is located near the high school.

The High School

All school facilities in the district are excellent, but Thomas Creek High School is clearly the "centerpiece" of the community's commitment to education. Although the building is nearly 30 years old, it has been kept in perfect condition. The latest multimedia technology—integrating voice, video, and keyed data—have been added throughout the facility.

The staff at the high school has been very stable. Most teachers have advanced degrees, and resignations for reasons other than retirement have been rare. In the past five years, for example, only three new teachers have joined the faculty. Only about 40 percent of the teachers at the high school belong to the teachers' association, and the relationships between the administration and the teachers have been very positive. An estimated 85 percent of the approximately 750 pupils enter a four-year institution of higher education within two years after graduation.

The Principal

Allen Miller became the principal of Thomas Creek High School four years ago. Prior to this assignment, he was the principal of a suburban high school near Cleveland. He is energetic and enthusiastic, frequently spending 10 to 12 hours a day at school or attending to school-related matters. Most parents, students, teachers, and other administrators describe him as competent, caring, and patient. They also see him as being "people-oriented," devoting much of his time communicating with students, teachers, and parents. Each week, for instance, he invites 10 to 15 parents to meet with him to discuss their views about public education and Thomas Creek High School. In order to devote so much time to meeting with people, he tries to avoid spending time with routine management responsibilities such as supervising lunch programs, dealing with discipline problems, and managing the maintenance staff.

Delegating management tasks to his assistant principal has not been difficult for Allen. He basically finds managerial work boring and recognizes that his real strengths are communication, human relations, and planning. In fact, he moved to Thomas Creek High School because the high school's modest enrollment would permit him to have greater control over his priorities as a principal.

The Assistant Principal

George Hopkins has worked at Thomas Creek High School for the last 27 years. He coached football and taught physical education for 22 of those years. He is quite popular with students who affectionately refer to him as the "enforcer" because he is in charge of discipline.

George Hopkins and Allen Miller are truly an odd couple. They are very different people. George prefers management functions, and he especially likes dealing with discipline. He believes that he has a special talent for reaching students who are having problems. Allen aspires to become a district superintendent, whereas George would be content as an assistant principal for the remainder of his career. The two administrators not only have different work preferences and career goals, they also look very different. The principal always wears a coat and tie to work, while George dresses very informally. His crewcut and wrinkled clothes lead school visitors to guess that he is still a coach.

Despite being very different people, Allen and George respect each other and have become friends. They believe that they constitute a highly effective partnership. In recognition of George's contributions, Allen has recommended him for merit salary increases in each of the last four years.

Key Central Office Administrators

Both the superintendent, Dr. Ronald O'Brien, and the associate superintendent for instruction, Dr. Valerie Daniels, have been in their positions for only two years. They had previously worked together in an Illinois school district. The other two central office administrators have worked in Thomas Creek for more than 15 years.

Dr. O'Brien has always worked in affluent suburban school districts. He became a superintendent when he was only 33 years old, and Thomas Creek is the fourth district in which he has held this post. The school board members have been very supportive of him, in part because he shares their philosophy about public education and administration. He is able to spend nearly 80 percent of his time as superintendent working with state and community groups because Dr. Daniels and the other two central office administrators essentially manage the district on a day-to-day basis.

Relationship between the High School Principal and the Superintendent

When he first arrived in Thomas Creek, Dr. O'Brien was concerned that Allen Miller did not have a doctoral degree. He expected the high school principal in this affluent community making over $100,000 to have this level of education. But after working with Mr. Miller for one year, his concern lessened because he received nothing but positive comments about the principal's performance. Just six months ago, he nominated Mr. Miller for the state's outstanding principal award. In the nomination letter, Dr. O'Brien wrote, "Allen Miller is an outstanding leader. He is a dedicated professional who provides a positive role model for the teachers and students. He represents the values and beliefs that make Thomas Creek High School one of the best secondary schools in the nation."

Although Dr. O'Brien has a very positive attitude toward the high school principal, his contact with him has not been extensive. Principals in the district report to the associate superintendent, Dr. Daniels. She visits each school about once a week and also conducts group meetings with the principals in her office once every two weeks. Dr. O'Brien only occasionally attends these sessions; he was present at five of them in the past year. In the last two years, Allen has had just three private meetings with the superintendent.

Evaluation Procedures

The associate superintendent completes performance evaluations for the school principals, and she presents the results in separate conferences with each of them. The superintendent typically attends these conferences because salary recommendations are also discussed. Administrative salary increases are based exclusively on merit and recommendations are based on the annual performance evaluation. Thus, the associate superintendent completes the evaluation and the superintendent determines a salary recommendation. For the most part, the administrative staff in the district likes the present procedure because they usually receive a higher percentage of pay increases in comparison to other employees.

Principals are required to evaluate their assistants and to present the results to the associate superintendent at their own evaluation conferences. Principals also make salary recommendations for their assistants at that time.

The Incident

Evaluation conferences for principals are scheduled in late March. Principals review their evaluations of their assistants before receiving their own evaluations. Allen assumed that this year's meeting with Dr. Daniels would be routine. His conference was scheduled for 9:40 A.M. and he expected to be back in his office at least by 11:00 A.M.

Allen entered the superintendent's office, greeted by the two administrators, and took his customary seat at the small, round table. As Allen anticipated, he was asked to summarize his assistant principal's evaluation.

The district's rating instrument includes 24 items. George Hopkins received 19 "excellent" ratings, 4 "above average" ratings, and 1 "average" rating. The lowest rating was for personal appearance.

"You know old coaches," Allen commented with a smile, "they never seem to stop looking like old coaches."

It was apparent to Allen that the superintendent and associate superintendent were not amused by his comment. He quickly retracted his grin. Then there was an awkward moment of silence. Allen sensed that something was wrong. He became uncomfortable, but he wanted someone else to break the silence.

Dr. Daniels finally did so. She looked directly into Allen's eyes and said, "This community is considered a great place to live, and Thomas Creek High School is considered to be a very effective institution. Clearly, your leadership has served to enhance the school's reputation. But when our administrators cease to look and act like competent leaders, our reputation suffers. Your own ratings reveal that George has a problem in this area. He rarely wears a tie or coat, and he just isn't very well groomed. Visitors to the school could easily mistake him for a custodian."

Allen was immediately concerned by this harsh assessment. While it was clear that George did not dress like other Thomas Creek administrators, he was puzzled why this matter had suddenly become so important. He directed that question to Dr. Daniels.

"George has always looked and dressed in the same manner. If this is such a critical issue, why did you approve my recommendation to give him a maximum merit raise last year?"

Dr. O'Brien did not wait for his associate to answer. "We did it for you, Allen. We weighed not supporting your recommendation against our concerns about George, and we decided that it was more important to support you. Don't forget we were both new to this district last year. It would have been quite awkward for us to overturn your recommendation. But now, things are different."

"So where are we?" Allen asked. "I'm again recommending George for the highest merit category. I think his overall performance has been outstanding."

"We think this matter goes beyond a question of merit salary," Dr. Daniels answered. "We believe George should be replaced as assistant principal. He can return to teaching at the High School, or he can be assigned to teach at the Middle School. He will have the option of teaching driver education during the summer, so he won't have much of a salary reduction."

Allen stared across the table in disbelief. After collecting his thoughts, he responded, "Please understand, I had no idea you felt this strongly about George. I really don't agree that he should be reassigned. George is a good administrator. In my opinion, he has never received the recognition he deserves. My job will become more difficult if he is no longer assistant principal. He has been as loyal and dedicated as any person with whom I have been associated. He doesn't deserve to be treated this way. I wish one of you would have discussed this with me earlier."

Dr. O'Brien again entered the conversation. "Allen, listen. You don't have to take the blame for this. I will explain to the board that Valerie and I made this decision. George won't be able to blame you. Any outrage will be directed at us—not you. We just don't want you fighting us publicly on this issue."

"He's right, Allen," Dr. Daniels interjected. "You have provided excellent leadership at the High School; but with an assistant who projects a proper image, you could be doing even more. Believe me—Dr. O'Brien and I have given this much thought. There are many administrators who can be as effective as George handling discipline and management responsibilities."

Dr. O'Brien reached over and put his hand on Allen's shoulder. "We want your assurance that you will not fight this decision."

THE CHALLENGE

Place yourself in Allen's position. After identifying alternative courses of action, select the one that you believe is most effective.

KEY ISSUES/QUESTIONS

1. Do you believe that the community environment is an important variable in this case? Explain your response.
2. What are some possible reasons for the personal appearance of the assistant principal?
3. Why do you believe the superintendent and associate superintendent are placing so much emphasis on personal appearance?
4. Do you believe that the superintendent and associate superintendent are behaving ethically?
5. To what extent is the principal responsible for what occurred in this case? What could he have done, if anything, to avert this confrontation?
6. In private corporations, standards for dress are typically tied to positions. For example, the president or a vice president of a bank is unlikely to come to work dressed casually. What values and beliefs cause organizations to have dress norms for executives?
7. Do you believe that there is a relationship between administrative appearance and job performance? Why or why not?
8. From reading the case, what judgments can you make about communication among administrators in this school district? What parts of the case provide clues about communication patterns?
9. Is personal appearance a valid criterion for evaluating administrative performance? Why or why not?
10. Should the overall effectiveness of a school be a factor in evaluating principals and assistant principals?
11. Typically, administrators learn dress norms through a process of socialization. What is socialization?
12. What are some possible reasons why socialization did not influence the behavior of the assistant principal in this case?
13. Is it appropriate to have different dress codes for administrators and teachers?

SUGGESTED READINGS

Calabrese, R., & Tucker-Ladd, P. (1991). The principal and assistant principal: A mentoring relationship. *NASSP Bulletin, 75*(533), 67-74.

Cantwell, Z. (1993). School-based leadership and the professional socialization of the assistant principal. *Urban Education, 28*(1), 49-68.

Duke, D. (1992). Concepts of administrative effectiveness and the evaluation of school administrators. *Journal of Personnel Evaluation in Education, 6*(2), 103-121.

Fulton, O. (1987). Basic competencies of the assistant principal. *NASSP Bulletin, 71*(501), 52.

Hamner, T., & Turk, J. (1987). Organizational determinants of leader behavior and authority. *Journal of Applied Psychology, 72*, 647-682.

Hess, F. (1985). The socialization of the assistant principal: From the perspective of the local district. *Education and Urban Society, 18*(1), 93-106.

Hoy, W., Newland, W., & Blaxovsky, R. (1977). Subordinate loyalty to superior, esprit, and aspects of bureaucratic structure. *Educational Administration Quarterly, 13*(1), 71-85.

Immegart, G. (1988). Leadership and leader behavior. In N. Boyan (Ed.), *Handbook of research on educational administration* (pp. 259-278). New York: Longman.

Kowalski, T., & Reitzug, U. (1993). *Contemporary school administration: An introduction.* New York: Longman (see chapters 7, 10).

Lang, R. (1986). The hidden dress code dilemma. *Clearing House, 59*(6), 277-279.

Marshall, C. (1992). *The assistant principal: Leadership chores and challenges.* Newbury Park, CA: Corwin.

Marshall, C. (1985). Professional shock: The enculturation of the assistant principal. *Education and Urban Society, 18*(1), 28-58.

Marshall, C., & Greenfield, W. (1985). The socialization of the assistant principal: Implications for school leadership. *Education and Urban Society, 18*(1), 3-8.

Norton, M., & Kriekard, J. (1987). Real and ideal competencies for the assistant principal. *NASSP Bulletin, 71*(501), 23-30.

Owens, R. C. (1998). *Organizational behavior in education* (6th ed). Boston: Allyn and Bacon.

Peterson, K. (1984). Mechanisms of administrative control over managers in educational organizations. *Administrative Science Quarterly, 29*, 573-597.

Case **6**

Using Committees to Make Key Decisions

BACKGROUND INFORMATION

At the very heart of leadership is the process of making decisions. For this reason, the science of decision has become increasingly important in professional preparation. Decision-making models may be predicated on normative (what should occur) or descriptive (what actually occurs) theory. Reviewing research on this topic, Estler (1988) outlined four models that were cogent to the practice of educational administration: rational-bureaucratic, participatory, political, and organized anarchy. The first two address desired conditions; the others seek to explicate behavior.

Research conducted in schools and districts reveals that several variables may influence the manner in which administrators make decisions. For example, behavior might be affected by

- personal biases, beliefs, and experiences
- a formal role stipulated by the organization
- norms associated with organizational culture
- political pressures exerted by individuals and groups
- personal and professional ethics

Through much of the twentieth century, management scholars recognized that personal, social, and political variables could influence organizational decisions, causing inconsistencies of behavior and ultimately inefficiency. Thus, they formulated rational and easily understood decision-making models intended to control individualism and errors. Peter Drucker (1974), for instance, reduced the act of organizational decision making to five critical steps: defining the problem, analyzing the problem, developing alternative solutions, selecting the best solution, and taking action. But researchers studying school and district administrators have found that such normative theories often have only a limited effect on behavior. In part this is because schools are sociopolitical systems in which power and authority is distributed among formal and informal groups. These entities vie for scarce resources so that their respective needs and wants can be addressed. Tensions created by this competition often deter rationality and democratic procedures (Kowalski, 1999).

This case centers on a new superintendent's decision to create a special committee to study a lingering problem in the district. Several administrators do not support the superintendent's action, and they speculate about his motives.

KEY AREAS FOR REFLECTION

1. Decision-making theories
2. Conflict and conflict resolution
3. Democratic decision making
4. Subordinate expectations of a new superintendent
5. Leadership style

THE CASE

The Community

Fullmer, a city of 45,000 residents, is the county seat of Oxford County (population 78,000). Located in the western part of a mid-Atlantic state, it is known for its scenic beauty. In recent years, the population has increased about 1 percent every two years. The growth is largely attributable to the development of condominiums and apartment complexes designed for retirees.

Over the past 20 years, most of the counties in this part of the state developed industrial parks, enterprise zones, and tax abatement programs in an effort to attract both foreign and domestic companies. This economic development tactic was not implemented in Oxford County, however, because many residents feared that increased industrial activity would change the county's character. There are only a handful of small companies scattered across the county—several of their executives have recently announced that they are considering relocating their companies in the industrial parks of neighboring counties.

In addition to Oxford County's natural beauty, three factors have attracted retirees. They are reasonable real estate costs, low taxes, and above-average health care. Six years ago, a new hospital was built in Fullmer offering modern medical care to county residents. The structure, costing more than $95 million, is considered one of the most modern in the state.

The School District

The Oxford County School District serves the entire county population. The system enrolls 19,700 students and operates the following attendance centers:

- Two high schools (grades 9–12)
- Four middle schools (grades 6–8)
- Thirteen elementary schools (grades K–5)
- One vocational school (also includes an alternative program for secondary students not enrolled in a regular high school program)

Enrollment in the school system has declined just about 1 percent over the past decade, but in the last two years, kindergarten enrollments have declined by 5 percent.

The district's central office staff has remained stable over the past 10 years. Data below show each staff member's name, position title, and length of service in the present position and in the school district.

		Length of Service	
Name	*Position*	*Position*	*District*
Bob Andrevet	assistant superintendent – curriculum	18	24
Pamela Davis	assistant superintendent – business	12	15
Jake Barnes	director of personnel	10	27
Neil Vickers	director of transportation	17	17
Iran Sults	director of maintenance	21	26
Anne Major	director of federal programs	16	19
Margo Jasik	director of special education	16	16

Superintendent Dr. Rudy Quillen is in his first year with the school district, having replaced Orville Cruthers who retired after having held the position for the previous 18 years.

The Incident

Dr. Quillen arrived in Oxford County in mid-July. For the past three years, he had been superintendent of a much smaller district (enrollment 2,400) in a neighboring state. Several Oxford County school board members met Dr. Quillen at a national convention when they attended a presentation he made on goal setting. Impressed with the topic and delivery, they encouraged him to apply for the impending vacancy in their district. At age 38, Rudy Quillen was in good health, experienced (he had already accumulated 12 years of administrative experience), and eager to provide leadership for a much larger school system.

A controversy that faced Dr. Quillen almost immediately when he arrived in Oxford County involved the use of petty cash funds by principals. These funds had existed for as long as anyone could remember. Recently, however, Dr. Davis, the assistant superintendent for business, challenged their necessity. Principals used these funds for emergencies or to purchase small items, and they were adamantly opposed to them being discontinued.

Dr. Davis had made several unsuccessful attempts to persuade the previous superintendent to eliminate petty cash funds. The employment of Dr. Quillen gave her another opportunity to pursue this objective. She raised the topic in her first meeting with the new superintendent. She told Dr. Quillen that auditors believed the potential risks associated with these funds far outweighed their benefits. In addition, she informed him that this topic had been considered by the previous superintendent and school board; and as a result of information she provided, two of the seven members openly supported her position.

Dr. Quillen's experiences with petty cash funds, both as a superintendent and principal, were not negative. Based on his discussion with Dr. Davis, he concluded that her opposition was premised on potential rather than actual problems. Even so, he told Dr. Davis that he would seek counsel regarding their use. He talked to the attorney for the school district, the attorney for the state school boards' association, and several officials in the school finance division of the state department of education. These individuals merely confirmed what Dr. Quillen already knew—petty cash funds were legal, but the funds could create problems if they were not managed properly.

Dr. Quillen met monthly with the principals and central office administrators, and he decided to discuss petty cash funds with them at the November meeting. Dr. Davis spoke first and she summarized her concerns. Dr. Quillen then shared comments he had received from the attorneys and the state department employees. Several principals reacted. They noted that petty cash funds served a useful purpose, and they opposed Dr. Davis's recommendation to eliminate them.

Even though she was clearly outnumbered, Dr. Davis did not back down. "You know that mistakes could be made. Having petty cash funds in each school is simply not good management. I'm willing to set up a district petty cash fund. This arrangement still allows you to respond to emergencies or to purchase small items immediately. One fund gives us greater management control."

"That's just the problem," one of the high school principals answered. "More control. Every time we turn around, things are being centralized in this district. What makes you think mistakes cannot be made in the central office?"

Judging that the issue was not going to be resolved quickly, Dr. Quillen announced, "Clearly, there are different opinions on this matter. Let's move on and we'll revisit the petty cash funds at a later date."

Pamela Davis feared that Dr. Quillen was essentially putting the topic on a back burner. Before the superintendent could begin discussion of the next agenda item, she spoke again. "There are some serious management questions surrounding this practice, and we accomplish nothing by pretending that the possibility of legal problems doesn't exist," she said with emotion. "Just because I may stand alone on this issue doesn't mean that you are right and I am wrong. At the very least, we need to study this issue objectively."

Before any of the other administrators could respond to her, Dr. Quillen spoke. "First, I want to make it clear that I'm not suggesting that we ignore this issue. Pamela has a job to do and she's trying to do it. I'm sure she is not enjoying this. Second, I agree with her that we should study this matter objectively and in greater detail. But the question is, who is going to conduct the study?"

Anticipating that Dr. Davis and the principals would have different answers to his question, the superintendent said he would take the matter under advisement and announce a decision at the next meeting of the administrative group in two weeks. He invited everyone present to send him recommendations or suggestions in the interim.

When the next meeting of the administrative group began, the administrators were anxious to hear Dr. Quillen's decision. Not only were they deeply interested in the matter at hand, but they also recognized that the decision would reveal how their new superintendent managed conflict. The principals were all guessing about the outcome. Some thought that Dr. Quillen would skillfully avoid dealing with the issue, even though he promised to pursue further study. Others were divided over whether his decision would favor Dr. Davis or them.

To no one's disappointment, the first agenda item was petty cash funds.

"I have looked at this matter carefully," the superintendent began. "I remain convinced that this issue should be thoroughly examined. If for no other reason, there are valid points being made on both sides of the argument. Some believe that this is a political and not a fiscal matter. Persons who hold this view have generally urged me to appoint Bob Andrevet to conduct the study. The rationale is that Bob is aware of the needs facing principals. Another suggestion is that Dr. Davis be appointed to conduct the study. This position has been endorsed by two of the school board members. Several others have urged me to appoint a committee consisting of individuals who can be objective. I have decided to pursue this alternative. I will be appointing an ad hoc committee consisting of two teachers, a parent who is an accountant, a high school senior, a parent who is an attorney, and Anne Major, the director of federal programs. Anne will chair the committee, and Bob and Pamela will be nonvoting advisors to the committee."

The room fell silent. After about 30 seconds, one of the principals asked, "How can you appoint a committee without any of the principals being involved? We're the ones most affected by any recommendation that will be made."

Dr. Quillen answered. "If we want an objective analysis, we can't have people who already have their minds made up serving on the committee. No doubt, principals will be asked to meet with the committee to share their views. Every person on this committee is sufficiently detached from the issue to ensure that they will be objective."

Immediately after the meeting, Dr. Davis spoke with Dr. Quillen in his office. She expressed disappointment with his decision. She was convinced that the principals would persuade the committee members that this was purely a political matter and—given their numbers—they would be able to sway the committee's conclusions and recommendations.

"If I knew that you would treat this matter by appointing a committee with parents, students, and teachers, I would never have raised this issue. There are two things that really bother me," she told the superintendent. "First and most importantly, I see this as a slap in the face. My office should handle fiscal matters. Otherwise, why have an assistant superintendent for business? Second, by creating this committee, you have reduced an important management issue to a political argument. Sooner or later we're going to have a real problem and when that happens, you can bet that Bob and the principals will not accept responsibility."

Dr. Quillen asked her to be patient and to give his approach an opportunity to work .

Bob Andrevet also visited the superintendent after the meeting. He noted that he and principals also were concerned about having teachers, parents, and students making a recommendation on such an important matter. He feared that Dr. Davis would be able to influence them by suggesting that serious legal problems would likely occur if the funds were continued.

THE CHALLENGE

Imagine that you are Dr. Quillen. Would you pursue the decision you announced to the administrative group? Would you alter the membership of the ad hoc committee? Would you abandon the idea of an ad hoc committee?

KEY ISSUES/QUESTIONS

1. Assume that the superintendent's objective was to eradicate the conflict over petty cash funds as soon as possible. How could he have done this?
2. What are the advantages and disadvantages of eliminating the conflict as soon as possible?
3. What are the advantages and disadvantages of allowing principals to have petty cash funds?
4. While the assistant superintendent for business frames the problem from a managerial perspective, the principals view it as a political matter. Describe the differences in these two perspectives.
5. Duties and responsibilities in school districts are commonly divided into distinct divisions. In this case, two divisions—curriculum and business—vie for jurisdiction over a decision on petty cash funds. What are the advantages and disadvantages of dividing functions into organizational divisions?
6. What is an ad hoc committee? What are the advantages and disadvantages of using such committees?
7. Evaluate the superintendent's decision not to place any principals on the ad hoc committee. Do you support this decision? Why or why not?
8. Dr. Davis apparently has the support of at least two of the seven board members. To what extent is this fact relevant to the case?
9. The principals believe that the decision on studying petty cash funds will reveal how Dr. Quillen will deal with conflict. Do you agree? Why or why not?
10. If you were a principal in this district, how would you interpret the superintendent's decision to appoint an ad hoc committee?
11. Will the use of a committee increase the likelihood that this issue will be resolved politically?
12. Evaluate the behavior of Dr. Davis. Was it appropriate for her to raise this issue so quickly with the new superintendent?
13. Dr. Davis offered to replace the existing petty cash funds with one district-wide petty cash fund that she would administer. The principals obviously did

not support her idea. Assess the merits of her suggestion. Is it a legitimate compromise?

14. One of the concerns voiced by the principals is excessive centralization. What does this mean? Why would principals be opposed to centralization?

SUGGESTED READINGS

Black, J., & English, F. (1986). *What they don't tell you in schools of education about school administration*. Lancaster, PA: Technomic (see chapter 1).

Boston, J. (1994). In search of common ground. *Educational Leadership, 51*(4), 38–40.

Brunner, C. (1998). The new superintendency supports an innovation: Collaborative decision making. *Contemporary Education, 69*(2), 79–82.

Conway, J. (1984). The myth, mystery and mastery of participative decision making in education. *Educational Administration Quarterly, 20*(3), 11–40.

Cunningham, W., & Gresso, D. (1993). *Cultural leadership: The culture of excellence in education*. Boston: Allyn & Bacon (see chapter 9).

Drucker, P. (1974). *Management: Tasks, responsibilities, practices*. New York: Harper & Row.

Estler, S. (1988). Decision making. In N. Boyan (Ed.) *Handbook of research on educational administration* (pp. 305–320). New York: Longman.

Feld, M. (1988). The bureaucracy, the superintendent, and change. *Education and Urban Society*, 417–444.

Gold, ., & O'Shea, C. (1990). A culture for change. *Educational Leadership, 47*(8), 41–43.

Iv 993). Shared decision making improves staff and efficiency. *NASSP Bulletin, 77*(550), 9.

. (1992). Shared decision making works! *Educational Leadership, 50*(1), 36–38.

i, T. J. (1999). *The school superintendent: Theory, practice, and cases*. Upper Saddle River, NJ: Merentice Hall. (See Chapter 13.)

ki, G. (1987). Values and decision making in educational administration. *Educational Administration Quarterly, 23*(4), 70–82.

ws, B. (1987). The influence of participants' values on group process and decision making. *North Central Association Quarterly, 61*(3), 440–443.

ws, B. (1990). The rewards and risks of shared leadership. *Phi Delta Kappan, 71*(7), 5

r, E. (1995). Shared decision making make for better decisions. T letter, 11(6), 1–4.

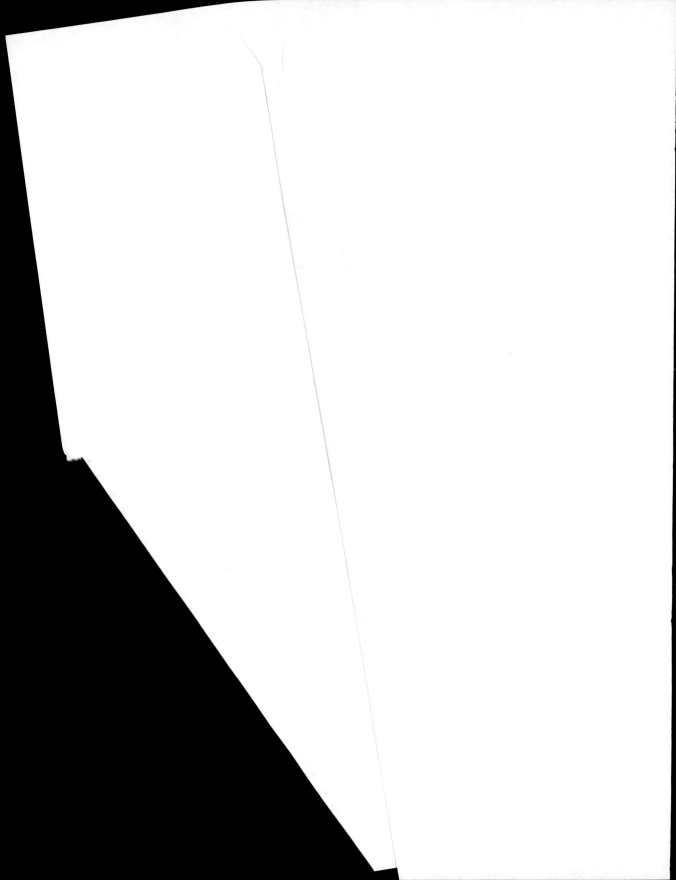

Case **7**

The Principal Changes Some Valued Rules

BACKGROUND INFORMATION

Past practices and the preponderance of evidence suggest that principals play a central role in school effectiveness. Thus, when a school is not functioning up to expectation, replacing this administrator is often the first action considered. However, schools are terribly complex organizations, and in some instances the ability of any one individual to restructure long-standing values, beliefs, and practices is limited.

Often when principals propose change, the processes they employ are at least as important as the ideas they promote. Teachers usually resent being coerced, and the fact that much of their work occurs behind a closed classroom door permits them to be highly resistant to "top-down" change initiatives.

This case is about an experienced urban elementary school principal who voluntarily transfers to a difficult assignment. Once there, he enacts a number of new rules concerning discipline and student retention in grade. Conflict between the principal's philosophy and the faculty leads to calls for his removal. As you analyze this case, pay particular attention to how the principal attempted to implement change as well as his specific initiatives.

KEY AREAS FOR REFLECTION

1. A principal's ability to impose change
2. Conflicting values and beliefs among educators
3. How groups and individuals interact and exchange power in schools
4. Communication processes between the principal and faculty
5. Organizational climate and culture

THE CASE

Oliver Wendell Holmes Elementary School is the third-oldest facility in this California city. Located in a neighborhood that has deteriorated substantially in the past three decades, the drab brick building and its rectangular shape exemplify the unimaginative nature of school facility design in the 1940s. The sidewalks around the school are cracked and soiled with endless works of graffiti, written in English and Spanish and displaying different bright colors. The playground is strewn with weeds and litter, and the broken swings and teeter-totters suggest that school officials have given up their attempts to keep the area functional.

John Lattimore has been the school's principal for the last three years. A veteran administrator, he previously served in the same capacity at three of the district's other elementary schools. He has been an educator for 31 years and a principal for 22 of them. When the position at Holmes became vacant, John was the only principal in the district who applied. His peers were puzzled by his decision. Why would an experienced principal want to leave a school in one of the district's best neighborhoods to go to a school in one of the district's worst neighborhoods? Also, why would John Lattimore want to leave a school where he had widespread support to go to a school where there was a revolving door on the principal's office?

Central office administrators who had the responsibility of selecting a new principal for Holmes also questioned John's motives. In his interview with the superintendent and assistant superintendent for elementary education, John gave the following brief and direct explanation: "I'm ready for a new challenge. I think Holmes will benefit from my leadership, and I will benefit from the change in scenery. I have always liked a challenge."

Dr. William Gray, the superintendent, had two choices. He could either oblige Mr. Lattimore by letting him transfer to Holmes Elementary School, or he could hire an inexperienced principal. Accepting the former alternative was an easy decision.

The three years at Holmes Elementary School passed quickly for John. During the first year, he tried to adjust to the school and neighborhood. He met with parents, got acquainted with students, and met frequently with the school's staff. The second year was marked by substantial changes in rules and regulations. In particular, John revamped the school's discipline program, which had relied heavily on corporal punishment and suspensions. He also altered the criteria for retaining students in first grade (Holmes had the highest percentage retention rate of any school in the district). At first, Mr. Lattimore sought teacher support for these changes, but after failing to do so, he implemented them anyway.

His third year at Holmes has been steeped in conflict. Mr. Lattimore is somewhat of an enigma to many of the teachers. On the one hand, they view his policies toward students as being too lenient but on the other hand they view his administrative style as being too dictatorial. One teacher summarized her feelings thusly, "He appears to be friendly and caring, but I'm not sure that he is really helping students. In the end, he does as he pleases, so I don't even bother arguing with him anymore."

Dissatisfaction with Mr. Lattimore's leadership style and decisions has clearly grown during the past year. Largely influenced by teachers, a group of approximately 50 parents signed a petition demanding that he be reassigned to another position in the district. Nearly 70 percent of the faculty signed a letter written to Dr. Janelle Danton, assistant superintendent for elementary education, stating similar sentiments. It read as follows:

Dear Dr. Danton:

Undoubtedly you receive many complaints from teachers who disagree with their principals. Please do not consider this letter to be frivolous. Over the past two and one-half years, the teachers at Oliver Wendell Holmes Elementary School have observed the leadership style of Mr. John Lattimore. While he is a friendly, industrious, and intelligent person, his approach to dealing with children at this school simply is ineffective.

Most of the children who attend Holmes come from one-parent families living below the poverty level. Many receive little or no direction with regard to their personal behavior outside of school. Even the parents and guardians of the students recognize that the school must be a major source of discipline. Since becoming our principal, Mr. Lattimore has

- weakened discipline rules and regulations
- prohibited the use of corporal punishment
- discouraged student suspensions
- encouraged social promotions

While we share his sentiment that many of our students lack love and understanding, we reject his apparent conclusion that the school can be parent, psychologist, social worker, and friend to every student. Allowing a disruptive child to remain in a classroom deprives other students of their opportunities to learn.

Unfortunately, we are never asked to join Mr. Lattimore in studying needed changes or to democratically participate in making decisions. Nor are we permitted to voice our concerns at faculty meetings. If we disagree with any of his proposed changes, we must state our objections privately in his office.

It is with heavy hearts that we must notify you that we have no confidence in Mr. John Lattimore as principal of Oliver Wendell Holmes Elementary School. Perhaps his talents can be utilized more productively in another assignment. He is a good person who means well. He cannot, however, effectively lead this school. We ask that he be removed as principal as soon as possible.

Respectfully,

(signed by 18 of the 26 teachers)

cc: Dr. Gray, superintendent
    School Board members
    Ms. Hutchins, president of the local teachers' union

Although John knew that some teachers objected to his leadership style, he had underestimated the intensity and extent of the discontent. His eyes were opened, however, when Dr. Danton showed him a copy of the teachers' letter and the parents' petition.

The school district has 87 elementary schools, most in inner-city neighborhoods. Complaints about principals were not uncommon, but a letter of no confidence signed by this many teachers was indeed rare. Dr. Danton met with John one day after having received the negative communications. John Lattimore told his supervisor that he was surprised and hurt by the petition and the letter. He also expressed anger. He felt that the teachers had acted unethically by trying to remove him as principal.

"You mean you had no idea there was this level of concern among your staff members?" Dr. Danton asked.

"Well," John responded, "several teachers voiced displeasure with my changing some rules and regulations related to discipline. You know how that goes, Janelle—you were a principal. Teachers don't always agree with you, and we have to respect the fact that everyone is entitled to an opinion. Unfortunately, someone has to be in charge; someone has to make the difficult decisions. No, I knew there was some displeasure. I just didn't think it was so widespread."

John Lattimore and Janelle Danton had been friends for many years. They served together as elementary principals in the district for nearly a decade, and John wrote a letter of support for Janelle when she applied for her current position. Their personal relationship made the meeting more difficult.

"John, is it true that you didn't discuss the rules and regulations with them before you made changes? Is it accurate that you didn't give them an opportunity for input?" Dr. Danton inquired.

"The changes were discussed in faculty meetings. We never voted on them, but I did explain the changes and my reasons for them. Very few teachers came to my office to voice opposition. Consequently, I thought that most of the teachers were willing to give my ideas a chance. Listen, I've been around these children for a long time—and so have you. Their lives are filled with grief and disappointments. Why should school become another enemy and just another miserable experience? Maybe, just maybe, by showing some love and compassion for these children we could turn a few lives around. Maybe we could convince a few children that someone cares. Isn't that important? What do we accomplish when we suspend a child from school? We're punishing the parent, not the child. How will we ever teach these children to be responsible for their own behavior if we constantly rely on negative reinforcements?"

"What about this issue of social promotions?" asked the assistant superintendent.

"Failing children who are already at risk simply does not work. They prefer to say that I favor social promotions. I prefer to say that I condemn failing children when doing so just makes it more likely they will never graduate from high school."

Dr. Danton looked at him and asked, "John, would you consider taking another assignment at this time? I can arrange for you to work with me here in the central office. I need a director of pupil personnel services. It would mean an increase in salary, and it would be a good way to resolve this problem. Now I don't want you to think that I'm just trying to get you out of the school. I really would like to have you here working with me in the central office. You've earned it. You have put in your time in the trenches. What do you think?"

"Janelle, you know the answer. I've had other opportunities to work in the central office. Being away from the students is not my cup of tea. No, I'm sorry. I'm not going to run away from this. I think I am right and if you give me time, I can turn the parents and teachers around. Why is everyone so sure that my changes won't be successful? I thought the principal was supposed to be the school's leader. All I'm asking for is the opportunity to do my job."

"But John, I don't know if we have time. Dr. Gray may demand that we resolve this right away. Let me think about it for a day or so. I'll call as soon as I make a decision. And John, you should know that I can't make any promises. Dr. Gray doesn't want another big fight with the union, and this whole thing is quickly becoming a political bomb." With that being said, John got up from his chair and nodded that he understood. He shook Dr. Danton's hand and left her office.

As soon as he departed, Dr. Danton thought about the fact that Mr. Lattimore also belonged to a union. The district's principals' union was nearly as powerful politically as the teachers' union. She concluded that the conflict at Holmes Elementary School had the potential of being a "no-win" situation. She sat at her desk and thought about what she would do concerning this matter when she met with the superintendent in several hours.

THE CHALLENGE

Assume the position of assistant superintendent for elementary education. What are your options for resolving this matter? Which course of action would you pursue?

KEY ISSUES/QUESTIONS

1. Do you consider Mr. Lattimore to be dictatorial? Why or why not?
2. Evaluate Mr. Lattimore's practices with regard to introducing change proposals and soliciting input. If you were the principal, what procedures would you have used?
3. Assume that the principal accepts the offer to be reassigned to the central office. Is this an acceptable resolution to the conflict? Why or why not?
4. Is the principal correct in his judgment that corporal punishment and suspensions provide negative reinforcement that deters the development of self-discipline?
5. Discuss the rights of the troubled child in relation to classmates. Are the teachers correct in their contention that permitting a disruptive child to remain in the classroom deprives other students of their opportunity to learn?
6. Did the teachers act ethically in asking parents to sign the petition? Did they act ethically in signing the letter?
7. Who should have the authority to determine policy over matters such as corporal punishment and retention?

8. Based on information presented in the case, the faculty at Holmes Elementary School played no role in employing a new principal. Do you support this practice? Why or why not?
9. What positive actions might bring the parents, teachers, and principal together to address this problem?
10. Do the goals of the principal justify his means in this case? Why or why not?
11. What role does school culture play in this conflict?
12. Based on information presented in the case, it appears that elementary schools in this district were able to set their own rules and regulations concerning discipline and student retention. If true, what are the advantages and disadvantages of this flexibility?
13. Often administrators do not adjust their behavior when they assume new positions. Why could this decision be troublesome?

SUGGESTED READINGS

Blase, J. (1991). The micropolitical orientation of teachers toward closed school principals. *Education and Urban Society, 23*(4), 356-378.

Blase, J. (1985). The phenomenology of teacher stress: Implications for organizational theory and research. *Administrator's Notebook, 31*(7), 1-4.

Blase, J. (1984). Teacher coping and school principal behaviors. *Contemporary Education, 5*(1), 21-25.

Docking, R. (1985). Changing teacher pupil control ideology and teacher anxiety. *Journal of Education for Teaching, 11*(1), 63-76.

Gaziel, H. (1990). School bureaucratic structure, locus of control, and alienation among primary teachers. *Research in Education,* (44), 55-66.

Hartzell, G., & Petrie, T. (1992). The principal and discipline: Working with school structures, teachers, and students. *The Clearing House, 65*(6), 376-380.

Houston, W. R. (1998). Innovators as catalysts for restructuring schools. *Educational Forum, 62*(3), 204-210.

Hoy, W., Tarter, C., & Witkoskie, L. (1992). Faculty trust in colleagues: Linking the principal with school effectiveness. *Journal of Research and Development in Education, 26*(1), 38-45.

Johnson, P. E., Holder, C., Carrick, C., & Sanford, N. (1998). A model for restructuring governance: Developing a culture of respect and teamwork. *ERS Spectrum, 16*(2), 28-36.

Johnston, G., & Venable, B. (1986). A study of teacher loyalty to the principal: Rule administration and hierarchical influence of the principal. *Educational Administration Quarterly, 22*(4), 4-27.

Kowalski, T., & Reitzug, U. (1993). *Contemporary school administration: An introduction.* New York: Longman (see chapters 9, 10).

Lane, B. A. (1992). Cultural leaders in effective schools: The builders and brokers of excellence. *NASSP Bulletin, 76*(541), 85-96.

Lowe, R., & Gervais, R. (1984). Tackling a problem school. *Principal, 63*(5), 8-12.

Maynard, B. (1983). Is your discipline policy part of your discipline problem? *Executive Educator, 5*(3), 26-27.

McDaniel, T. (1986). School discipline in perspective. *Clearing House, 59*(8), 369-370.

Menacker, J. (1988). Legislating school discipline: The application of a systemwide discipline code for schools in a large urban district. *Urban Education, 23*(1), 12-23.

Menacker, J., Weldon, W., & Hurwitz, E. (1989). School order and safety as community issues. *Phi Delta Kappan, 71*(1), 39-40, 55-56.

Neuman, S. (1992). Editorial: The negative consequences of the self-esteem movement. *Alberta Journal of Educational Research, 38*(4), 251-253.

Prestine, N. (1993). Shared decision making in restructuring essential schools: The role of the principal. *Planning and Changing, 22*(3-4), 160-177.

Reitman, A. (1988). Corporal punishment in schools— The ultimate violence. *Children's Legal Rights Journal, 9*(33), 6-13.

Rosen, M. (1993). Sharing power: A blueprint for collaboration. *Principal, 72*(3), 37-39.

Sashkin, M. (1988). The visionary principal: School leadership for the next century. *Education and Urban Society, 20*(3), 239-249.

Sikes, P. (1992). Imposed change and the experienced teacher. In M. Fullan and A. Hargreaves (Eds.), *Teacher development and educational change* (pp. 36-55). Bristol, PA: Falmer Press.

Slavin, R., & Madden, N. (1989). What works for students at risk: A research synthesis. *Educational Leadership, 46*(5), 4-13.

Smylie, M. (1992). Teacher participation in school decision making: Assessing willingness to participate. *Educational Evaluation and Policy Analysis, 14*(1), 53-67.

Thomas, W. (1988). To solve "the discipline problem," mix clear rules with consistent consequences. *American School Board Journal, 175*(6), 30-31.

Wager, B. (1993). No more suspension: Creating a shared ethical culture. *Educational Leadership, 50*(4), 34-37.

Case **8**

An Effort to Study Site-Based Management

BACKGROUND INFORMATION

Criticisms of public education during the last two decades of the twentieth century prompted a number of conclusions about elementary and secondary schools. They included the following:

- Because authority in public education has remained highly centralized, states have controlled local districts and districts have controlled individual schools. This bureaucratic-like arrangement has prevented meaningful change.
- Schools could not improve significantly by simply doing more of what they were already doing; organizational restructuring and cultural transformation were necessary.
- If schools and teachers were more independent, more individualization of instruction could occur. This individualization would increase productivity.
- Public schools should reflect the society they serve. Hence, community participation and democratic decision making should be central to school improvement.

These judgments provide a foundation for current reform efforts that pursue greater liberty and excellence simultaneously.

The concept of site-based management (SBM) has become the most popular approach to decentralization. Although it may be applied in different ways, the idea basically seeks to create councils that play an instrumental role in governance and decision making. Not all educators, however, support SBM. Opposition ranges from philosophical objections, such as fears of inequalities among and within districts, to legal concerns, such as the potentialities of violating employment or special education laws. Some educators, however, oppose decentralization because it broadens administrative responsibility. That is, concepts such as SBM require important policy decisions to be made at the district and school levels.

This case involves a superintendent who wants to decentralize governance in the school district. Key staff members resist. Both the change process (i.e., how the superintendent attempts to achieve change) and the primary objective (i.e., getting schools to adopt SBM) are cogent to analyzing their resistance.

Although change is encountered in all school districts, albeit to varying degrees, the ways in which these institutions react to, encourage, and manage the process vary substantially (Kowalski & Reitzug, 1993). In one district, massive change can be pursued with little conflict, whereas in another district, efforts to produce even minor alterations spawn substantial conflict. Aspects of organizational culture and climate that determine receptivity to change are responsible for this variance. Thus, our understanding of how organizations treat change is facilitated by asking these questions:

- What is to be changed?
- Why is the change being proposed?
- How will the change occur?
- How will change affect individuals and groups?
- To what degree is the change supported and likely to be sustained?

As you read this case, try to identify elements of organizational life that either encouraged or discouraged change. Try to understand why some administrators even opposed studying the implementation of SBM. As you complete your analysis, separate procedural issues from substantive issues.

KEY AREAS FOR REFLECTION

1. Processes for studying possible change in school
2. Why principals and other administrators may oppose decentralization
3. Why administrators and teachers may not be ready for change
4. Why certain elements of organizational culture and climate are unique and how this condition affects responses to proposed change
5. The advantages and disadvantages of decentralization

THE CASE

Lora Mipps has been secretary to the superintendent of the Lewis Public Schools for 31 years. In that period, she has outlasted eight superintendents, all of whom had unique personalities and leadership styles. She thought about that fact as she listened to the shouting coming from behind the closed door of the superintendent's office. As the voices became louder, Lora started to wonder if she was about to see the ninth superintendent depart during her tenure.

Dr. George Pisak arrived in Lewis, a quiet community of 18,000 located in the "sunbelt," just 15 months ago. He accepted the superintendency in this district because he wanted new challenges and opportunities for personal and professional growth. For the previous 12 years, he was an assistant superintendent for instruction in a large urban school system located in a neighboring state. George believed that contemporary superintendents had limited job security; however, since their two children had now graduated from college, George and his wife, Estelle, thought that they could now afford to take risks.

The Pisaks moved to Lewis well aware of the school system's history. The longest tenure of a superintendent in recent times was five years, and in the past six years, three different individuals have occupied this post. In part, the instability was linked to turnover on the school board—no incumbent has been re-elected in the past three elections. Typically, there have been three or more candidates for each seat on the school board.

When George was contacted initially by a former professor, Ken Hollman, about the Lewis superintendency, he said he was not interested. Largely because of the district's reputation, George concluded that this position would be more difficult than most. Dr. Hollman, who had been retained as a search consultant after the school board had difficulty attracting candidates, asked George to reconsider. The two met for lunch a week later to discuss the Lewis School District job.

During their meeting, Dr. Hollman tried to persuade George to apply for the Lewis position. He outlined five reasons why the position had become more attractive:

1. The school district desperately needed someone who could provide fresh leadership ideas. Of the four most recent superintendents, three were promoted from within the district. Each of these "insiders" found themselves in conflict with newly elected board members.
2. The board members have agreed that stability in the school system is necessary. They want to employ a person who can be both an effective manager and an instructional leader—an individual who will lead the process of change.
3. The board members believe that because of the district's recent problems with superintendents they will have to offer a highly competitive salary to attract the type of administrator they desire.
4. Lewis is a heterogeneous community, especially with respect to economics and politics. Over the past decade, the school district has shifted from having a predominately "blue collar" board to having a predominately "white collar" board. Five current board members are either professionals or corporate executives.
5. The board is willing to let the superintendent replace any and all of the current administrative staff if such decisions are deemed necessary.

George listened attentively to his former professor's comments. He told Dr. Hollman that he and his wife were interested in relocating, preferably to a city smaller than the one in which they were living. He also admitted that he wanted to become a superintendent. Although the Lewis position would accommodate both interests, he remained concerned about the school district's history of changing superintendents frequently.

The two men knew each other well. Dr. Hollman had been George's doctoral program adviser. The professor perceived his former student to be intelligent, capable, and industrious—but very cautious. He knew that if he was going to persuade George to apply for the Lewis position, he had to balance the positives and negatives associated with the job. During the two-hour meeting, he did just that. He repeatedly emphasized that opportunities outweighed problems. His strategy worked; George agreed to submit his application.

Dr. Hollman described Dr. Pisak to the Lewis school board members as a "perfect candidate." During a first interview with the board, George did nothing to contradict that assessment. Most board members were very impressed with him, and they invited him to return for a second interview. Meeting the board members and hearing their thoughts about the future reduced some of George's apprehensions. He was particularly impressed with the fact that the board recognized the negative consequences of leadership instability. They repeatedly mentioned that they intended to give their new superintendent considerable authority and leeway to pursue reforms.

Three days after the second interview, the board president called George and offered him the position. Before answering, George asked if the board was united in its decision to hire him. He was told that one board member may vote against his appointment purely for political reasons—that board member was a close friend of the previous superintendent and had publicly objected to his dismissal. After discussing the offer with his wife, George agreed to accept the Lewis position.

George received a three-year contract at a salary approximately $20,000 greater than the previous superintendent received. One board member, Dan Foster, voted against the motion to employ Dr. Pisak. In an interview with the local newspaper reporter following the board meeting, Mr. Foster called the new superintendent's salary "outrageous." He said, "We have families in Lewis who have to cut every corner just to pay their property taxes. Yet, we pay a school superintendent over $100,000. I don't think this will set well with many voters in this district. We have highly qualified administrators who have spent their entire careers in this district. They would have taken the position for much less money. Now having said that, I want everyone to know that I think Mr. Pisak is a fine man. I'll certainly try to work with him."

The four board members who supported Dr. Pisak's appointment arranged for him to be very visible in the community during his first few months on the job. They introduced him to community leaders and arranged for him to speak to local service clubs and civic groups. During this adjustment period, Dr. Pisak became aware that economics and politics almost evenly divided the school district's population into two distinct groups—one being much more affluent and politically conservative than the other. This separation was made even more obvious by the fact that the lower-income families were concentrated in the southern half of the district's boundaries. Because all board members were elected on an at-large basis, equal representation for the two factions was not assured. The four board members who had voted to hire Dr. Pisak lived in the northern half of the district and were politically aligned with the conservative and more affluent segment of the population. Just four years ago, however, the balance of power was different—that board consisted of three members from the south and two from the north.

Each portion of the district's population having its own high school made the line of demarcation even bolder. Lewis North High School was constructed 12 years ago to accommodate enrollment growth in the district. It enrolls about 1,200 students and approximately two-thirds of its graduates attend college. Lewis South High School, housed in a much older building, was originally the district's only high school. Located near the city's business district, it serves about 1,300 students. Only about 20 percent of the Lewis South graduates enter college. Ever since Lewis North opened, the two high schools have been bitter rivals.

Dr. Pisak thought that the divided school community was both the cause of school board instability and an enormous barrier to meaningful reforms. He also believed that most residents in the southern portion of the district viewed him and the four board members who supported him as political adversaries. These views were instrumental in Dr. Pisak's determination to implement site-based management. But before announcing his intent to decentralize publicly, he wanted to know if the school board and administrative staff supported the initiative.

The superintendent's argument in favor of site-based management was predicated on the general conclusion that meaningful school improvement was more likely if it were pursued on a school-by-school basis. Dr. Pisak indicated that three factors contributed to this judgment:

1. Most Lewis citizens identified with individual schools rather than with the district.
2. Any centralized reform efforts would probably be attenuated by the district's economic and political schism.
3. Faculty, students, and parents would be more likely to support change if they were involved in planning the changes and if the changes directly addressed the real needs and wants of individual schools.

He presented his position to board members individually, and all of them reacted positively. His presentation to the administrators occurred during the March staff meeting. The reactions from them were mixed. About one-third claimed that they did not have enough knowledge about site-based management to formulate an opinion. An almost equal number expressed opposition to the idea because they thought that school councils would erode administrative authority. The remaining administrators said they supported the concept.

Despite knowing that many of the district's administrators were opposed or apprehensive, Dr. Pisak moved forward with his idea. At the March school board meeting, he received approval to employ two consultants to complete a feasibility study if he thought such a study was necessary. He sent administrative staff copies of journal articles favorable to SBM, and he offered to have administrators, especially those who were not supportive, visit SBM schools.

At the May administrative staff meeting, Dr. Pisak engaged the staff in another conversation about SBM. Neither the visits to SBM schools nor the journal articles had increased support for SBM. Disappointed by the lack of progress, Dr. Pisak told the administrators, "You have been very open with me about my idea, and I appreciate your candor. But I still believe we should pursue site-based management. Therefore, I am going to recommend to the school board that we move forward. Essentially, our two consultants will lead a committee consisting of parents, teachers, and administrators. The committee's task is to issue recommendations for policy and resources so that site-based management can be implemented after the next school year. Keep in mind that no final decision would be made until we have had ample time to study their report."

Reactions to the announcement were immediate. Clearly, many of the administrators, including all of the secondary school principals, were opposed to even studying the feasibility of adopting SBM. Dr. Pisak, however, was not dissuaded. He told the administrators that he would inform the school board of his decision at their next meeting.

Keeping his word, the superintendent prepared the following recommendation that he sent to board members and administrators several days prior to the board meeting:

Topic: Feasibility Study for the Implementation of Site-Based Management

Superintendent Recommendation: A special committee, consisting of three administrators, three teachers, and three district residents, should be formed to study the feasibility of implementing site-based management. The committee shall work with Dr. Jane Jones and Dr. Milton Brown, the consultants who have been retained by the school district. The committee shall present a report to the superintendent and school board within 10 months.

Background Information: I have concluded that site-based management offers the greatest promise for achieving school improvement in this district. The approach permits schools to pursue their own reform agendas, and to do so with the active participation of taxpayers, teachers, and students. The feasibility study will better prepare you to make a final decision on this critical matter. The committee will be looking at potential policy changes, structural changes, and resources. I want to stress two points. First, you should know that a significant portion of the administrative staff—maybe as many as 60 percent of them—do not support this study. Second, I want to stress that you will be voting to approve the study and not to implement the concept. A vote on that issue would come after the study is completed over the next 10 months or so.

After having received the recommendation, the principal at Lewis South High School telephoned all the other principals in the district and asked them to attend a meeting at his house. All but two of them did so. A petition was circulated at the meeting asking the superintendent to withdraw his recommendation. It read as follows:

Dr. Pisak,

As principals in Lewis, we respectfully request that you reconsider your recommendation regarding a feasibility study for implementing site-based management in our district. Our request is based on four concerns:

- We believe that site-based management could seriously diminish administrative control in our schools.
- There is little evidence that site-based management has resulted in real improvements in teaching and learning.
- We believe that the money and human resources that will be used to complete this study could be better utilized to meet facility and equipment needs.
- Nearly all of the principals oppose the feasibility study.

Accordingly, we request that you withdraw your recommendation and consider other alternative approaches to school improvement.

The petition was signed by 11 of the district's 14 principals.

After receiving the petition, Dr. Pisak asked his two assistant superintendents to join him in his office. He showed them the petition and asked if they knew who had organized the effort. They said that the meeting had occurred at the home of one of the high school principals. Dr. Pisak first called the principal at Lewis South High School. He asked if he had organized the meeting, and the principal said that he had. The principal was then instructed to meet with the superintendent at 5:00 P.M. that afternoon. The principal requested to bring at least two other principals with him to the meeting; the request was denied.

The face-to-face encounter between the superintendent and principal was not pleasant. As their meeting progressed, their voices became louder and their words became harsher. Sitting outside the closed door to the superintendent's office, Mrs. Mipps, the secretary, had recollections of other such heated arguments. That is why she wondered if yet another superintendent was about to have a short stay in Lewis.

THE CHALLENGE

Place yourself in Dr. George Pisak's position. What would you do at this point?

KEY ISSUES/QUESTIONS

1. Do you agree that the political and economic division in the school district has been responsible for instability on the school board? Why or why not?
2. Is instability on a school board likely to affect turnover in the superintendency? What evidence do you have to support your response?
3. Assess the composition of the present school board. What are the advantages and disadvantages of having members elected on an at-large basis?

4. Evaluate Dr. Pisak's decision to pursue SBM after having been in the school district for only six months.
5. Arguments for and against decentralization are not new to public education. What are the primary arguments?
6. What are the advantages and disadvantages of adopting SBM given the political and economic conditions in the school district?
7. Do you think that the superintendent did an adequate job of trying to educate the administrative staff about SBM?
8. Was it ethical for the high school principal to convene a meeting of the principals and ask them to sign the petition? Did the principals who signed the petition act ethically?
9. What are the advantages and disadvantages of the superintendent withdrawing his recommendation?
10. If you were superintendent in this district and wanted to pursue site-based management, what other tactics might you have used?
11. Is it common for school districts to be divided by economics and politics? What evidence do you have to defend your response?
12. How can the conflict in this case be used to improve conditions in the school district?

SUGGESTED READINGS

Bechtel, D. (1998). *Principal perceptions of restructuring: Is there a 'deal' between districts and schools?* (ERIC Document Reproduction Service No. ED 423 591)

Black, J., & English, F. (1986). What they don't tell you in schools of education about school administration (pp. 15–17). Lancaster, PA: Technomics.

Caldwell, S. (1988). School-based improvement: Are we ready? *Educational Leadership, 46*(2), 50–53.

Caldwell, S., & Wood, F. (1992). Breaking ground in restructuring. *Educational Leadership 50*(1), 41, 44.

Cawalti, G. (1989). The elements of site-based management. *Educational Leadership, 46*(8), 46.

David, J. (1989). Synthesis of research on school-based management. *Educational Leadership, 46*(8), 45–53.

Golarz, R. J. (1992). School-based management pitfalls: How to avoid some and deal with others. *School Community Journal, 2*(1), 38–52.

Guthrie, J. (1986). School based management: The next needed education reform. *Phi Delta Kappan, 68*(4), 305–309.

Herman, J., & Herman, J. (1992). Educational administration: School-based management. *The Clearing House, 65*(5), 261–263.

Kowalski, T. J. (1994). Site-based management, teacher empowerment, and unionism: Beliefs of suburban school principals. *Contemporary Education, 65*(4), 200–206

Kowalski, T., & Reitzug, U. (1993). *Contemporary school administration: An introduction.* New York: Longman (see chapters 9, 13).

Kritek, W., & Schneider, G. (1993–94). Site-based management and decentralization. *National Forum of Educational Administration and Supervision Journal, 11*(1), 3–20.

Leithwood, K., & Menzies, T. (1998). A review of research concerning the implementation of site-based management. *School Effectiveness and School Improvement, 9*(3), 233–285.

Smith, S. (1998). School by school. *American School Board Journal, 185*(6), 22–25.

9

Different Perceptions of Effective Teaching

BACKGROUND INFORMATION

The term "teacher empowerment" is interpreted in several different ways. All definitions, however, are anchored in the concept of professionalism; that is, they focus on a professional orientation to teaching (Ponticell, Olson, & Charlier, 1995). Some reformers believe that meaningful school improvement requires an intricate combination of state deregulation, district decentralization, and teacher empowerment. This is because the real needs of students are not constant across local districts, schools, or even classrooms. But despite the merits of individualized instruction, not everyone is comfortable giving teachers substantial latitude to determine what should be taught and how it should be taught in their classrooms.

In large measure, apprehension about total deregulation or decentralization is related to the inevitable tension that exists between liberty and equality—two metavalues that have historically guided the formulation of educational policy. For example, giving schools within a district the freedom to experiment with curriculum could lead to real or perceived inequalities (e.g., a course or special program is offered in one school but not in others). For this reason, total empowerment—allowing teachers to have absolute control over their practice—is highly improbable. Rather, sociopolitical arrangements that represent compromises between liberty and equality are more likely.

Many administrators remain apprehensive about giving teachers substantial control over instructional decisions. Consider three of the possible reasons for their trepidation:

1. Administrators may fear being held accountable if a teacher fails to comply with state laws and regulations.
2. Administrators may fear criticism from parents and students who disagree with a teacher's decisions.
3. Some teachers prefer to work under a tight network of policies and rules; they may react negatively toward the principal if they are required to assume greater responsibility for their practice (Kowalski, 1995).

Decisions made by educators are political as well as professional. This is especially noteworthy because parents and taxpayers often have different priorities and philosophies. Thus, any decision made by school officials is likely to result in some criticism or overt opposition. Both decentralization and teacher empowerment—conditions that diminish reliance on centralized policies and rules—increase the likelihood that these philosophical differences will surface and generate conflict.

Conflict emerges in this case when a third-grade teacher's philosophy about homework is challenged by a group of her students' parents. The principal is asked to intervene. His situation is exacerbated by the fact that he transferred the teacher from first grade (where her position on homework was not controversial) to third grade (where it was).

KEY AREAS FOR REFLECTION

1. The concept of teacher empowerment
2. Role conflict in the principalship
3. Conflict sparked by different philosophies of education
4. Effective communication with parents
5. Establishing instructional policies

THE CASE

The Community

Ocean County has a diverse population. About 20 percent of the families live at or below the poverty line, but about 10 percent have annual incomes in excess of $300,000. Approximately 43 percent of the population are members of racial minorities, and the native language of about one in three residents is something other than English. In addition, nearly half of the population has migrated to the county in the last 20 years.

The low-income and minority families are concentrated in Rio Del Mar, the county seat of Ocean County. High-income families own properties on or near the oceanfront, and the remainder of the county is composed of middle-class housing developments and small towns.

The School District

There is only one public school system in Ocean County, the Ocean County School District. It has doubled in enrollment since 1975, requiring the construction of 12 new schools in the past decade. About half of the district's schools are in Rio Del Mar.

A seven-member school board, representing various geographic sections of the county, governs the school system. Four of the seven board members are from Rio Del Mar. Board members are elected to four-year terms in nonpartisan elections. With approximately 75,000 students, there are 83 attendance centers that include:

- 10 high schools
- 20 middle schools
- 52 elementary schools
- 1 alternative high school

The central office staff consists of over 100 professionals.

Since 1982, the school system has implemented an in-district-busing plan to achieve racial balance. Approximately 25 percent of the minority children in Rio Del Mar are bused to schools in other parts of the district. No students are required to be bused to schools in Rio Del Mar; however, they may choose to attend any of these schools if room is available.

Dr. Elizabeth Eddings is the district's superintendent. She came to Ocean County two years ago, after serving as superintendent in a 12,000-student district in another state. Most teachers and administrators have responded positively to her leadership style. She is a proponent of site-based management and teacher empowerment, and she has encouraged principals to increase parental involvement in school governance.

The School

Seminole Elementary School, enrolling just over 800 students, is one of the newest schools in the district. Opened just four years ago, it serves an unincorporated area about four miles north of Rio Del Mar. Three of the most expensive housing developments in the county are served by this school; however, approximately 100 students are bused from low-income neighborhoods on the northwest side of Rio Del Mar.

Nearly 40 professional staff members work at the school. They include three kindergarten teachers (each teaches two half-day classes), six first-grade teachers, and five teachers in each grade level 2 through 5. Specialized teachers in art, music, physical education, learning disabilities, speech and language therapy, and computers augment the standard educational program. Additionally, the school has a full-time guidance counselor, an assistant principal, and a half-time nurse. Both psychological services and social work services are provided through central office personnel.

Overall, the faculty members at Seminole Elementary School are quite young and inexperienced. Their average age is only 31 and the average level of teaching experience is just five years.

The Principal

Howard Carlsburg has been the principal of Seminole Elementary School since it opened. Prior to receiving this assignment, his professional experience included two years as an assistant principal and eleven years as a fifth-grade teacher. As principal, his performance evaluations have been consistently above average.

The teachers view the principal as a "hands-on" leader who spends time visiting classrooms and talking to teachers about their work. He makes himself available to teachers and occasionally does some direct teaching (about once a month he serves as a substitute teacher). To create a schedule that permits these activities, he delegates many of the routine administrative responsibilities to his assistant principal. These tasks include such functions as taking attendance, managing the lunch program, supervising bus loading and unloading, handling student discipline, and supervising the custodial staff.

The principal and superintendent have a positive relationship. Dr. Eddings has visited Seminole Elementary School many times, and she considers it to be one of the district's most innovative schools. Mr. Carlsburg is one of the superintendent's most vocal supporters.

The Teacher

Alicia Comstock, age 29, has been teaching at the school for two years. She previously taught for three years in another state. She is an even-tempered, positive person. Other teachers and the principal like her. When you walk into her classroom, you get a warm feeling; the walls are covered with the students' work and the bulletin boards are brightly decorated. She appears to like children very much and she often comments about her love of teaching.

Alicia was initially employed to teach first grade at Seminole Elementary School, but after one year, the principal asked her to accept an assignment teaching third grade. The principal explained that he had an opportunity to hire a woman who had just graduated from college, and she would only accept the position if she could teach first grade. He went on to explain that it was difficult to find good teachers, and he did not want to loose this applicant.

Alicia asked him, "Why do you want me to take a new assignment? How about the other first-grade teachers? Why don't you move one of them to third grade?"

"I asked them if they would be willing to move, and they said no," he answered.

"Well, what if I say no too? I much prefer to stay where I am. All of my teaching experience has been at the first-grade level."

"Alicia, I'm asking you to do this for the good of the school. I have to look at the big picture. If a first-grade assignment becomes available in the future, you'll be first in line."

Alicia finally agreed to teach third grade, but she did so reluctantly. She felt that Mr. Carlsburg was really not being fair with her.

Performance Evaluations

School district policy requires that principals complete annual performance evaluations of professional staff under their supervision. This evaluation culminates with a formal conference between the principal and teacher sometime in mid- to late March. Principals must follow policy guidelines that specify using an evaluation calendar and a standard evaluation instrument.

Mr. Carlsburg has tried to make the evaluation process more formative than summative. He often tells teachers, "Since we have to do this, let's try to make it a growth experience for both of us." He avoids confrontation and he attempts to influence the performance of teachers by gaining their confidence.

The Problem

Just two months after Mrs. Comstock started teaching third grade, Mr. Carlsburg received three complaints from parents about her. The first was from a mother who displeased because her son was not being assigned homework.

"My daughter was in third grade last year and brought work home almost every day. Now my son is in Mrs. Comstock's class and he never has homework. I'm very concerned about this," she told the principal.

Mr. Carlsburg asked the parent if she had talked to Mrs. Comstock and she said she had not. He encouraged her to do so, and added that he would look into the matter. But before he had an opportunity to discuss this complaint with Alicia, he received two others. Both were from parents expressing the same concern. After these calls, he immediately went to Alicia's classroom and asked her to step out into hallway. There he told her about the three telephone calls.

She reacted by saying that she did not believe homework was appropriate for third-grade students.

"These children have a long school day, and they work hard while they are here. I don't think it is in their best interest to give them more work to do at home."

The two agreed to meet after school to discuss the matter further. The principal then visited briefly with each of the other third-grade teachers and asked them if they assigned homework. They all responded affirmatively, although the amount of work they assigned ranged from 30 to 60 minutes.

When Alicia and the principal met later that day, he suggested a compromise position. He asked her to assign homework occasionally, perhaps twice a week. His rationale was that the other third-grade teachers were assigning homework and this made her even more vulnerable to parental complaints.

She told the principal, "If you think this is best, I'll do it."

About six weeks later, more parents called the principal complaining about Mrs. Comstock. Now, the concerns were broader than homework. They were also displeased because they thought she set low expectations for students and gave them too much freedom. One father put it this way, "My son has never been happier about school. But why shouldn't he be? He's never had a teacher who lets him do whatever he wants to do."

In total, the principal had received nine separate complaints about Mrs. Comstock. Several parents threatened to take the matter to the superintendent and school board if something was not done to improve conditions in her classroom. Rather than tell Alicia about the most recent complaints, Mr. Carlsburg observed her class three times during the following week. None of his observations revealed the lack of structure and purpose suggested by the complaining parents.

The principal never revealed to the parents that he had essentially pushed Alicia into the third-grade assignment—possibly because he felt some responsibility for the ensuing conflict. Mr. Carlsburg concluded that the parents had a very narrow perception of schooling. They viewed teaching the basics as the school's only responsibility. As such, they were misinterpreting Alicia's teaching style.

The holiday vacation was near, and the principal decided not to meet with the parents until school resumed in January. He also decided it would be better to invite all of the parents to a meeting; he hoped that many of them would have positive things to say Mrs. Comstock. His letter inviting them to the meeting indicated that the purpose was to discuss some concerns that had been voiced. On the last day of school before the holiday break, the principal finally told Alicia about the additional phone calls and indicated that he would be meeting with parents in several weeks. He assured her that he did not find the complaints to be valid, and thus, he preferred that she not attend the meeting with the parents.

The meeting was held just three days after school resumed in January. It was not well attended; parents of fewer than half of the students in the class (11 of 24) were there. The principal began by saying that he wanted the meeting to be positive. He explained that he asked Mrs. Comstock not to attend. He then emphasized the following points:

- Since October, Mr. Comstock has been assigning some homework to her students.
- He had observed her teaching five times during the first semester, and on each occasion, he found her performance to be acceptable.
- He explained that all teachers were evaluated formally in accordance with district policy, and he had not yet completed her final evaluation for the current school year.

He concluded his comments by expressing support for Mrs. Comstock. "In my opinion, Mrs. Comstock is a competent, sensitive, and caring teacher. She tries to meet all the needs of her students. This includes social adjustment, development of a positive self-image, and, of course, educational progress. Because she does things to help students like school, that doesn't mean she is ignoring teaching the basics."

His comments were not well received by some of the parents. Ben Rodius, a stockbroker, spoke on behalf of the concerned parents.

"Mr. Carlsburg, let me first say that I left work several hours early to be here today with my wife. We obviously think this problem is serious. Two years ago when we moved here from Vermont, I put my children in the public schools because I was told they were very good. My daughter, Betsy, who is now in Mrs. Comstock's class, started going to a private preschool program when she was three years old. By the time she entered kindergarten she could read. When we attended the parent-teacher conference, Mrs. Comstock spent most of time telling us what a happy child we had. I don't think it's Mrs. Comstock's responsibility to see that Betsy is happy. My wife and I will worry about that. It is her job to set high expectations for our daughter—to see that Betsy is challenged to do her best. Public schools cannot solve all the problems of society. I pay taxes so my daughter can receive a good education. Schools are not equipped to solve social or psychological problems, and if teachers try to do so, they only neglect their real duties."

The principal reacted that he thought it was unfair to characterize Mrs. Comstock as someone who did not care about learning. He pointed out that some children in her class came from families living below the poverty level, and he explained that academic, personal, and social needs could not be cleanly separated as distinct tasks.

After listening to the principal's explanation, Mr. Rodius asked, "Do you think it is unreasonable for parents to expect a teacher to challenge students to do the best they can?" Before the principal could answer, he asked him another question, "Well, forget that. Just tell us if our concerns will be reflected in the formal evaluation you make of this teacher?"

"It would be inappropriate for me to discuss her formal evaluation. And besides, the process will not be completed until March. If you are asking me whether I think she is doing a good job—given what I know now—my answer is 'yes'."

At that point, one parent defended Mrs. Comstock. She said, "My son has never shown interest in school before. He talks about Mrs. Comstock all the time. I don't want to argue with these other parents, but from what I know, she is a great teacher."

The principal concluded the meeting with the following comments, "When some of you complained about your children not being assigned homework, I urged Mrs. Comstock to change her practices—and she did. I don't believe that she sets low expectations for students, nor do I believe that she lets students do whatever they want. Perhaps she doesn't push her students as hard as some other teachers, but that does not make her incompetent. I encourage you to visit her classroom so you can observe her teaching. I encourage you to talk to her directly about your expectations. I think everyone will benefit."

Most of the complaining parents were not satisfied. Mr. Rodius told the principal that he was going to present the concerns to the superintendent and school board.

THE CHALLENGE

Assume the position of the principal. Would you do anything more to try to resolve the conflict? If so, what?

KEY ISSUES/QUESTIONS

1. Why do parents often have different beliefs about the purposes of public education?
2. Some school districts have policies requiring the assignment of homework. What are the advantages and disadvantages of such a policy?

3. If you were an elementary principal in a district that did not have a homework policy, would you institute a rule for your school? Why or why not?
4. Evaluate the principal's decision not to tell Mrs. Comstock about the additional complaints until the last day before the holiday break. Should principals immediately tell teachers about parental complaints?
5. If you were the principal, what would you have done differently after receiving the first complaints from parents in October?
6. The principal emphasizes that the formal evaluation process should be both formative and summative. Is there any information in the case that suggests he is using the evaluation process to improve the teacher's performance?
7. Was it a good decision to exclude the teacher from the January meeting with parents? Why or why not?
8. Consider the fact that parents of only 11 students attended the meeting, and at least one parent openly supported the teacher. What, if any, relevance do you assign to these facts?
9. Is it relevant that several of the students in Mrs. Comstock's class are bused to the school from low-income neighborhoods? Why or why not?
10. The principal did not tell the parents that he basically coerced Mrs. Comstock to take the third-grade teaching assignment. Was he behaving ethically when he withheld this information? Why or why not?
11. To what extent is teacher empowerment an issue in this case?
12. Analyze the leadership style of this principal. What are his strengths and weaknesses?
13. Analyze the leadership style of this principal. What are his strengths and weaknesses?

SUGGESTED READINGS

Cascaddem. D. S. (1998). Principals and managers and leaders: A qualitative study of the perspectives of selected elementary school principals. *Journal of School Leadership, 8*(2), 137–170.

Deutsch, M. (1992). Typical responses to conflict. *Educational Leadership, 50*(1), 16.

Epstein, J. (1988). Parents and schools: How do we improve programs for parent involvement? *Educational Horizons, 66*(3), 59–95.

Goldring, E. (1990). Elementary school principals as boundary spanners: Their engagement with parents. *Journal of Educational Administration, 28*(1), 53–62.

Johnson, P. E., & Short, P. M. (1998). Principal's leader power, teacher empowerment, teacher compliance and conflict. *Educational Management & Administration, 26*(2), 147–59.

Kowalski, T. J. (1995). Preparing teachers to be leaders: Barriers in the workplace. In M. O'Hair & S. Odell (Eds.), *Educating teachers for leadership and change: Teacher Education Yearbook III* (pp. 243–256). Thousand Oaks, CA: Corwin.

Kowalski, T., & Reitzug, U. (1993). *Contemporary school administration: An introduction.* New York: Longman (see chapters 5, 8, 11).

Margolis, H., & Tewel, K. (1988). Resolving conflict with parents: A guide for administrators. *NASSP Bulletin, 72*(506), 26–28.

McEwan, E. K. (1998). *How to deal with parents who are angry, troubled, afraid, or just plain crazy.* (ERIC Document Reproduction Service No. ED 422 639)

Moo, G. (1987). Communicating with the school publics. *NASSP Bulletin, 71*(501), 142–144.

Polardy, J. (1988). The effect of homework policies on student achievement. *NASSP Bulletin, 72*(507), 14–17.

Ponticell, J. A., Olson, G. E., & Charlier, P. S. (1995). Project MASTER: Peer coaching and collaboration as catalysts for professional growth in urban high schools. In M. O'Hair & S. Odell (Eds.), *Educating teachers for leadership and change: Teacher Education Yearbook III* (pp. 96–116). Thousand Oaks, CA: Corwin.

Reetz, L. (1990-91). Parental perceptions of homework. *Rural Educator, 12*(2), 14–19.

Ribas, W. B. (1998). Tips for reaching parents. *Educational Leadership, 56*(1), 83–85.

Sagarese, M. M., & Giannetti, C. C. (1998). Turning parents from critics to allies. *Educational Leadership, 55*(8), 40–41.

Sapone, C. (1982). Appraisal and evaluation systems: What are the perceptions of educators, board members? *NASSP Bulletin, 66*(458), 46–51.

Shen, J. (1998). Do teachers feel empowered? *Educational Leadership, 55*(7), 35–36.

Short, P. M. (1998). Empowering leadership. *Contemporary Education, 69*(2), 70–72.

Tschannen-Moran, M., Hoy, A. W., & Hoy, W. K. (1998). Teacher efficacy: Its meaning and measure. *Review of Educational Research, 68*(2), 202–48.

Turner-Egner, J. (1989). Teacher discretion in selecting instructional materials and methods. *West's Education Law Reporter, 53*(2), 365–379.

Watkins, D. (1993). Five strategies for managing angry parents. *Principal, 72*(4), 29–30.

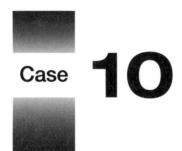

Case **10**

A Matter of Honor

BACKGROUND INFORMATION

It is virtually impossible to shape administrators into mechanical figures who consistently make rational, objective, and predictable decisions—despite values expressed in some normative theories. Researchers who have studied practitioners commonly discover that real behavior is shaped by a myriad of variables. For example, professional knowledge may provide insights suggesting that a routine or prescribed response is inappropriate; emotions, ethical concerns, or political conditions may likewise affect decisions.

Sergiovanni (1992) aptly observed that there are three dimensions to leadership behavior. He labeled them the *heart,* the *head,* and the *hand.* The first involves personal beliefs, values, dreams, and commitments; the second pertains to professional knowledge; and the third to actions or leadership styles. Perhaps the greatest difficulties for practitioners arise when these dimensions are in disharmony. For instance, professional, political, and legal factors may direct principals to certain decisions, but from a moral perspective, they *feel* that different courses of action may be best.

In this case, a minority student is caught plagiarizing a book report for her English class. Invoking school district policy, the teacher recommends that the student be given a failing grade for the semester. This student happens to be a gifted athlete who has received an appointment to one of the service academies. A failing grade in English would almost certainly mean that her appointment would be rescinded.

As the case unfolds, the principal finds that he must choose between enforcing the district's policy as demanded by the teacher, and a political compromise suggested by the student's attorney and supported by the school system's attorney. Although he personally favors the compromise he fears repercussions from the teachers' union if he fails to enforce the policy.

Howlett (1991) wrote that "ethics begin where laws and doctrines of right and wrong leave off" (p. 19). Hodgkinson (1991) noted that "values, morals, and ethics are the very stuff of leadership and administrative life" (p. 11). In the real world of school administration, ethics can take several forms. These include nonroutine issues of morality and nonroutine issues of professional practice (Kowalski & Reitzug, 1993). For instance, a principal may face intense pressure to dismiss a teacher because students and parents do not like her. Yet, the principal believes that the teacher is effective and can improve her skills in human relations if given proper guidance. Should he make a political decision or a moral decision?

Matters of student discipline often entail political, professional, and ethical entanglements. How does one know whether the punishment is just and ethical? How does one know whether the punishment will really help the student? The school? Society? What considerations need to be given to setting precedent? What obligations does a principal have to follow a teacher's recommendation on punishment? Consider these questions as you read this case.

KEY AREAS FOR REFLECTION

1. The ethical and moral dimensions of practice
2. Student discipline
3. The political nature of controversial decisions
4. Balancing personal feeling with professional obligations

THE CASE

The Community

Newton, Michigan has fallen on hard times in recent years. The local economy was devastated when two automobile-related factories, a transmission plant and a battery plant, closed. Union strife, lower domestic automobile sales, high labor costs, and automation contributed to their demise. The parent companies diverted much of the work from Newton to new operations they opened in Mexico—a pattern that had become all too common and exasperating for Michigan residents.

As might be expected, this industrial retrenchment spawned an exodus of citizens, and the city's population dropped from 45,500 to slightly over 38,000 in the past nine years. Many who remained were bitter. Some displaced workers were fortunate enough to qualify for early retirement, but many others were forced to either leave Newton or take jobs that paid only a fraction of the salaries they had made previously. Present-day Newton stands in sharp contrast to its glory days.

During the glory days following World War II, Newton grew rapidly. High salaries in emerging industries attracted a steady stream of new residents. Many of the immigrants came from southern states such as Tennessee and Alabama—

places where industrial growth had been minimal. Others came from large industrial cities such as Chicago, Detroit, and Pittsburgh. Many of these new residents were of eastern European extraction. During the 1960s and 1970s, a number of Hispanic families also settled in Newton. They had come to Michigan originally as migrant farm workers, but other job opportunities were sufficient to induce them to stay. Hence, Newton became a mini-Detroit or Pittsburgh—a melting pot of racial and ethnic backgrounds.

The Union Influence

In the mid-1960s, the vast majority of the labor force in Newton worked in factories that had ties to the automobile industry. Virtually all factory workers were loyal union members, and the autoworkers' union was the most powerful political, social, and economic force in the community. During that period, union leaders often had more political influence than either the mayor or city council members, and they enjoyed widespread support because they got things done.

Beyond protecting worker rights and negotiating contracts, the autoworkers' union played a positive social role in the community. This was most evident in the area of building racial harmony. For example, its leaders operated the union hall as if it were a community center—making sure that everybody was welcome and treated equally. The union also was a mechanism for forging friendships that crossed racial and ethnic lines.

In the early 1980s, jobs in Newton started to disappear, and as they did, the union started losing members and power. After two factories closed, membership dropped by over 50 percent. The loss of income resulted in fewer social and civic activities. Gone were the once-a-month socials that provided free kegs of beer, the annual Fourth of July picnic, and the annual Christmas party that provided gifts to the children and grand-children of union members. The union leaders now had to concentrate on their own organization's survival.

A New Mayor

In the midst of all of its economic and social problems, Newton residents looked to the past when they elected a new mayor. Stanley Diviak, a 63-year-old retired tool-and-dye maker, was something of a folk hero in the town. From 1965 to 1978, he served as president of the local autoworkers' union, and many residents fondly remembered those years as the very best.

Stanley was viewed as a tough, hard-working individual. During his tenure as union president, he wielded considerable power and he had few public enemies. He personified the values that many residents held important. He kept his word, he helped his friends, he was a devoted father and grandfather, he went to church regularly, and he was not afraid to express his convictions.

During the election, in which Stanley faced only token opposition from a 26-year-old lawyer who was the Republican candidate, no one doubted the outcome. Rather than discussing the merits of the candidates and the issues, voters focused on stories that established Mr. Diviak as a hero in the community's dominant culture. Many believed that things would have been different had Stanley not given up the union presidency. Blaming the global economy or changing market trends for automobiles for Newton's economic woes was usually not tolerated, especially after everyone had had a few beers.

Following his election, Mayor Diviak appointed many of his former union associates to key positions in the city administration, and he made sure that his appointees reflected Newton's cultural diversity. Second, he appointed a special committee to examine prospects of attracting new industry. And third, he announced that the traditional Fourth of July picnic would be back—this time sponsored by city government.

Newton High School

If you were to ask someone about the Newton public schools, chances are great that the response would somehow involve the district's athletic teams. The high school still occupies a two-story building erected in 1958 just four blocks from the center of town. The first thing you see as you walk through the front entrance, is a huge trophy case that is overflowing with tarnished cups and plaques. Pictures of athletes from years past line the hallways.

The school's principal, Nick Furtoski, has lived in Newton virtually all of his life. Except for the time he spent going to college and two years in the Army, he has lived in the same house that was built by his parents prior to World War II. He played football for Newton High in the 1950s and helped the school earn its first state gridiron championship. Over time, he has become an authority on Newton High School history.

The principal's love for his school is obvious, but his greatest pleasure comes from bragging about the athletic heroes of the past. No visitor can escape without hearing about the seven graduates who made it all the way to the National Football League, or the three who played professional baseball. He will take you down the hall and show you Ann Smith's picture—she won a silver medal in the 1972 Olympics. And before you say good-bye, he will puff up his chest and tell you about the 13 graduates who last year received full or partial athletic scholarships. But beyond all the bravado and enthusiasm, one can detect that even Nick Furtoski realizes that the best days of Newton High are probably in the past.

The Newton School District

Overall the school district has declined from about 8,500 to just over 6,000 students. Superintendent Andrew Sposis has survived seven difficult years. During his time in office, three schools have been closed due to declining enrollments. And in each of the last seven years Mr. Sposis has had to reduce staff. But problems involving employee unions have caused him the most political damage. During his time in office there have been three strikes—two by the teachers and one by the custodians.

Virtually all administrators in the district obtained their positions through internal promotions. This includes Superintendent Sposis who has never worked in another school system. Over the past 29 years he has been a teacher, elementary school principal, assistant superintendent for business, and superintendent.

The school board is composed of five members selected through nonpartisan elections. Members serve three-year terms. In the past 10 years the entire board has changed. Only one member who was in office when Superintendent Sposis was employed remains on the board. The current board consists of the following members:

Casmir Barchek, a postal worker

Yolanda Cody, a nurse

Matthew Miskiewicz, a mechanic

Angela Sanchez, a housewife

Darnell Turner, a dentist

Mr. Miskiewicz is president of the board and Dr. Turner is the vice-president. Mrs. Cody and Dr. Turner are African American; Mrs. Sanchez is Hispanic. Mr. Miskiewicz is Mayor Diviak's brother-in-law.

The Incident

Nancy Allison, a senior at Newton High School, is a *B* student, an outstanding athlete, and one of the most popular students in the school. She is an African American. By the end of her junior year she had been named to the all-state basketball team and was inundated with scholarship offers from more than 40 universities. In the fall of her senior year, she was elected homecoming queen, but this honor was far less important than the one she received some five months later. In early March, a special delivery letter came to her home from the United States Naval Academy. Nancy had received an appointment to the prestigious Annapolis institution.

The news of Nancy's appointment to Annapolis spread throughout Newton. Her picture appeared on the front page of the local newspaper above the story giving all the details. She was quoted as saying, "There is no doubt in my mind that I'm going to go to the Academy. I look forward to it." Nancy's selection was cause for rejoicing in a community desperate for good news.

However, about two weeks after Nancy received her good news, her life took a dramatic turn. On March 15, Janice Durnitz, an English teacher at Newton High School, entered the administrative office and requested to see the principal. At the time Mr. Furtoski was in the cafeteria having lunch with several teachers. Sensing the urgency of the situation, the receptionist went to the cafeteria to get him. She apologized for interrupting his lunch and told him that Mrs. Durnitz insisted on seeing him immediately. On returning to his office, the principal greeted the teacher with his usual smile.

"Hi, Janice. What could be so important as to take me away from my lunch?" he asked.

"I've got some bad news," she responded.

The smile left the administrator's face as he motioned for her to enter his office. Once she was inside, he quickly shut the door.

Janice had not even settled in a chair before she said, "Nancy Allison is in my honors English class and up until last week was doing quite well."

"Well, what's the problem?" inquired the principal.

"Students are expected to complete a critique of a contemporary novel. The assignment was given at the beginning of the semester. The deadline for submitting the critique was two days ago. Nancy was the last one in class to give me her work. In fact, she was a day late. I read her paper last night, and that's when I discovered a problem."

"Well, what exactly is it?" Mr. Furtoski inquired.

"There is no doubt in my mind that Nancy is guilty of plagiarism. Her critique was copied from another source," responded the teacher. "I checked it carefully."

"Then you're absolutely sure about this?" asked the principal. "There is no possibility of coincidence?"

"It's no coincidence," asserted Mrs. Durnitz. "Her work was copied from a review that appeared in a literary magazine three months ago. Unfortunately for her, it is a magazine I read regularly. I compared her work to the review three times—hoping I was mistaken. I was not. As you well know, the school district policy clearly states that a student caught cheating or plagiarizing in an honors class automatically fails."

"What does Nancy say about this?" the principal asked.

"She doesn't deny that she took the material from the magazine. She says she did not know that doing so was wrong. I don't believe her. Nancy is bright. She knows that you can't copy something word for word and claim it as your own work. She said that since she agreed with the review, she saw no harm in restating the content."

A pained look came over Mr. Furtoski's face and he stared off into space. The teacher could see he was at a loss for words. Suddenly, he looked directly at the teacher and asked, "Well, what do you plan to do about this?"

"I have no choice, Nick. Nancy has to fail the course. That's the policy," she answered.

"Janice, we have worked together for over 15 years. We have never had a student at Newton High School flunk a course because of plagiarism. Hell, half the people in this town don't even know what the word means. Isn't there some other solution? Can't we give her the benefit of the doubt? Maybe she is telling you the truth when she claims she didn't know she was breaking a rule. You know that if you give her an *F,* and especially an *F* for plagiarism, her appointment to the Academy will probably be withdrawn. At the very least she will have to go to summer school in order to graduate, and she can't do that and report to the Academy in late June. Couldn't we just give her some form of discipline and let her make up the work?" the administrator pleaded.

"Look, Nick. I didn't make this rule, but I certainly agree with it. Plagiarism is cheating. It is a serious offense. What will we be saying to other students if we just slap her wrist? I feel just as badly as you do, but I can't let my feelings interfere with my duty. If enforcing the policy means she doesn't get into the Naval Academy, so be it. She should have thought about the consequences before she copied someone else's work." With those parting comments, the teacher turned and walked out of the principal's office.

Mr. Furtoski shut the door to his office and slumped in his chair. He sat quietly looking out his window and thinking. After about 15 minutes he called the superintendent. He was still unsure what he would say as he waited for Mr. Sposis to come on the line. The easiest thing for him would be to support Mrs. Durnitz; he too could say that he was just doing his job. But something inside of him made him feel that failing the student was excessive punishment. Maybe he was being influenced by the fact that he knew Nancy and her parents quite well. They were a close, solid family, and Nancy not going to the Academy would devastate them. He was troubled by the possibility that Nancy's life might be ruined by one mistake. When the superintendent came on the line, however, the principal decided to relate the facts and not to take a position immediately.

Mr. Sposis listened and then responded, "This is just what I need, Nick! Do you know what will happen if Nancy doesn't get to go to the Naval Academy? The mayor has been talking about her appointment every chance he gets. He had the whole Allison family to city hall for pictures a week ago. There has got to be a way around this without failing her. Don't you agree, Nick?"

"I know Mrs. Durnitz and she is not going to back down. She can be real stubborn. I don't know about her personal relationship with Nancy, but I don't think her decision is affected by personal issues. She made it clear to me that she plans to follow the policy and give her an *F.* Neither of us may be able to talk her out of it."

"Can't you come up with some alternative that everyone will accept?" Mr. Sposis asked.

"I suggested giving Nancy the benefit of the doubt. But Mrs. Durnitz rejected my suggestion immediately. I pointed out that giving Nancy an *F* would cause all kinds of problems in the community. Nancy is popular, and then there is the racial element."

The conversation between the two administrators lasted another 10 minutes. Nick shared his emotions and noted that he was inclined to find a way out, but he just couldn't see how that could be done. The conversation concluded with Mr. Sposis saying that he would inform the school board about the problem when they met in a few days.

The principal did not reveal the charge of plagiarism to the high school faculty, and he asked Mrs. Durnitz and Nancy Allison not to talk to anyone about the incident. Both agreed to remain silent until a final decision had been reached.

When Mr. Sposis informed the school board about the plagiarism accusation, the attorney for the district, June VanSilten, was present. She was annoyed that the superintendent had not told her about this matter prior to the meeting. After listening to the superintendent's report, she made the following comments:

- She warned that there would be serious problems if Nancy failed the course, but she did not indicate if the problems would be legal or political.
- She cautioned the board members not to talk about the matter because if the student were given a failing grade and appealed that decision, the board members would have to become involved officially.
- She recommended that the board and superintendent not commit themselves until the principal had made a formal recommendation.

After the meeting, Superintendent Sposis called the principal and told him to submit a formal recommendation. Mr. Furtoski would have to decide whether to support the teacher's decision. The superintendent explained that everyone needed to be careful about violating procedures since litigation was certainly possible.

The principal again met with Mrs. Durnitz and asked her to reconsider an alternative punishment. The teacher presented the principal with a written statement indicating that the student would receive a failing grade as per district policy for having plagiarized a book report. A copy of the statement was sent to teachers' union president.

The following day, the union president telephoned the principal to tell him that the teachers' union expected him to support Mrs. Durnitz. Two reasons were given for this expectation. First, the union took the position that teachers, not administrators, determine student grades; second, the decision being made by the teacher was in compliance with district policy which administrators are required to enforce.

Feeling trapped, the principal confided in two trusted friends who were influential in the teachers' union. They both advised the principal to support Mrs. Durnitz. Although he remained convinced that a compromise would be better, he decided to follow their advice.

News of the incident quickly spread through the community. The reactions were mixed—largely along racial lines. Mr. and Mrs. Allison were furious with the teacher and the principal arguing that had the student been white, the decision would have been different. In accordance with established procedures the parents appealed the decision to give Nancy a failing grade to the superintendent.

Her parents and their attorney represented Nancy at the appeal hearing; the principal and Mrs. Durnitz represented the high school. After listening to both sides, the superintendent upheld the decision to give Nancy a failing grade. He did so on the grounds that the policy was clear and that the student had not denied copying the report; she merely argued that she had not been properly instructed about plagiarism.

Following the hearing, a newspaper reporter interviewed Mr. and Mrs. Allison and their attorney. They suggested that the decision made by Mrs. Durnitz and supported by Mr. Furtoski and Mr. Sposis was racially motivated.

Mr. Allison said, "If this had been a white football player, do you think this would be happening? Isn't it strange that when they decide to make an example of someone, it just happens to be an African-American female who is probably the best known student in the school?"

The school board discussed the case in detail in an executive session after the superintendent made his decision. The board members were divided; three supported the decision to fail the student; the other two, both African Americans, did not. The two dissenting board members also made statements to the media hinting that race was a central issue. The plagiarism case divided the community, the school board, and even students and teachers at the school.

According to school policy, the next level of appeal open to Nancy Allison was to the school board. Her parents decided not to do so believing that a majority of the board would support the teacher and administrators. Rather, their attorney filed a lawsuit naming the teacher, principal, superintendent, and school board as defendants.

The school system's attorney, who had already warned the board that there would be problems if the student received a failing grade, implied that the district might not win the lawsuit. None of the board members, however, changed positions on the matter.

Three weeks after initiating legal action, the attorney representing the Allison family contacted the attorney for the system and proposed an out-of-court settlement. Fearing that the litigation might affect Nancy's enrollment at the Academy, Mr. and Mrs. Allison offered to withdraw the lawsuit if the school officials would allow Nancy to retake the English class with another teacher. Phillip Jones, an African American member of the English department, offered to direct an independent study for Nancy. She would complete the work after school and on weekends allowing her to graduate with her class in late May. Nancy would not be allowed to participate in any spring sports as part of the settlement.

The attorney representing the school district urged the board and the administrators to accept the settlement. She said that it would be difficult to prove that Nancy knowingly committed plagiarism since there was little or no evidence indicating that her teachers sufficiently advised her of the nature of this offense. In addition, she argued that a settlement was in the best political interest of the community.

"This litigation could cost the school district a great deal of money. And there is a good chance that we won't win. Here is an opportunity for everyone to walk away with heads held high. Mayor Diviak knows about this offer, and he asked me to tell you that he supports it," she told them.

The superintendent and three board members who had steadfastly supported Mr. Furtoski said they could accept the proposed settlement provided that the principal agreed to the terms.

"Nick, what do you think?" the board president asked. "We don't want to put you on the spot, but this proposed settlement may be best for everyone."

THE CHALLENGE

Place yourself in the principal's position. What would you do?

KEY ISSUES/QUESTIONS

1. Identify the possible alternatives that the principal may pursue in this matter. Evaluate the merits of each of them.
2. Assess the behavior of Mrs. Durnitz in this case. Did she behave professionally? Ethically?
3. To what extent do you think the community's economic and political environment are critical variables?
4. Identify the moral and ethical dilemma facing the principal.
5. Most of the administrators in Newton acquired their positions via internal promotions. Do you think this has any bearing on this case?
6. What, if anything, would you have done differently if you were principal after first learning about the charges of plagiarism?
7. As principal, what weight would you give to the following in reaching a decision?
   a. Division on the school board
   b. Advice from the school system's attorney
   c. The superintendent's status with the school board and community

      d. The disposition taken by the teachers' union

      e. Concerns for race relations

8. Was it advantageous for the principal to propose a compromise as soon as the problem was brought to his attention? Why or why not?

9. What is your assessment of the superintendent's behavior in this matter?

10. Do you think it is important to this case that the principal is a "hometown boy"? Why or why not?

11. Do you think moral convictions and professional ethics influence most administrative decisions? What evidence do you have to support your answer?

12. Evaluate the school board policy regarding plagiarism in an honor's class. If you were the principal, would you propose that the policy be changed? Why or why not?

13. What is likely to occur if the principal refuses to accept the proposed settlement?

14. Evaluate the charge made by the parents and their attorney that the decision to fail the student is influenced by race. If you were the principal, how would you respond to this charge?

15. Should the principal and superintendent have consulted with the school attorney before discussing this matter with the school board?

SUGGESTED READINGS

Bartlett, L. (1987). Academic evaluation and student discipline don't mix: A critical review. *Journal of Law and Education, 16*(2), 155-165.

Browlee, G. (1987). Coping with plagiarism requires several strategies. *Journalism Educator, 41*(4), 25-29.

Curtis, J. (1996). Cheating—Let's face it. *International Schools Journal, 51*(a), 37-44.

Drum, A. (1986). Responding to plagiarism. *College Composition and Communication, 37*(2), 241-243.

Fass, R. A. (1986). By honor bound: Encouraging academic honesty. *Educational Record, 67*(4), 32-36.

Fennimore, B. S. (1997). When mediation and equity are at odds: Potential lessons in democracy. *Theory-into-Practice, 36*(1), 59-64.

Fris, J. (1992). Principals' encounters with conflict: Tactics they and others use. *Alberta Journal of Educational Research, 38*(1), 65-78.

Hobbs, G. J. (1992). The legality of reducing student grades as a disciplinary measure. *The Clearing House, 65,* 284-285.

Hodgkinson, C. (1991). *Educational leadership: The moral art.* Albany, NY: State University of New York Press.

Howlett, P. (1991). How you can stay on the straight and narrow. *Executive Educator, 13*(2), 19-21, 35.

Ingram, W. B. (1998). Calling the shots: When it comes to school governance, who makes what decisions? *Our Children, 23*(7), 36-37.

Kaleva, E. A. (1998). *The trouble with academic discipline.* (ERIC Document Reproduction Service No. ED 426 464)

Kowalski, T. J., & Reitzug, U. C. (1993). *Contemporary school administration: An introduction.* New York: Longman (see chapters 9, 15).

Peterson, P. (1984). Plagiarism: It can happen to you. *Quill and Scroll, 58*(4), 15.

Sergiovanni, T. J. (1992). *Moral leadership: Getting to the heart of school improvement.* San Fransisco: Jossey-Bass. (See Chapters 7 and 8).

Shea, J. (1987). When borrowing becomes burglary. *Currents, 13*(1), 38-42.

Sterling, G. (1991). Plagiarism and the worm of accountability. *Reading Improvement, 28*(3), 138-140.

The Closed-Door Policy

BACKGROUND INFORMATION

Research on leadership behavior reveals how administrators can facilitate or hinder goal attainment in educational institutions. At the district level, for example, the superintendent usually plays a pivotal role in determining behavior norms and in communicating what is to be accomplished. Early leadership studies were premised largely on the assumption that great leaders possessed unique qualities. Examples included case biographies and trait theory research. The latter, popular following World War II, sought to link effectiveness to selected psychological characteristics such as personality type. More recently, research has focused on examining behavior in conjunction with situational factors (i.e., the settings in which the behavior occurs) (Hanson, 1996).

The behavior of a superintendent or principal is the product of many influences, one of which is a normative disposition toward organizational life. If a principal, for instance, embraces the tenets of classical theory, this conviction is apt to influence most or all administrative decisions. In the school administration profession, where practitioners are likely to change positions and organizations several times, this is a weighty consideration. When a principal moves to a new school or district, for example, he or she will likely encounter somewhat different values, beliefs, practices, and expectations. Success often depends on recognizing these differences and making appropriate adjustments to them (Kowalski, 1999).

Contingency theory stresses that there is a middle ground between the opposing views that organizations are totally unique and that organizations are all the same (Hanson, 1996). Accordingly, neither universal principles of management nor the total rejection of theory is viewed as appropriate. Some scholars (e.g., O'Toole, 1995), however, have criticized the contingency philosophy as an amoral approach to administration that "stands on the quicksand of relativism" (p. 105). This critique is based on the belief that contingency theory is normative, encouraging leaders to be guided solely by political motives associated with the conditions in which they find themselves. But before rejecting contingency theory, we should ask ourselves the following questions: Is contingency theory both normative and descriptive? Is it possible for administrators to be both value-driven and flexible?

In this case, a newly employed superintendent in a relatively small school district isolates himself from his staff. Employees and even central office administrators have difficulty communicating with him. Two queries are central to the case: What are the symbolic effects of the superintendent's behavior? What are implications of his behavior on organizational effectiveness?

KEY AREAS FOR REFLECTION

1. Leadership behavior
2. Analysis of behavior in an organizational context
3. Communication processes
4. Conflict between personal and organizational interests
5. Delegation of authority

THE CASE

The Community

Placid Falls is a suburban community that began being developed in the early 1950s. Located approximately 35 miles from New York City, it is considered a community of choice by many upper-class families. Market values for houses in the community are approximately $450,000 to $1,200,000. The 1990 census set the population at 7,631 residents, and the average family income is over $250,000 per year.

All of the land suitable for single-family dwelling in the community has been developed. A five-member city council, mayor, and city manager govern Placid Falls. The council members and mayor serve four-year terms. The city has never had a "full-time" mayor and the current occupant of the position is a retired physician. The city manager is a professional administrator who has a master's degree in public administration. He works closely with the council and mayor and performs the day-to-day management functions of city government.

The School District

The Placid Falls Public School District consists of four schools: two elementary schools (grades K–5), a middle school (grades 6–8), and a high school (grades (9–12). The district's enrollment has declined about 1 percent per year during the past decade; the current enrollment is approximately 1,800.

The local public schools have always been a source of pride for residents. Many families located in the community because of the perceived quality of elementary and secondary education. Approximately 90 percent of the high school graduates enroll in four-year institutions of higher learning, with about one-third of them enrolling in highly selective, prestigious colleges and universities. Thus academic competition among students, especially at the high school, is usually intense. Precollegiate programs are stressed and few students take vocational courses (most of which have to be taken at an area vocational school located 20 miles away).

Both local residents and officials in the state department of education perceive the professional staff in the Placid Falls Public School District to be among the very best; per-pupil expenditures in the school system are in the top two percent in the state. Nearly 15 percent of the teachers and 75 percent of the administrators have completed doctoral degrees. Excellent salaries are a primary reason why the district receives literally dozens of applications for every vacancy. Only a handful of the school district's employees, however, can afford to live in Placid Falls.

The Superintendent

Three years ago when the Placid falls school board searched for a new superintendent, they received 123 applications. Most came from highly qualified and experienced administrators. Dr. George Frieman, a well-known professor and placement consultant, was retained to assist with the search. Among the ten candidates he recommended for interviews were some of the best-known superintendents in the United States—a noteworthy accomplishment given the relatively small size of the district.

Although the board members were impressed with all the candidates they interviewed, Dr. Andrew Sagossi, a superintendent of a large county school system in North Carolina, was their unanimous choice. When offered the job, Dr. Sagossi said he would accept the position provided that the board and his attorney could construct a contract agreeable to both parties. Having to negotiate with an attorney was a novel, but not disturbing, experience for the board. One member said it was like hiring a professional athlete and having to deal with his agent; another was quite impressed that Dr. Sagossi would pay an attorney to perform this service. Within a week, the parties agreed to a four-year contract with generous fringe benefits and an annual salary of $148,000.

Twenty years ago, success in the superintendency was often measured by one's ability to move to progressively larger school systems. Today, that is not necessarily the case. Dr. Sagossi left a 25,000-student school system to move to Placid Falls for several reasons which mainly included:

- The salary was over $20,000 more than he had received in North Carolina.
- He was originally from New York and had relatives, including his mother, who lived near Placid Falls.
- He needed five more years of service in New York to reach maximum benefits in the state retirement system.

Dr. Sagossi never mentioned salary, family, or retirement as reasons for accepting the job in Placid Falls. Instead he told the board members and media that he was attracted by the community's commitment to quality education. In his final interview he said, "I have been superintendent in several large school systems. I no longer equate success with the size of the organization I manage. The quality of the work experience is now much more important to me. In a district such as Placid Falls, the superintendent has more opportunities to work with community and state leaders to achieve excellence in our schools. Quite frankly, I don't want to spend the remainder of my career justifying why public schools should exist. I'd rather work in a school system where good administrators and good teachers are appreciated."

The Administrative Staff

At the time of Dr. Sagossi's appointment, the administrative staff in the district included the following individuals:

> Dr. Al Yanko, assistant superintendent for business
> Dr. Joan Myers, assistant superintendent for instruction
> Dr. Neil Larson, high school principal
> Mr. Joe O'Bannion, middle school principal
> Dr. Wilma Tucko and Ms. Andrea Kline, elementary principals

Dr. Myers was employed in the middle of the school year to replace a person who had resigned to become superintendent in another district. Thus, she had been in the district only about six months prior to Dr. Sagossi's arrival. All other administrators were former teachers in the district.

The Assistant Superintendent for Instruction

Joan Myers was born and raised in a suburban community in neighboring New Jersey. She is the oldest of three children. Her parents are now retired. Her father practiced dentistry for 37 years and her mother was a marketing executive for a large department store. Her upper-middle-class home life offered many cultural and educational opportunities. As an undergraduate, she attended a prestigious liberal arts college in New England. It was during her sophomore year there that she decided to major in social science education—a decision that was accepted but not cheered by her parents. They had hoped that she would pursue dentistry and enter the family-owned practice.

While teaching for six years in a high school, Joan finished her master's degree in school administration in Philadelphia. After completing her studies and receiving a principal's license, she accepted a position as an assistant principal in a large high school. After just two years there, she resigned to accept a doctoral fellowship at a large state university.

Doctoral study was an exciting experience for Joan. She enjoyed the campus culture and the opportunity to go to school without working full-time. One year after starting doctoral studies, she married Robert, a practicing attorney who taught part-time at the university. She ultimately spent two and a half years completing her graduate studies.

Joan Myers was attracted to the assistant superintendent position in Placid Falls for three reasons. Her husband was now working for a Manhattan law firm; she preferred to have a position that focused on curriculum and instruction; and Placid Falls had few problems compared to most other school districts. Although she had considerably less administrative experience than other candidates, she was selected because of her immediate availability (being able to start the job in January), her potential for professional growth (she had now completed the doctorate), and her ability to work effectively with others.

Although her title in the school system is "assistant superintendent," Dr. Myers is basically a staff administrator. That is, she does not have line authority for the principals. She works cooperatively with administrators and teachers on curriculum projects and serves as a resource person to assist with the development of instructional materials.

The New Superintendent

During the first two to three weeks in Placid Falls, Dr. Sagossi held several administrative staff meetings and met with administrators individually. During these sessions, he outlined expectations and developed several organizational goals that he had for the school system. In general, he appeared to the administrative staff to be much like his predecessor—confident, articulate, and capable.

After those first weeks, however, the administrators had only limited contact with Dr. Sagossi. Even the central office secretaries commented that he spent very little time in his office. And when he was there, he either had appointments or worked with his personal secretary behind a closed door. This lack of visibility in the central office separated Dr. Sagossi from his predecessor. The former superintendent not only spent a considerable amount of time in his office, he frequently joined secretaries and other administrators for coffee in the office lounge.

Unaccustomed to the superintendent being gone so much, the principals started asking questions about his work habits. Dr. Yanko, the assistant superintendent for business, tried to provide some answers. He said that the new superintendent was "community oriented." That meant that he preferred to spend most of his time working with civic and governmental leaders. He told the principals that Dr. Sagossi delegated considerable authority to him and to Dr. Myers.

Just three months after becoming superintendent in Placid Falls, Dr. Sagossi was indeed highly involved in community activities. For example, he had been appointed to the board of directors for a local bank and board of directors for the local United Way. In addition, he continued to serve as a member of the alumni council at his alma mater, and he was the president-elect of a large national administrators' group.

The Problem

In December, Dr. Myers attended a national conference on gifted and talented education. There she met Maggie Zerich, a program officer for a foundation. Ms.

Zerich's interest in gifted and talented education was tied to a project her employer had funded in six school districts. The project involved mentoring relationships for highly talented middle-grade students. Dr. Myers met Ms. Zerich purely by chance as they were seated next to each other at a luncheon.

During their initial encounter, Dr. Myers learned that Ms. Zerich was seeking proposals from school districts in an effort to expand the middle-school mentoring project.

"What can you tell me about this program?" Dr. Myers asked the foundation official.

"The primary purpose is to examine the benefits of taking students in the seventh grade and linking them with mentors for two years," Ms. Zerich answered. "The mentors are usually government officials, business leaders, physicians, engineers, and lawyers who live in the community. The students spend approximately three hours per week working with their mentors on approved projects. Our major interest is to find out if these encounters have a positive effect on the students. For example, did they affect curricular choices later in high school? Did they affect career choices?"

Ms. Zerich could see that Dr. Myers was highly interested in the project. After learning about the Placid Falls School District, she encouraged Dr. Myers to submit a proposal. Dr. Myers left the conference excited about the opportunity. She could hardly wait to share the information with Dr. Sagossi. Getting the grant would benefit the district and it would be a feather in her cap—proof to the new superintendent that she could make positive contributions. Her one concern about developing the proposal was the time lines. The proposal had to be received by the foundation within five weeks so that it could be reviewed for the upcoming funding cycle.

When Dr. Myers returned to Placid Falls, she immediately outlined what needed to be done to complete the proposal. The list included the following tasks:

1. Talk to Joe O'Bannion, the middle school principal, to ensure his support and cooperation.
2. Develop a method for selecting students to participate in the program.
3. Construct a list of prospective mentors.
4. Identify a consultant who would complete the research portion of the project (the foundation required that the investigator be a person not employed by the school district).
5. Get Dr. Sagossi's approval to appropriate $30,000 in matching funds.

The first four were accomplished with little difficulty; the final one proved to be a problem.

The first day back from the conference, December 7th, Dr. Myers walked across the hall to Dr. Sagossi's office in hopes of seeing him. Miss Halston, his secretary, told her that he was out of town at a conference and would not return until December 12th. Fearing that not seeing the superintendent until then would delay her planning, she then went to see Dr. Yanko. She explained the proposal and asked if he could approve a commitment for the required matching funds.

"Only the boss and the school board can approve the appropriation," Dr. Yanko told her. "Besides, all proposals for outside funding must be approved by the school board before they are submitted to funding agencies. And as you know, nothing goes to the school board for consideration unless Dr. Sagossi decides to recommend it. When do you have to submit this?"

"I think the last date is January 12th," Dr. Myers replied.

"Well, you still have the January board meeting. Let's see; the first Wednesday in January is the 3rd. You'll be okay."

After the conversation, Dr. Myers went back to Miss Halston to set an appointment with the superintendent after he returned to the district. The secretary scheduled it for 10:00 A.M. on December 13th. She explained that December 12th would not be possible because the superintendent had a standard practice of not scheduling appointments on the day he returns after an absence of more than two days.

Dr. Myers continued working on the proposal. She concluded that the delay in seeing the superintendent would actually be beneficial because her work on the project would be nearly completed by the time she met with him. This would permit her to discuss the proposal in detail.

Dr. Myers saw Dr. Sagossi briefly on Wednesday the 12th, the day he returned to Placid Falls. The two exchanged greetings in the hallway of the administrative office, but she did not mention the proposal. The following morning, they both attended an administrative staff meeting at 8:00 A.M. Such meetings were not regularly scheduled and were held only when Dr. Sagossi determined they were necessary. The meeting on the 13th was devoted to a series of state-level reports that the superintendent wanted to share with the administrators. The meeting ended at approximately 9:30 A.M. At promptly 9:55 A.M., Joan arrived at Dr. Sagossi's office for her 10:00 A.M. appointment.

Miss Halston said, "I was just getting ready to call you, Dr. Myers. I'm afraid I'm going to have to change your appointment. Dr. Sagossi just received a telephone call that his mother is quite ill. He said he will be back in the office on Monday and he recommended that you meet with him sometime that morning. His calendar is pretty clear, and I'm sure he'll be able to chat with you then."

On Monday morning about 9:00 A.M., Dr. Myers again tried to see the superintendent. This time Miss Halston told her that the board president was with the superintendent and that she didn't know how long they would be together. Dr. Myers reminded the secretary that Dr. Sagossi was supposed to see her and asked that she be informed as soon as the two men finished their conference.

At about 10:30 A.M., Miss Halston called Dr. Myers and apologized on behalf of the superintendent. She told Dr. Myers that a problem had surfaced and that it would be necessary to schedule an appointment for the next day, Tuesday. Dr. Myers looked at her calendar and realized that she had to go to a meeting regarding textbook adoptions in the state capital that day.

"How about Wednesday?" asked Dr. Myers. "Is he available on Wednesday?"

"No," the secretary answered. "He is scheduled to be at the university for an alumni board meeting all that day. He will be back on Thursday."

At this point, Dr. Myers was both frustrated and angry. She told Miss Halston, "Look, this is important. This is not General Motors. I don't understand why I can't arrange to see the superintendent for just 30 minutes. There are thousands of dollars and an excellent educational opportunity at stake. I'm sure that if Dr. Sagossi knew why I wanted to see him, he would find time."

"Dr. Myers," replied the secretary, "I'm just doing my job. Let me talk to Dr. Sagossi again. Maybe he can see you before the end of the week."

Fifteen minutes later the secretary called back and informed Dr. Myers that she should talk to Dr. Yanko about the grant.

"Tell Dr. Sagossi that I have already done that and Dr. Yanko told me I had to talk to the superintendent," Joan impatiently responded.

After putting down the telephone, Dr. Myers realized that school would be dismissing for the holiday break in just four days. She knew that the agenda for the January 3rd board meeting was already being prepared. She went to the superintendent's office to see when board materials would be distributed for the January 3rd meeting. The secretary said that the packets, including the agenda, would be distributed as always one week before the meeting. Because Dr. Sagossi was going on vacation to Florida for 10 days commencing the 23rd of December, he intended to complete the board packets by the afternoon of Friday the 22nd. Once again, Dr. Myers pleaded her case, indicating that it was extremely important to see the superintendent about the grant proposal. Again she was told that she would have to make an appointment.

"Look, the only possible date left is Thursday, December 21st. What if something else comes up and he cancels the appointment again?" Dr. Myers asked.

The secretary looked at her and said slowly, "Dr. Sagossi is a busy person. You cannot expect that he will see you whenever you like. If you have deadlines on a grant proposal, you should have talked to him about it weeks ago."

Dejected, Dr. Myers walked back to her office.

THE CHALLENGE

Place yourself in Dr. Myers's position. What would you do at this point?

KEY ISSUES/QUESTIONS

1. How do you characterize Dr. Sagossi's leadership style?
2. Assess the climate in this school system based on what you learned from reading this case. Is the climate typical for a public school district?
3. In a school district of this size, what would you consider to be an ideal communication style for a superintendent?

4. Although Dr. Myers has the title of assistant superintendent, she functions in a staff capacity. What does this mean? Is it relevant to the problem presented in this case? Why or why not?

5. Is there any evidence in this case suggesting that Dr. Sagossi's relied on contingency theory to guide his behavior?

6. Is it possible for a superintendent to spend most of his or her time away from the school district and still be highly effective? What evidence do you have to support your response?

7. What values and beliefs might contribute to a superintendent isolating himself from other administrators?

8. What alternatives does Dr. Myers have to resolve this matter?

9. Do you believe there is a nexus between Dr. Sagossi's motives for taking the position in Placid Falls and his subsequent behavior? Why or why not?

10. Did Dr. Sagossi behave inappropriately when he did not tell the school board members all of his motives for taking the job in Placid Falls? Why or why not?

11. If you were a new superintendent in Placid Falls, how much time would you devote to working directly with your administrative staff during the first year?

SUGGESTED READINGS

Abrams, J. (1987). How superintendents can work better with others. *Education Digest, 52*(10), 26–28.

Akenhead, J. (1986). Use staff chats to build your schools' team spirit. *Executive Educator, 8*(10), 22–23.

Brunner, C. C. (1997). Exercising power. *The School Administrator, 54*(6), 6–9.

Chalker, D., & Hurley, S. (1993). Beastly people. *Executive Educator, 15*(1), 24–26.

Comer, D. (1991). Organizational newcomers' acquisition of information from peers. *Management Communication Quarterly, 5*(1), 64–89.

DeRoche, E. (1985). *How administrators solve problems.* Englewood Cliffs, NJ: Prentice-Hall (see chapter 3).

Diggins, P. B. (1997). Reflections on leadership characteristics necessary to develop and sustain learning school communities. *School Leadership and Management, 17*(3), 413–425.

Duke, D. L. (1998). The normative context of organizational leadership. *Educational Administration Quarterly, 34*(2), 165–195.

Duttweiler, P. (1988). The dysfunctions of bureaucratic structure. *Educational Policy and Practice,* Issue 3.

Eblen, A. (1987). Communication, leadership, and organizational commitment. *Central States Speech Journal, 38*(3–4), 181–195.

Geddes, D. (1993). Empowerment through communication: Key people-to-people and organizational success. *People and Education, 1*(1), 76–104.

Goldman, E. (1998). The significance of leadership style. *Educational Leadership, 55*(7), 20–22.

Hanson, E. (1996). *Educational administration and organizational behavior* (4th ed.). Boston: Allyn & Bacon (see chapter 9).

Hoy, W., Newland, W., & Blaxovsky, R. (1977). Subordinate loyalty to superior, esprit, and aspects of bureaucratic structure. *Educational Administration Quarterly, 13*(1), 71–85.

Immegart, G. (1988). Leadership and leader behavior. In N. Boyan (Ed.), *Handbook of research on educational administration* (pp. 259–278). New York: Longman.

Kelly, D. G. (1997). Turnover at the top. *American School Board Journal, 184*(4), 46, 48.

Kowalski, T. J. (1998). Critiquing the CEO. *American School Board Journal, 185*(2), 43–44.

Kowalski, T., & Reitzug, U. (1993). *Contemporary school administration: An introduction.* New York: Longman (see chapters 7, 10).

Loose, W., & McManus, J. (1987). Corporate management techniques in the superintendent's office. *Thrust, 16*(7), 11–13.

O'Toole, J. (1995). *Leading change: Overcoming the ideology of comfort and the tyranny of custom.* San Francisco: Jossey-Bass.

Shelton, M. M., & Powell, T. (1997). The ethics question. *American School Board Journal, 184*(12), 36–37.

Spaulding, A., & O'Hair, M. J. (2000). Public relations in a communication context. In T. J. Kowalski (Ed.), *Public relations in schools* (pp. 137-164). Upper Saddle River, NJ: Merrill, Prentice Hall.

Vroom, V., & Jago, A. (1988). *The new leadership: Managing participation in organizations.* Englewood Cliffs, NJ: Prentice-Hall (see chapter 7).

Captain Punishment

BACKGROUND INFORMATION

Role theory is concerned with variables that shape work behavior; it is a conceptual framework that describes and analyzes job performance in an organizational context in relation to performance expectations (Gaynor, 1998). Role conflict is one dimension of role theory. A common problem for school principals, it stems from individuals and groups—in and outside of the organization—expressing divergent expectations for administrative performance. Variables that contribute to this condition may be personal (e.g., philosophy, needs, biases, and wants), organizational (e.g., job descriptions, organizational culture), and environmental (e.g., parent expectations, community expectations).

One form of role conflict results from individuals and groups making different demands on a single role. For example, some parents, students, and faculty want the principal to be caring, understanding, and nurturing when dealing with discipline; others prefer the principal to be stern and uncompromising. Ambiguity—a condition caused by the role not being clearly defined or by the person occupying it not comprehending expectations—is a primary cause of this friction (Hanson, 1995). Role conflict also may exist within a single individual (Owens, 1998). For example, the formal job description may require a principal to be primarily a manager when his or her personality needs lean toward creativity and risk taking.

When confronted with role conflict, a principal may behave in several different ways. He or she may select the following options:

- Choose one expectation over others
- Withdraw from the situation (e.g., resign from the principalship)

- Seek to reconcile expectation differences
- Attempt to satisfy all expectations
- Seek protection from policy and rules (acquiesce to behavioral norms established by the formal organization)
- Ignore expectations and behave according to personal convictions

The effectiveness of each option usually depends on variables surrounding a specific situation.

This case involves a middle school principal facing different role expectations. For example, some mothers who are raising their children alone encourage the principal to be a father figure; they support his use of corporal punishment. Others, including some of the faculty in the school, expect the principal to behave professionally; they want him to rely on professional knowledge and to be understanding and compassionate when disciplining students. Not surprisingly, such divergent expectations contribute to vastly different conclusions about the principal's effectiveness.

As you read this case, try to identify personal, organizational, and environmental variables that contributed to role conflict for this principal. Also, think about your experiences with role conflict. How did you deal with role conflict? What have you observed with regard to others responding to role conflict?

KEY AREAS FOR REFLECTION

1. Role expectations
2. Role conflict
3. Relationship between behavior and organizational outcomes
4. Alternative approaches to discipline
5. The effects of community environment on the normative behavior of principals

THE CASE

The School

Rogers Middle School is located in a major city in a southwestern state. The school was built nine years ago to accommodate population growth in low-cost housing areas. The building is attractive and well maintained, and it is a source of pride for many families in the neighborhoods surrounding it. Although the houses in these neighborhoods are less than 25 years old, they are inexpensive, prefabricated structures already showing signs of deterioration.

Many students at Rogers Middle School are bilingual. A statistical report prepared for the central administration of the school system included the following racial-ethnic profile:

Hispanic – 41 percent

African American – 15 percent

Caucasian – 24 percent

Native American – 9 percent

Asian American – 9 percent

Other – 2 percent

The profile of the school's professional staff is quite different. About two-thirds of the teachers, counselors, and administrators identify themselves as Caucasian.

Rogers Middle School contains grades 6–8 and accommodates a total enrollment of 1,150. Compared to other schools in the district, Rogers is considered by many to be highly effective. Average scores on the state proficiency test are the highest among the district's middle schools, and athletic teams and other extracurricular programs have an established record of success. In addition, Rogers has fewer suspensions and expulsions than other middle schools. Much of the credit for these accomplishments has been directed at the school's principal, Pete Sanchez.

The Principal

Ever since he was in third grade, Pete Sanchez knew that he wanted to be a teacher. One of nine children reared in a poor family living in the southwest, he could not afford to go to college after graduating from high school. He instead worked in a local factory. Over a span of seven years while he worked full-time, he drove 45 miles twice a week to take night classes at a state university. He completed the first three years of study in this manner. Then he quit his job, obtained a student loan, and finished his degree as a full-time student.

Several of Pete's professors encouraged him to go directly to graduate school. His grades were quite good, especially during his final year of undergraduate study. But Pete wanted to start teaching. He was married, his wife was pregnant, and he needed the income. So he accepted a high school teaching position in a neighboring state. There he taught mathematics and assumed two coaching responsibilities—assistant football coach and head track coach. During a period of 12 years he taught at this school, occasionally took graduate courses, and eventually completed a master's degree in educational administration. The following year, Pete was hired as an assistant high school principal in another district.

Pete's primary assignment as assistant principal was to oversee the student discipline program. According to the school's principal, Pete excelled at the job. He set high expectations and helped students who got in trouble. But he also relied on corporal punishment, because he believed that some students only listened when they got their bottoms paddled. It was this element of his performance that earned him the nickname "Captain Punishment."

After acquiring three years of administrative experience, Pete applied to be principal of a new middle school in the district. During his interview for the position, he indicated that he preferred to work with students from low-income families. He also stated his discipline philosophy. It was predicated on the following beliefs:

- Many students living in low-income families did not receive guidance and direction outside of school.
- These students often did not take advantage of their educational opportunities because they did not respect authority and did not exercise self-control.
- Discipline for these students had to be consistent and meaningful; occasionally corporal punishment was the most effective means of correcting their negative behavior.

His interview was successful and he was selected to be the first principal of Rogers Middle School.

Within two months after the new school opened, Mr. Sanchez had formed a parent association. He appointed members to serve on various school committees with teachers and administrators. One of these committees—the Student Discipline Committee (SDC)—consisted of seven parents, three teachers, and an assistant principal. In the past two years, the SDC has received requests from parents or teachers to review the school's use of corporal punishment. On both occasions, Mr. Sanchez appeared before the committee requesting that the current rules not be changed. Both times, the SDC members voted 9 to 2 to support the practice of paddling students provided that the discipline was administered legally.

During his tenure at Rogers Middle School, Mr. Sanchez has been the subject of numerous feature stories done by the local media. He was portrayed consistently as an effective administrator whose "no nonsense" approach had contributed to the school's success. Two of the stories referred to the principal's nickname, Captain Punishment. The most recent of these profiles was conducted by a television station. Several parents were interviewed and each expressed strong support for the principal. One mother said, "Mr. Sanchez understands my children. He teaches them that they have to obey rules. They don't have a father at home, so I'm glad they get discipline at school. My kids have a lot of respect for Mr. Sanchez."

Not everyone, however, supported Mr. Sanchez's discipline philosophy. One teacher who did not was Aaron Carson. A social studies instructor, Mr. Carson relocated in the Southwest after teaching in Virginia for three years—a move prompted by chronic asthma.

Mr. Carson first challenged the principal's use of corporal punishment about four years ago in a faculty meeting. At the time, he received little support from his colleagues and his comments were basically ignored. Two years later, he again raised the issue at a faculty meeting. This time he was armed with articles from professional journals criticizing corporal punishment. Two other teachers who were relatively new members of the faculty supported him. Most of the other teachers, however remained unwilling to discuss the issue. A teacher who said, "If you have differences with Mr. Sanchez, you ought to discuss them with him at some other time," summarized their feeling.

Mr. Carson had two subsequent meetings with the principal to discuss his concerns about corporal punishment. But the principal was not persuaded to change his practice.

The Incident

Every student at Rogers Middle School knew Jimmy Longbow. He was a gifted athlete prone to getting into trouble. His father had died several years ago, and he lived with his mother and two sisters. Jimmy was in Aaron Carson's social studies class. It was one of the few classes in which he was making a better than average grade. Aaron liked Jimmy. Maybe he saw a little of himself—a rebellious child, growing up in poverty, without a father, and with a big chip on his shoulder. Aaron remembers all too well his own childhood in Brooklyn, New York. Life was tough, and you had to grow up in a hurry.

Jimmy's least favorite class was English. The teacher, Mr. Draycroft, made the students diagram sentences, study grammar, and read poetry—all things Jimmy found boring and irrelevant. One day, when Mr. Draycroft was in an especially bad mood, he was giving Jimmy a tongue-lashing for not doing his homework. When the three-minute diatribe ended, Jimmy looked directly at the teacher and said, "This stuff is all crap. Why don't you teach us something important?"

The students could see the veins pop out the teacher's neck. Mr. Draycroft shook his finger at Jimmy and said, "You, young man, are going to the office. I have had it with you. Maybe a dozen good whacks will teach you not to be so impudent."

The teacher escorted Jimmy to the office and then told the principal what had happened. Jimmy and Mr. Sanchez were not strangers. According to the school grapevine, Jimmy had gotten hit with the paddle more than any other student in the school.

"Jimmy," Mr. Sanchez began, "when are you going to learn? You mess up, you're going to get it. You can't shoot your mouth off any time you feel like it. It's time for you to grow up. But as we see by this incident, you're not there yet. You have no respect for authority, so, I have to treat you like a second-grader."

The principal then directed the student to empty his back pockets, to bend over, and to hold his ankles. But this time Jimmy refused to comply.

"You're not going to hit me with that paddle again," he told the principal. "You can take your school and shove it."

With that, Jimmy ran from the office and the school building. Before anyone could catch him, he was nowhere in sight. The principal called Jimmy's mother, who worked as a waitress in a restaurant near the school. She left work immediately to see if she could find her son, but the effort proved fruitless. Jimmy did not come home that night, or the next, or the next.

Various accounts of the incident spread quickly through the school. When Aaron Carson found out about it, he called Jimmy's mother and asked if he could talk to her. The two had met previously at parent-teacher conferences. Mrs. Longbow trusted Mr. Carson. When they met, she shared with him the details of the incident given to her by the principal. Mr. Carson said that he would try to find Jimmy and indicated he planned to talk to the principal as well.

The meeting between Aaron Carson and Pete Sanchez the next day took place in the principal's office. Unlike previous encounters between the two, this one was not very civil. The teacher was angry and blamed the principal for the student's disappearance. After making his feelings known to Mr. Sanchez, Mr. Carson then complained to Dr. Penelope Mackee, an assistant superintendent who had supervisory responsibility for secondary school principals. She indicated that the principal had not violated policy, and that philosophical differences between the two of them should be settled at the school level. Mr. Carson judged that Dr. Mackee was unwilling to take action against a principal because he had become somewhat of a legend and hero in the city.

Concluding that school officials would only protect Pete Sanchez, Aaron Carson decided to state his case in the media. He wrote the following letter to the editor of the major newspaper in the city:

The public needs to know the story of Jimmy Longbow, a young Native American student at Rogers Middle School who is now a runaway. Jimmy is no angel, but neither is he some type of second-class citizen who should be whipped every time he does something improper. Corporal punishment is a practice that has been discontinued in most American public schools, but it is alive and well at Rogers Middle School. Jimmy Longbow is now somewhere on the streets because his teachers and his principal thought that brutality was more effective than counseling and constructive behavior modification. Parents of Rogers Middle School students and citizens of this community, wake up! Wake up before it is too late. Let your school board members know what you think about corporal punishment. Let's put a stop to this. Hopefully, Jimmy Longbow will come home, reenter school, and prove that he can be successful. Let's do something before there are more tragic stories.

Sincerely,

Aaron Carson,

Social studies teacher, Rogers Middle School

The letter generated dozens of calls from angry citizens to the school board supporting Mr. Carson's position. The newspaper then provided a three-part report on the incident involving Jimmy Longbow and the use of corporal punishment at Rogers Middle School. The publicity prompted many citizens, most of them parents of students at Rogers Middle School, to publicly defend Mr. Sanchez. They paid for a newspaper ad praising Mr. Sanchez and pledging to support him in the future. The ad contained the signatures of nearly 100 parents.

The controversy and negative publicity bothered most of the school board members. They asked the superintendent to provide a full report on the matter at the next school board meeting. After learning that the school board would be looking into the matter, the parent association at Rogers Middle School formulated the following petition:

We the undersigned fully support the leadership of Principal Pete Sanchez. He has made Rogers Middle School the most successful school in our district. Clearly, the incident involving Jimmy Longbow is unfortunate, but we do not agree with those who claim that Mr. Sanchez is to blame. We urge you, our representatives on the school board, to join us in supporting a great principal. Further, we believe that in the best interest of Rogers Middle School, teachers who try to discredit our principal should be transferred to other schools.

In one week, nearly 70 percent of the Rogers parents signed the petition. Copies were mailed to each board member and to the superintendent, Dr. Fred Lopson, prior to the board meeting.

The meeting drew more than 400 supporters of Mr. Sanchez. Dr. Lopson's report included the following points:

- Existing policy did not prohibit corporal punishment.
- Rogers Middle School was considered to be one of the most effective schools in the district.
- Parental involvement in the school was outstanding.
- The vast majority of parents supported the principal and his discipline procedures.

Board member George Manulita, a Native American, asked to be recognized after the superintendent concluded his remarks.

"I think we are all aware of Mr. Sanchez's successes," he said. "That is, in my opinion, not the real issue here. I want to know what we are going to do about allowing corporal punishment in our schools. It's unfortunate that this incident with the student at Rogers Middle School occurred. Hopefully, he will be found and he will return to school. But our action as board members should be directed to the future. I want to know, Dr. Lopson, what you recommend with regard to policies governing corporal punishment. Do you think we should continue to permit such activity? Should we pass new policy to prohibit it?"

Mr. Manulita's last question was answered with shouts of "no" from most in the audience.

Darren Marshall, another board member, was next to speak.

"Let's keep in mind that we're talking about one of our best schools. Do we want to present yet another barrier to our administrators, especially when this administrator, Mr. Sanchez, is certainly getting the job done? I'm more concerned about a teacher who writes derogatory letters to the newspaper about his principal. What are we going to do about this teacher, Mr. Superintendent?"

This time the crowd applauded and started to chant, "Mr. Sanchez, Mr. Sanchez."

THE CHALLENGE

Place yourself in the superintendent's position. What would you do?

KEY ISSUES/QUESTIONS

1. Behavior in schools is affected by three critical factors: individuals, groups, and structure. Discuss how each plays a part in the behavior detailed in this case. How is each of these likely to influence the superintendent's decision?

2. What are your impressions of Mr. Sanchez? Would you like to be a teacher in this school?

3. In what ways might the principal's personal life affect his philosophy toward discipline?

4. What are your impressions of Mr. Carson, the teacher who wrote the letter to the newspaper? Is he a hero or troublemaker?

5. The case suggests that most of the teachers and most of the parents in this middle school supported the practice of corporal punishment. Should this have any influence on the decision made by the superintendent and school board? Why or why not?

6. What does the literature say about the effectiveness of corporal punishment?

7. Analyze this case from the following perspectives: professional behavior, ethical behavior, political behavior, legal perspective.

8. Are corporal punishment and the middle school philosophy compatible?

9. Should discipline policies be developed collaboratively between a principal and faculty? Why or why not?

10. Do you believe that every school district should have a policy on the use of corporal punishment? Why or why not?

11. Mr. Sanchez's philosophy and practices in the area of student discipline were known in the district prior to his being named principal at Rogers Middle School. Is this fact relevant to the case? Why or why not?

12. Mr. Sanchez used committees to involve parents in the educational process. Do you consider this to be a good idea for a middle school? Why or why not?

13. In your opinion, do most principals attempt to integrate research and theory into their practice? What evidence do you have to support your response?

14. How would you describe the culture of this school? To what extent does the community environment affect the school's culture? To what extent does the principal influence the school's culture?

15. Evaluate the presumed nexus between the principal's leadership style and the success of the school.

SUGGESTED READINGS

Andrews, R,. & Soder, R. (1987). Principal leadership and student achievement. *Educational Leadership, 44*(6), 9-11.

Ashbaugh, C., & Kasten, K. (1984). A typology of operant values in school administration. *Planning and Changing, 15*(4), 195-208.

Barbour, N. (1991). Ban the hickory stick. *Childhood Education, 68*(2), 69-70.

Borelli, J. (1997). A schoolwide discipline plan that empowers teachers and gives principals time for instructional leadership. *NASSP Bulletin, 81*(588), 68-75.

Campbell-Evans, G. (1990). Nature and influence of values in principal decision making. *Alberta Journal of Educational Research, 37*(2), 167-178.

Carey, M. (1986). School discipline: Better to be loved or feared? *Momentum, 17*(2), 20-21.

Curwin, R., & Mendler, A. (1988). *Discipline with dignity.* Arlington, VA: Association for Supervision and Curriculum Development.

Eberts, R., & Stone, J. (1988). Student achievement in public schools: Do principals make a difference? *Economics of Education Review, 7*(3), 291-299.

Erickson, H. (1988). The boy who couldn't be disciplined. *Principal, 67*(5), 36-37.

Gaynor, A. K. (1998). *Analyzing problems in school and school systems: A theoretical approach.* Mahwah, NJ: Lawrence Erlbaum Associates.

Glassman, N. (1986). Student achievement and the school principal. *Education Evaluation and Policy Analysis, 7*(2), 283-296.

Glickman, C. (1991). Pretending not to know what we know. *Educational Leadership, 48*(8), 4-10.

Gordon, J. A. (1998). Caring through control. *Journal for a Just and Caring Education, 4*(4), 418-440.

Grasmick, H. (1992). Support for corporal punishment in the schools: A comparison of the effects of socioeconomic status and religion. *Social Science Quarterly, 73*(1), 177-187.

Gusky, D. (1992). Spare the child. *Teacher Magazine, 3*(5), 16-19.

Hanson, E. M. (1996), *Educational administration and organizational behavior* (4th edition). Boston: Allyn and Bacon.

Henley, M. (1997). Why punishment doesn't work. *Principal, 77*(2), 45-46.

Hyman, I. A. (1997). *The case against spanking: How to discipline your child without hitting.* San Francisco: Jossey-Bass.

Hyman, I. A., & Snook, P. A. (2000). Dangerous schools and what you can do about them. *Phi Delta Kappan, 81*(7), 488-498, 500-501.

Hyman, R., & Rathbone, C. (1993a). *Corporal punishment in schools: Reading the law.* NOLPE Monograph Series, No. 48.

Hyman, R., & Rathbone, C. (1993b). *The principals's decision: A teaching monograph on corporal punishment.* NOLPE Monograph Series, No. 48a.

Kowalski, T., & Reitzug, U. (1993). *Contemporary school administration: An introduction.* New York: Longman (see chapters 11, 14).

Maurer, A. (1981). *Paddles away: A psychological study of physical punishment in schools.* Palo Alto, CA: R & E Research Associates.

McDaniel, T. (1986). School discipline in perspective. *Clearing House, 59*(8), 369-370.

McFadden, A. (1992). A study of race and gender bias in the punishment of children. *Education and Treatment of Children, 15*(2), 140-146.

Nolte, M. (1985). Before you take a paddling in court, read this corporal punishment advice. *American School Board Journal, 173*(7), 27, 35.

Owens, R. G. (1998) *Organizational behavior in education* (6th ed.). Boston: Allyn and Bacon.

Paquet, R. (1982). *Judicial rulings, state statutes, and state administrative regulations dealing with the use of corporal punishment in public schools.* Palo Alto, CA: R & E Research Associates.

Pearce, A. (1992). Investigating allegations of inappropriate physical punishment of students by school employees. *School Law Bulletin, 23*(2), 15-21.

Pitcher, G., & Poland, S. (1992). *Crisis intervention in the schools.* New York: Guilford Press.

Rose, T. (1984). Current uses of corporal punishment in American public schools. *Journal of Educational Psychology, 76*(3), 427-441.

Slavin, R., & Madden, N. (1989). What works for students at risk: A research synthesis. *Educational Leadership, 46*(5), 4-13.

Zirkel, P., & Gluckman, I. (1988). A legal brief: Constitutionalizing corporal punishment. *NASSP Bulletin, 72*(506), 105-109.

The Stepping Stone

BACKGROUND INFORMATION

The concept of administrative career patterns has been studied in both business and education. Part of this research has focused on regularities found in pathways from lower-level to higher-level positions (Miklos, 1988). This particular subject has received considerable attention in school administration because vertical career mobility has been the norm. That is to say, principals and other administrators typically advanced in their careers by moving to a sequentially higher position, often in different school districts.

Practical and ethical questions evolve when the careers of school administrators are analyzed. For instance, is it proper to accept a position with the intent of only remaining in the job until a better position is secured? Should an individual accept a position solely to gain visibility in the profession? Are administrators legally and ethically bound to fulfill the terms of an employment contract before accepting another position?

Although such questions certainly are not new, their relevance has been heightened by efforts to reform public education. Concerns have been expressed in several ways. Consider the following criticisms:

- Upwardly mobile administrators allow personal ambitions to take precedence over the interests of schools and children.
- Superintendents or principals who resign after only a year or two to accept more lucrative positions attenuate the prospects for school improvement.

- Often quality candidates willing to make long-term commitments to a position are bypassed for upwardly mobile candidates who are not candid about their career goals during the selection process.
- Ambitious administrators frequently pursue reforms that enhance their reputations regardless of whether such changes benefit schools and children.

Administrators who have been subjected to such charges have often countered with arguments such as these:

- School administrators have little job-related security, therefore, they must be concerned with their own careers.
- The political environment in general, and school boards in particular, are often more responsible for leadership instability than are administrators.
- Gaining two or three years of leadership from dynamic and capable administrators is more advantageous for a school or district than is suffering through 15 years of service from a mediocre or ineffective administrator.

This case involves an ambitious young man who tries to advance his career by accepting a superintendency in a small rural community. Attempting to emulate his former superintendent, the individual generates substantial conflict because his behavior and the climate of the community and school district are incongruent.

As you read the case, think about the ways that career goals and past experiences may influence leadership behavior. Also consider how organizational climate, and especially the component of organizational culture, create the boundaries for acceptable and unacceptable administrative behavior.

KEY AREAS FOR REFLECTION

1. Career patterns of school administrators
2. Ethical and moral dimensions of career development
3. Influences on leadership behavior
4. The importance of community and organizational contexts with regard to leadership behavior
5. Human relations within organizations
6. Organizational climate and culture in relation to administrative behavior

THE CASE

The Community

Hallville is located in northern Iowa. It is a friendly town of about 2,500 residents, many of whom have never lived anywhere else. Besides the bank, the Sears outlet store, Dotty's restaurant, an IGA grocery store, two taverns, and Klink's Farm Implements, there is not much else downtown. Being only 17 miles from the county seat, a community of 65,000, Hallville's residents have become accustomed to traveling elsewhere to meet most of their special needs.

Most everyone in Hallville knows everyone else. The town picnics, one in early June and one in late August, are the social highlights of the year. Loretta Helmich, the town's part-time mayor, works at the bank. The town's largest employer is the corn processing plant. It employs about 175 local residents. Farms surround the town—many of them are rather large (400 or more acres).

The Schools

Hallville Community School District serves residents of Hallville and two adjoining townships. There are only two schools in the district: Hallville Junior/Senior High School and Hallville Elementary School. The basic information for each school is as follows:

Hallville Junior/Senior High School

- Grade levels: 7 through 12
- Enrollment: 440
- Principal: Oscar McCammick
- Assistant principal: Judy Buschak
- Number of teachers: 26
- Number of counselors: 1
- Number of secretaries: 2
- Number of custodians: 3
- Other personnel (e.g., cooks, aides): 9

Hallville Elementary School

- Grade levels: kindergarten through 6
- Enrollment: 407
- Principal: Denise Fischer
- Number of teachers: 18
- Number of counselors: 1
- Number of secretaries: 2
- Number of custodians: 2
- Other personnel (e.g., cooks, aides): 13

The junior/senior high school is housed in a new structure that was built just six years ago. The elementary school operates in a much older facility, built in 1955. The elementary school is located in town; the junior/senior high school is located just outside of town on a state highway.

The Need for a New Superintendent

Last year Wilbur Stineman, the superintendent, was killed in an automobile accident on his way home from a meeting in Des Moines. He had spent his entire career in the Hallville school district as a teacher, coach, counselor, principal, and superintendent. His death stunned the community. He was well-liked and respected by those who knew him.

Most everyone took for granted that Oscar McCammick, one of the two principals, would become the next superintendent. But the veteran administrator told the school board members that he was not interested in the job. He preferred to remain at the junior/senior high school because he enjoyed being a principal. In fact, no employee in the district applied for the position of superintendent. Therefore, for the first time in more than 50 years, the school board had to look outside the district to find a superintendent.

The five school board members invited the two principals, the mayor, and the president of the Hallville Elementary School Parent-Teacher Association to participate in the search process. The selection team received 18 applications, and after reviewing them, four candidates were invited to interview for the job. All nine individuals participating in the selection process supported the appointment of Rob Zelker.

The New Superintendent

Just 31 years old when he arrived in Hallville, Rob had spent three years as principal of an elementary school in a large city. He recently had completed his specialist's degree and obtained his superintendent's license. Rob grew up in a farming community in western Iowa much like Hallville—a factor that was weighed positively by members of the search team.

Three issues influenced Rob's decision to move to Hallville:

- Although neither Rob nor his wife, Alice, preferred to live in a small town, they were willing to do so to advance his career. They came to Hallville intending to stay no more than three or four years. Rob saw Hallville as a stepping stone to a larger community; he ultimately wanted to be a big-city superintendent.
- Hallville was just 38 miles from a university where Rob could pursue his doctoral degree without going to school full-time. He planned to use much of his vacation to attend summer school classes.
- Rob's role model, Dr. Nolan Smythe, recommended that he take the Hallville job. Dr. Smythe was the superintendent in the district where Rob had been a principal. The two men were friends and Rob idolized the older, more-experienced administrator. Rob thought that Dr. Smythe dressed and acted like a corporate executive—a characteristic Rob admired. Dr. Smythe once told Rob, "You have to look the part to be an effective leader."

The Zelker family moved to Hallville in July. They rented a house from a retired couple who had just moved to Florida. Alice, a registered nurse, was hired by a local physician to work part-time in his clinic. The Zelker's only child, Amy, was enrolled in first grade at Hallville Elementary School.

The First Year

The district offices are located in a wing of the Junior/Senior High School. Only three persons are employed for the central office—a secretary, a bookkeeper, and the superintendent. The secretary, Bonnie Stutz, is the sister of one of the school board members. The bookkeeper, Norine Dawson, is the widow of a former teacher and coach at the high school. Both Bonnie and Norine have lived in Hallville their entire lives, and each has worked for the school district for over 20 years.

After starting his new job, Rob immediately took steps to improve the appearance of the superintendent's office. The existing furniture was over 20 years old, and the walls had not been painted for some time. The board members unanimously approved his recommendation to spend $6,000 on office improvements.

During his first week on the job, Rob devoted much of his time to touring the two schools and visiting the principals. School would open in about six weeks and Rob wanted to make sure that the buildings were ready. These initial encounters produced several negative perceptions that Rob shared with his wife.

"You know, Alice, I expected things to be informal here. But you wouldn't believe just how informal they are. Two days ago, I spent about two hours with Oscar McCammick. He appears to be a pretty good guy. But when I first got to his office, the secretary was not there. So I walked around the counter and looked into Oscar's office. He was talking with several teachers. The door was open and when saw me, he motioned for me to enter. He was leaning back in his chair and his feet were on his desk. He was wearing a tee shirt and pair of shorts. He told me he was taking a half-day of vacation to play golf with two of the teachers that afternoon. Could you imagine what would have happened if Dr. Smythe walked into my office and I was dressed like that?"

"Well," his wife answered, "it is July and this is Hallville. Maybe he didn't have to see students or parents. When school starts, he'll probably be wearing a coat and tie."

"You never know when someone is going to walk into a school, even in July. I think principals should look more presentable when they are working. I hope you're right about how he will dress when school is in session."

Rob then told her about the visit to the elementary school.

"When I got to the elementary school, the secretary was listening to the radio and reading *People* magazine. When I asked to see Mrs. Fischer, she said she would be back in an hour or two. She was getting her hair done. I'm not sure the secretary knew who I was. She didn't ask. In any event, it seemed she didn't care."

During the next two months Rob had several other experiences that led him to conclude that the casual manner he had observed in early July was not atypical. Even school board meetings were informal. Board members and patrons addressed each other using first names; members of the audience frequently interacted freely with the board members. These meetings were substantially different than those he observed prior to coming to Hallville. In addition, everyone, including employees, addressed him as "Rob" and not as "Mr. Zelker." He considered this to be disrespectful, and thought that his young age was responsible for the way he was being treated. By late October, Rob decided to deal with the excessive informality.

First, he met with the other two central office employees and the two principals. He stated that he was troubled by their lack of decorum. He cited several examples of what he considered improper behavior. One involved a telephone conversation between Mrs. Stutz and a parent; during the conversation, he overheard the secretary repeatedly refer to him as "Rob." The other involved a memorandum the elementary principal sent to the faculty in which she wrote, "Our new superintendent will be visiting the building on Tuesday. Please join me in making Rob feel welcome." The superintendent told them that this level of informality was excessive and uncharacteristic of what one would find in other districts. Before the meeting ended, Rob distributed a list of guidelines and asked the four to follow them.

- He preferred to be addressed as Mr. Zelker, especially in the presence of other employees, parents, and students.
- All employees were expected to dress professionally at work.
- Employees were not to leave work for personal reasons unless an immediate supervisor approved the absence. When such approvals were granted, employees would be required to make up the lost time.
- Principals should discourage their own office staff from addressing them by their first names during office hours.
- Formal titles should be used in writing memoranda.

The four employees were surprised by the superintendent's comments. They explained that they intended no disrespect by addressing him by his first name. They said they simply were in the habit of doing this, and no one had been concerned in the past. Rob said he was not angry; he noted that he simply wanted to improve the district's image and operations.

Next, Rob shifted his attention to the school board. He wrote a lengthy memorandum recommending procedural changes for school board meetings. He included these recommendations:

- Formal roll-call votes should be taken on all motions.
- Items addressed during the meeting should be restricted to those included on the formal agenda prepared by the superintendent.

- Comments from the audience should be restricted to a specific portion of the meeting and no patron should be allowed to speak for more than three minutes unless the board grants permission for extended comments.

Rob also suggested that the board members should consider other ways of making their meetings more formal.

Dale Klink, president of the school board, owns a farm implement business. The other board members look to him for leadership; however, he has not used this influence to intrude into administration. Mr. Klink believes that the superintendent and principals should be left alone to perform their duties. Thus, he rarely initiated meetings with the superintendent, but Rob Zelker's memorandum prompted him to do so.

Dale Klink went to see Rob on a dreary mid-November day. After getting a cup of coffee and saying hello to Bonnie Stutz and Norine Dawson, he walked into Rob's office and shut the door. They shook hands, and Dale spoke first.

"Rob, what the hell possessed you to send this memo to the board members? Don't you think that it would have been better to talk to me first? You know, your memo is a little embarrassing."

The board president's demeanor and tone put Rob on the defensive. He had never heard Dale speak this way. Normally, he is soft-spoken and friendly. He collected his thoughts before responding.

"Dale, I certainly didn't want to embarrass you. I'm just trying to improve things. I thought that was what you expected from me. If I was out of line sending the memorandum, I'm sorry. But even now, I don't think I was wrong in trying to improve the way we run our board meetings."

"Rob, you've been here four months. In that short time, you've told the principals and the women in this office to start doing things differently. Yes, the board members know about your guidelines even though you didn't bother to tell us about them. Don't forget, this is a real small town," the board president said.

Reference to the guidelines caused Rob to be even more defensive. "I know people here think this is a very good system, and in many ways it is," he responded. "But it could become a lot better. I know some people think that my concerns about informality are trivial. They're not. I just want to increase efficiency."

"What's efficiency got to do with calling you Mr.?" Dale asked.

"It's not the informality that bothers me. It's the attitudes associated with employee behavior. For example, some key staff go to the bank, buy groceries, or get their hair done on school time. And when the administrators and central office staff do this, they're symbolically telling other employees that it is okay for them to do the same things. I believe that good examples have to start with us—the superintendent and school board. That's one reason why I suggested that we make our board meetings more formal and businesslike."

The board president took a drink of his coffee and stood up. He looked out the window for a moment and then turned to face the young superintendent.

"Rob, I've got to get back to my store. But let me give you some advice before I go. This is a nice community and you have a good job. We've never fired a superintendent. You have to admit, board members don't interfere with how you manage the schools. All five of us want you to be successful, and we will help you in any way we can. But you have got to understand that people are not going to sit still if you try to change everything in a few months. So we're not going to change the board meetings—at least not now. Maybe you should think about the need for you to change. Forget that you ever wrote this memorandum to the board. I'm going to suggest to the board members that they do the same. We all make mistakes. What causes serious problems is our unwillingness to recognize them."

That said, Dale Klink walked out of the office. Rob's heart was beating and he had little beads of perspiration on the back of his neck. He knew he was in trouble, and he was not sure what he should do. He picked up the telephone and called his trusted advisor, Dr. Nolan Smythe, but his secretary indicated that he was on a trip to Russia with a group of educators for the next two weeks.

THE CHALLENGE

Analyze the behavior of Rob Zelker in this case. What do you believe he should do at this point?

KEY ISSUES/QUESTIONS

1. Consider Rob's motives for taking the position in Hallville. Did his motives influence his behavior once he was in the job?
2. Assess the selection committee's judgment that Rob would understand the culture of Hallville because he grew up in a similar community. What other factors should the committee members have weighed in selecting a superintendent?
3. Assume you were the new superintendent in Hallville. Would you have reacted to the informality? If so, in what manner?
4. In this case, Rob attempts to emulate Dr. Smythe. Is emulation common among administrators? What evidence do you have for your answer?
5. Rob expects employees to respond to his directives because he is the superintendent. Thus he relies on legitimate power—that is, power associated with his position in the organization. What are the advantages and disadvantages of relying on legitimate power?
6. Should a superintendent be making recommendations about improving school board meetings? Why or why not?
7. Rob appears to link informality with inefficiency. Do you agree? Why or why not?
8. What is the common pathway to the superintendency in your state?

9. Discuss the ethical dimensions of a superintendent taking a position without any intention of staying very long.
10. Evaluate the recommendations Rob made for improving school board meetings.
11. Compare indicators of the climate of the Hallville School District presented in this case with your personal experiences with rural and small town districts. Is Hallville typical?
12. Assume that Rob's perceptions about Dr. Smythe are accurate. Why is it advantageous or disadvantageous to try to duplicate his leadership style in Hallville?
13. Based on information in the case, do you believe Rob was adequately prepared to be a school superintendent? Why or why not?
14. Should Rob have told the school board members about the guidelines he gave to the principals and other two central office employees? What is the difference between a guideline and a rule? What is the difference between a guideline and a policy?
15. Rob assumes that people use his first name because he is young. Is there any information in the case that suggests that he may be wrong?

SUGGESTED READINGS

Anderson, S. (1989). How to predict success in the superintendency. *The School Administrator, 46*(7), 22, 24, 26.

Black, J., & English, F. (1986). *What they don't tell you in schools of education about school administration* (see pp. 293–307). Lancaster, PA: Technomic.

Burnham, J. (1989). Superintendents on the fast track. *The School Administrator, 46*(9), 18–19.

Chance, E., & Capps, J. (1992). *Superintendent instability in small/rural schools: The school board perspective* (ERIC Document Reproduction Service No. ED 350 121)

Clark, D., & Astuto, T. (1988). Paradoxical choice options in organizations. In D. Griffiths, R. Stout, and P. Forsyth, (Eds.), *Leaders for America's schools* (pp. 112–130). Berkeley, CA: McCutchan.

Grady, M., & Bryant, M. (1991). School board presidents describe critical incidents with superintendents. *Journal of Research in Rural Schools, 7*(3), 51–58.

Hart, A. (1991). Leader succession and socialization: A synthesis. *Review of Educational Research, 61,* 451–474.

Immegart, G. (1988). Leadership and leader behavior. In N. Boyan (Ed.), *Handbook of research on educational administration* (pp. 259–277). New York: Longman.

Jacobson, S. (1988a). Effective superintendents of small, rural districts. *Journal of Rural and Small Schools, 2*(2), 17–21.

Jacobson, S. (1988b). The rural superintendency: Reconsidering the administrative farm system. *Research in Rural Education, 5*(2), 37–42.

Johnson, S. M. (1996). *Leading to change: The challenge of the new superintendency*. San Franciso: Jossey-Bass (see chapter 6).

Kowalski, T., & Reitzug, U. (1993). *Contemporary school administration: An introduction*. New York: Longman (see chapters 10, 15).

Oberg, T. (1986). The ecstasy and the agony: Administrative success on one level does not guarantee success on another. *Journal of Educational Public Relations, 9*(2), 28–31.

Schmidt, L. J., Kosmoski, G. J., & Pollack, D. R. (1998). *Novice administrators: Personality and administrative style changes* (ERIC Document Reproduction Service No. ED 427 387)

Sergiovanni, T., Burlingame, M., Coombs, F., & Thurston, P. (1987). *Educational governance and administration* (2nd ed., pp. 206–219, 384–416). Englewood Cliffs, NJ: Prentice-Hall.

Sharp, W., & Newman, I. (1990). *Boards of education: Trust, confidence, and communication: A study of first year superintendents* (ERIC Document Reproduction Service No. ED 325 931)

Stephens, E. (1987). The rural small district superintendent: A position at risk. *Planning and Changing, 18*(3), 178–191.

Stronge, J. H. (1998). Leadership skills in school and business. *School Administrator, 55*(9), 21–24, 26.

Yukl, G. (1989). *Leadership in organizations* (2nd ed.). Englewood Cliffs, NJ: Prentice-Hall (see chapter 8).

Case **14**

The One-Skill Superintendent

BACKGROUND INFORMATION

In the present age of school reform the ideal role of school superintendent spans a number of different job requirements. They range from providing visionary planning leadership to managing an organization with a multimillion-dollar budget. In actual practice, however, most superintendents assume a narrower range of responsibilities either because of personal or school board preferences.

One widely used approach for classifying administrative skills is a three-skill taxonomy (Yukl, 1989) that includes the following categories:

- *Technical skills.* This category includes knowledge related to certain procedures and methods required in administering schools; application examples include budget development and administering a transportation program.
- *Human relations skills.* This category focuses on knowledge of human behavior, motivation, attitudes, communication, and other facets of organizational life; application examples include school-community relations and communications.
- *Conceptual skills.* This category includes analytical and problem-solving skills; application examples include visioning and planning.

Job responsibilities also have been expressed in general categories. Kowalski and Reitzug (1993), for example, discussed eight components of administrative work: representing, planning, organizing, leading, managing, facilitating, mediating, and evaluating.

In addition to generic responsibilities, administrators are expected to respond to specific roles that are shaped by the contextual job variables. They often include the climate and culture of the school or district, current goals and problems, and the individual occupying the position. These expectations tell a principal or superintendent what he or she should do in relation to fulfilling the responsibilities of a particular position; they also explain why success is not defined universally across positions in all school districts (Gaynor, 1998). Although all administrators experience conflicting role expectations, the degree of conflict varies from being very minor to being very severe.

In this case, an experienced superintendent assumes a new position and devotes much of his time and energy to community relations. He does so primarily because of school board member expectations; however, his limited role conflicts with expectations held by his deputy superintendent. The deputy concludes that she is doing much of the superintendent's work because the superintendent is self-centered and uses other administrators to advance his own career. She also suspects that the superintendent is manipulative and inconsiderate toward her because she is a woman. As you read this case, think about how role conflict can affect job performance and how it can destroy relationships among individuals in a school or district.

KEY AREAS FOR REFLECTION

1. Responsibilities of the school superintendent
2. Community and school district cultures as determinants of ideal and real roles
3. Role conflict
4. Male and female administrator relationships
5. Resolving personal conflict

THE CASE

The City

One of Peter Farley's earliest memories of Wellington involved a demolition project in the downtown area, a scene he observed on his first trip to this city. He was there to interview for the job of school superintendent. As he drove his new Buick down Main Street searching for the administrative office, he saw two large stores, each more than 100 years old, being flattened by a swinging steel ball.

Wellington is one of the larger cities in this New England state. It is an industrial community that fell on hard times in the past 20 years; however, things have started to improve recently. An upward economic trend started about the time that Dan Ferriter was elected mayor. An energetic and popular attorney who previously served two terms in the state legislature, Mayor Ferriter campaigned on the promise to bring new businesses to the city. Since his election just 18 months ago, two technology-based corporations have located in Wellington.

After becoming mayor, Mr. Ferriter also got involved in the search for a new school superintendent. One of his law partners, John O'Dell, was on the school board. Working through O'Dell, the mayor was able to influence the direction of the search. He convinced the board members to seek a person who had exceptional communication skills and a proven record of working closely with the community and city government.

The Search for a New Superintendent

The composition of the Wellington school board has changed substantially after the last two elections. The same political groups that had supported Mayor Ferriter became active in school board elections, and they managed to get four new individuals into that office. These new board members enthusiastically endorsed the mayor's notion that the district needed a superintendent who would help enhance the city's image.

The board retained a search consultant to assist them in finding a new superintendent. An impressive brochure was prepared listing the following desired qualifications:

- Candidates for the position should possess outstanding public relations skills because the superintendent represents the school district to multiple publics.
- Candidates for the position should be able to deal with all elements of the community and be willing to participate actively in community functions. Above all, candidates should be committed to working closely with other local governmental agencies.
- Candidates should have outstanding communication skills.
- Candidates should know how to delegate authority effectively.

Although other qualifications were listed, the school board members and the mayor placed the greatest degree of importance on these four. As a state legislator, Mayor Ferriter thought that local school districts often were recognized more on the basis of reputation than on the basis of actual achievements. He was convinced, therefore, that a superintendent with good public relations skills would be able to improve the district's image in a relatively short period of time.

When first contacted by the search consultant about the vacancy in Wellington, Peter Farley was ambivalent. He had never been to the city, but he was aware of its past economic problems. On the other hand, he respected the search consultant who told him that this was a good job. He decided to apply. Meeting the school board members during an interview removed many of his doubts. He perceived the board members to be uniformly positive, well-educated, and sincere—just as the search consultant had described them. When the school board narrowed the search to only two candidates, Peter was asked to return to Wellington for a second interview.

Prior to the second interview, Peter and his wife were invited to have dinner with Mayor and Mrs. Ferriter. The next morning, the mayor telephoned John O'Dell and said, "This is the guy we want. He's perfect. Do whatever it takes to get him, and if I can help, let me know." The board members agreed, but they were concerned that he might not be able to persuade Dr. Farley to leave his job as superintendent of an affluent suburban school district in eastern Pennsylvania. They eventually offered him a $150,000 salary and a lucrative fringe benefits package. They also pledged to support his efforts to rebuild the school district's reputation. Dr. Farley then agreed to move to Wellington.

The School District and Central Office Staff

Wellington City Schools is a large district consisting of 3 high schools, 7 middle schools, and 22 elementary schools. Overall, the district enrolls about 22,000 students. The central office has a professional staff of 24.

After arriving in Wellington, Dr. Farley reorganized the central office. The most notable change was the promotion of Dr. Teresa Howard, one of the three associate superintendents, to the newly created position of deputy superintendent. A veteran-administrator who was respected by administrative staff and other employees, she had been employed by the school district for over 20 years. In structuring the position of deputy superintendent, Superintendent Farley told the district's administrative staff that his deputy would be responsible for managing day-to-day operations. A second major element of restructuring was the creation of a division of public relations. Dr. Farley employed Tad Evans, a person who worked for him previously in Pennsylvania, to be the director. When the organizational changes were completed, Tad Evans and Dr. Howard were the only two administrators who reported directly to the superintendent.

The Superintendent's Behavior

The superintendent and mayor worked well together, especially in efforts to re-create the image of the city and the school district. Both men were adept at public relations, and both knew how to use information for image-building purposes. The two were frequently seen together in public and viewed as political allies. They also became personal friends, a factor that further enhanced the superintendent's stature with the school board.

Central office staff learned quickly that Dr. Farley was not a "hands-on" administrator. Much of his time was spent on community activities; he became a member of the Chamber of Commerce board; he was deeply involved in the mayor's efforts to recruit new industry; and he accepted every invitation to speak before local, state, and national groups.

During the first two years of Dr. Farley's tenure in Wellington, the district executed a successful public relations campaign. Local and state media produced dozens of positive stories about academic and athletic programs. Under the direction of Tad Evans, each of the district's accomplishments, no matter how minor, was turned into a media event. Mr. Evans knew how to stage press conferences and how to keep positive accomplishments before the public's eye. And he always made sure there were plenty of photographers there to take pictures of Dr. Farley shaking hands with students or staff.

The Problem

Dr. Farley and his deputy met every Monday morning for about two hours to go over issues that Dr. Howard felt needed the superintendent's attention. During these sessions, she tried to get him more involved in the district's day-to-day operations. But she never succeeded. For example, when she asked him if he could attend a budget meeting that was scheduled with the principals, he responded, "Teresa, you know a lot more about our budget than I do. I'm confident that you don't need me there." The superintendent displayed the same level of disinterest in other management functions. He always deferred to his deputy's judgments.

About midway through his second year in Wellington, Dr. Farley detected a change in his deputy's behavior. She seemed irritated and began to complain about work overload. He was concerned about her behavior shift because he depended on her to manage the school system. He eventually asked her if she was experiencing problems. She responded by telling him that she did not know if she would continue as his deputy.

"Why? Are you ill?" he asked.

"No. My health is fine. Telling you how I feel is going to take quite a long time, and I'm not sure you're willing to listen," Dr. Howard responded.

"Look, I will listen. There is no one more valuable on the administrative staff than you. I'll listen as long as you want me to listen."

The two agreed to have lunch the next day in the superintendent's office. Dr. Farley started the conversation by reiterating his positive feelings about her as deputy. He reminded her that he convinced the board to give her a 10 percent salary increase last year—the highest salary increase that was given to an administrator. She did not respond to his comment, so Dr. Farley reminded her why they were meeting.

Dr. Howard then looked at him and said, "I really don't know where to begin. But here goes. Staff members in the central office are concerned—no, let me rephrase that. I am concerned about the fact that you don't get involved in critical administrative functions. I have to give you detailed briefings so you can present recommendations to the school board, recommendations that I developed. Some people around the office are speculating that you don't know how to manage a school district this big. Personally, I don't believe that. Everyone knows that you basically delegate everything except public relations to me."

He asked her, "This concern is being expressed by most of the central office staff?"

"Yes, I believe it is. The administrators in this district are not used to having a superintendent who is gone most of the time. They don't know what you do with your time, and as a result, they form their own conclusions."

"What else are they, or you, concerned about?" he asked.

"I don't want to speak for the staff, but I guess I might as well lay the cards on the table as far as I'm concerned," she said. "I feel I'm running this district and you're getting all the credit. Last week at the annual Chamber of Commerce meeting, Mayor Ferriter gave you a plaque recognizing your leadership in the school district and the community. You never once acknowledged how much help you received from your staff. Then there's the matter of salary. I'm making $44,000 less than you, and I'm the one who is actually managing the school district. If you were in my shoes, would you think that this arrangement is fair?"

"Teresa, the board brought me here to improve the image of the district. I believe I have done that. You knew when I asked you to be my deputy that you would manage the day-to-day operations. I never misled you, and I have not tried to take advantage of you."

"I work darn hard, Peter, and you know it. I get here early and leave late every day. I have no idea how many hours you work. Some of the secretaries don't even know who you are. You rarely visit any of the schools; and when you do, it is usually for an awards ceremony or some other staged public relations event."

At that point Dr. Howard began to lose her composure. Dr. Farley sat quietly until she began to speak again.

"Look, Peter, let me be blunt. I don't think you would treat a man the way you have treated me. You probably know that I wanted to be the superintendent, but the board did not even extend the courtesy of giving me an interview. Yet, I am considered competent enough to manage this district. If you want me to continue in this job, two things have to happen. First, I want a salary increase—and I don't mean just a couple of thousand dollars. Second, I want to be recognized for what I do to make this district function well. Maybe I should be making some of the recommendations to the board and presenting some of the reports about positive accomplishments. You think about these two matters, and let me know if you want me to continue in this job." Dr. Howard then got up and left the office before the superintendent could respond.

The meeting left Dr. Farley wondering if he really wanted to retain his deputy. He tried imagining himself in her position. Would he react in the same way? What concerned him even more were Dr. Howard's comments about the perceptions of central office employees. He believed that he had worked very hard to accomplish what the mayor and school board wanted. Now his deputy was suggesting that most of his staff thought that he was self-centered, egotistical, and manipulative.

THE CHALLENGE

Analyze the relationship between the superintendent and his deputy. Is he being fair with her? Is she being fair with him?

KEY ISSUES/QUESTIONS

1. Do you believe that the deputy superintendent is being treated unfairly? Why or why not?
2. What are the advantages and disadvantages of having the superintendent focus on just one or two responsibilities?
3. What are the advantages and disadvantages of the superintendent giving his deputy what she wants?
4. What are the advantages and disadvantages of reassigning the current deputy and selecting someone else for this critical position?
5. Do you think that the deputy's gender is a legitimate issue in this case? Why or why not?
6. In your opinion, how much time should a superintendent spend on community relations? What is the basis of your opinion?
7. The superintendent makes a substantially higher salary than the deputy. Given their roles in the district, is this a problem? Why or why not?
8. Is the superintendent's relationship with the mayor relevant to this case?
9. Analyze the behavior of the superintendent and the deputy superintendent from an ethical-moral perspective. Has either or both behaved inappropriately?
10. According to the deputy superintendent, the superintendent rarely visits schools. Assuming this is true, how do you assess this aspect of the superintendent's behavior?
11. Could the deputy superintendent have addressed her concerns differently? If so, how?
12. Evaluate the superintendent's behavior in light of the direction he has received from the school board members.
13. Do you agree with the mayor's contention that the school superintendent can play a major role in improving the city's image? Why or why not?

SUGGESTED READINGS

Black, J., & English, F. (1986). *What they don't tell you in schools of education about school administration.* Lancaster, PA: Technomic (see chapter 12).

Duke, D. L. (1998). The normative context of organizational leadership. *Educational Administration Quarterly, 34*(2), 165–195.

Gaynor, A. K. (1998). *Analyzing problems in schools and school systems: A theoretical approach.* Mahwah, NJ: Lawrence Erlbaum Associates.

Gill, B. A. (1997). *Becoming a leader: Strategies for women in educational administration* (ERIC Document Reproduction Service No. ED412 594)

Gupton, S. L., & Slick, G. A. (Eds.) (1996). *Highly successful women administrators: The inside story of how they got there.* Thousand Oaks, CA: Corwin Press (see chapters 1 and 4).

Hirsh, S., & Sparks, D. (1991). A look at the new central office administrators. *School Administrator, 48*(7), 16–17, 19.

Irby, B. J., & Brown, G. (Eds.) (1995). *Women as school executives: Voices and visions.* Austin, TX: Texas Council of Women School Executives (see chapters 5 and 18).

Joy, L. (1998). *Why are women underrepresented in public school administration? An empirical test of promotion discrimination* (ERIC Document Reproduction Service No. EJ568 552)

Kowalski, T. J. (1999). *The school superintendent: Theory, practice, and cases.* Upper Saddle River, NJ: Merrill, Prentice Hall (see chapters 9, 10, 11, 12).

Kowalski, T. J., & Reitzug, U. (1993). *Contemporary school administration: An introduction.* New York: Longman (see chapters 10, 14).

Rist, M. (1991). Opening your own doors. *Executive Educator, 13*(1), 14.

Shakeshaft, C. (1989). *Women in educational administration* (updated edition). Newbury Park, CA: Sage Publications (see chapter 6).

Steller, A., & Kowalski, T. J. (2000). Effective programming at the district level. In T. J. Kowalski (Ed.), *Public relations in schools* (pp. 183–202). Upper Saddle River, NJ: Merrill, Prentice Hall.

Worner, R. (1989). Thirteen ways to help your inherited staff keep you afloat. *Executive Educator, 11*(5), 19–21.

Yukl, G. (1989). *Leadership in organizations* (2nd ed.). Englewood Cliffs, NJ: Prentice-Hall (see pp. 153–157).

Who Will Censure This Board Member?

BACKGROUND INFORMATION

Relationships between superintendents and school board members often affect more than the individuals directly involved. If these associations are contentious, many facets of the school-community could be affected negatively. Superintendents build and maintain positive relationships with board members by:

- being honest
- providing knowledge and assistance
- using two-way communication
- building mutual respect
- cooperating
- earning trust (Kowalski, 1999)

Although the superintendent, as a professional educator, has the primary responsibility for creating positive working associations, good intentions or acts do not ensure desired outcomes. Some board members may simply be unwilling to work with or support the superintendent.

Common negative behaviors among school board members include pursuing personal gain (i.e., using his or her office to benefit a personal cause) and intruding into the domain of school administration. This case reveals a situation in which a school board member appears to be guilty of both offenses. He reacts to a personal situation by trying to create problems for the school district. His behavior is deemed unethical by both the superintendent and board president;

however, the board president wants the superintendent to be the one who reprimands the offender.

KEY AREAS FOR REFLECTION

1. Relationships between school boards and superintendents
2. Ethical, legal, social, and political dimensions of board membership
3. Conflict resolution
4. Scope of superintendent responsibilities
5. Knowledge and skills in interpersonal relationships

THE CASE

The School District and School Board

The Richmond County School District covers 420 square miles of predominantly rural land. There are 7,800 pupils enrolled in two high schools, five middle schools, and ten elementary schools. The area has been experiencing modest growth in the past decade largely because of the county's proximity to the state capital, which is only 35 miles away. Land costs and taxes in Richmond County have made it an attractive site for small manufacturing companies. Although there have been nearly 500 new homes built here in the last decade, most have been in a rural subdivision. The county seat, Collins, with a stable population of about 20,000, is the only city or town of any size in the county.

The school board has seven members who are elected from designated geographic areas to ensure balanced representation among the 12 townships. At one time, virtually all school board members resided on farms, but that condition has changed in the last 20 years. The current board members are as follows:

John Mosure (president), a farmer

Iris Dembica, a homemaker

Elizabeth Highland, a real estate broker

Elmer Hodson, a farmer

Norman Salliter, an accountant and state employee

Martin Schultz, an attorney

Alicia Waddell, a pharmacist

Mr. Hodson is serving his third three-year term in office; Mr. Mosure and Ms. Highland are serving their second three-year terms; and the remaining board members are serving their first terms.

Politically, the board is not factious and votes on key policy issues are often difficult to predict. Elmer Hodson is the member least likely to support the superintendent's recommendations; his voting record shows that he did not support the superintendent about 30 percent of the time. Mr. Hodson tends to be very protective of the townships he represents, and he has been the most fiscally conservative board member. He has opposed every tax increase initiative since he has been on the board. Socially, however, Mr. Hodson has not had problems with either the superintendent or other board members.

The Superintendent

Matthew Karman became superintendent in Richmond County three years ago. His prior job was as superintendent of a smaller district in the same state. He is a friendly, somewhat reserved person. Unlike his predecessor in Richmond County who had been dismissed largely because of poor relations with the school board, Mr. Karman worked well with school boards and employees. He attributes his success in this area to the following activities:

1. He has lunch with the school board president twice each month.
2. He has at least two social events involving the school board at his house each year.
3. He tries to have lunch with each of the board members at least once each year.
4. He always makes himself accessible to board members, and he instructed his staff to always put board member phone calls directly through to him.
5. He personally delivers materials for school board meetings to their homes or places of business.

Just a few months ago when his contract was renewed for another three years, all seven board members supported the action. Several of them commented in the public meeting that they were extremely pleased that Superintendent Karman had kept them informed and that he had exhibited a sincere interest in their opinions on school matters. All the evidence indicated that he had succeeded in establishing a trusting and cooperative relationship with the board.

The Problem

Superintendent Karman was driving on a remote country road as the winds swirled across barren cornfields partially covered by snow. He was completing his monthly task of personally delivering school board packets three days before a meeting. The packets included recommendations and background information for the agenda items. Although it was only mid-November, the chilling temperatures made it feel more like January. The fields were dotted with corn stalks cut about two inches above the ground that looked like wooden spikes someone had arranged to discourage trespassers.

After about 20 minutes of driving, Mr. Karman pulled into the driveway beside a large three-story farmhouse. A German shepherd running alongside his car greeted him. The dog's barking summoned John Mosure from his barn where he was working on one of his tractors. The farmer had oil and grease all over his bib-overalls and hands.

"Greetings, John. I brought your board packet for our next meeting," Mr. Karman said as Mr. Mosure walked toward him wiping his hands on a soiled rag.

"Come in the house and we'll have a cup of coffee," the farmer said as he waved his hand indicating that the superintendent follow him.

Although John Mosure has been on the board for nearly five years, this was his first year as president. The two men had become good friends, and they worked well together. Their wives also had become friends, and about every two months, the four of them did things together socially.

"John, I hope you've got some time today. I want to discuss a sticky issue with you, and it may take a little while."

The board member responded, "Well, we'll just make time. I'm not sure I'm going to be able to fix that tractor anyway. There is something wrong with the transmission, and I may have to take it to the dealer to get repaired."

The two sat back enjoying the warmth of the kitchen and their coffee as Mr. Karman began telling him about the special problem.

"Two days ago, one of our high school principals, Bob Dailey at North Richmond High, received a telephone call from a friend who is the assistant commissioner of the state high school athletic association. This friend asked Bob if he knew a person named Elmer Hodson."

There was a moment of silence as John looked at the superintendent and then said, "Oh, no!"

Although they got along with Mr. Hodson, both men knew that he was often a troublemaker. And despite the fact that John Mosure and Elmer Hodson are both farmers, their philosophies and political preferences differed. John, who has three children still enrolled in the schools, has been supportive of program expansion and has voted for two building-related referenda since being on the board. By contrast, Elmer openly opposed both initiatives and worked closely with the county taxpayers' association to try to defeat them.

The superintendent continued with his story. "So, Bob tells his friend at the athletic association that Elmer is on our school board. This guy then informs Bob that Elmer's sitting in his outer office waiting to file a complaint against Bob and coach Yates, the football coach at North Richmond High."

"A complaint about what?" asked the board president.

"Well, Bob's friend didn't know at the time because he had not talked to Elmer yet. He just knew he was there to lodge a complaint. So he told Bob he was going to talk to Elmer and then call back before he did anything. About an hour later, Bob got another call. His friend said Elmer was all upset about the fact that the quarterback at North Richmond no longer lived with his parents. It seems the student, Jeb Boswell, is now living with Coach Yates. So Elmer wants the athletic association to take action against North Richmond High School because they are playing this student even though Elmer claims he is no longer a legal resident of our school system. At the very least, he wants the athletic association to ban the student from playing in the future."

"Is there any merit to his charge?" John Mosure asked.

"First," the superintendent answered, "there is no question that the student is living at the coach's house. The boy's parents moved to Colorado this past June. The boy and Coach Yates are pretty close, so Jeb asked his parents if it was okay to stay with Coach Yates to finish his senior year. He wants to graduate from North Richmond, and besides, Coach Yates is trying to get him a college scholarship to play football. Coach Yates and his wife agreed to work something out with the boy's parents to cover his room and board. So, since late June, Jeb has indeed been living in the Yates home."

"Can a student do that and still be eligible for athletics?"

"Apparently so," the superintendent answered. "Before the final decision was made to have the student stay here, Coach Yates asked the athletic director at North Richmond to write a letter to the state athletic association asking if this arrangement would be a violation. He was told that students whose parents moved out of a district could remain to finish their senior year without jeopardizing their eligibility so long as the parents and the school officials agreed to the arrangement. Bob Dailey, the athletic director, and the parents told Coach Yates that they had no objections to the boy staying here and continuing to play football."

"So, Elmer's complaint is meaningless. What's the problem?"

"John, we have to put this in perspective. Here we are one week before the state football tournament. North Richmond has a 9 and 1 record and is one of the favorites to win the championship in their division. Jeb Boswell, the student in question, is the star of the team—he may even end up being all-state. You know who the backup quarterback on the North Richmond team is?"

The board president said he had no idea. "You have to remember, Matt, that I don't live in the North Richmond area. I'm a South Richmond booster [the other high school in the district]."

"The second string quarterback is a senior named Ron Hodson."

The two looked at each other and John smiled. The superintendent continued, "You got it, John. The second string quarterback is none other than the grandson of Elmer Hodson. Get the picture? Elmer's got an axe to grind because he feels this other kid has deprived his grandson from playing quarterback. At the very least, Elmer selfishly wants to see his grandson play in the state tournament. Mr. Dailey tells me, however, that the grandson doesn't know anything about what Elmer is doing. He's supposedly a pretty good kid and probably would be embarrassed if he knew."

"You know, I just remembered something," commented John. "You recall last summer when we were approving contracts for employing driver education teachers. Elmer opposed Coach Yates being hired to teach driver education. He said he had heard that he was not a good instructor. Do you think that was linked to his feelings about his grandson as well?"

"Who knows. With Elmer, it's hard to tell. He votes against a lot of things. But what's on my mind is what we do about Elmer. I think his going to the athletic association without informing the board or the administration was unethical and divisive. As a board member, he should have voiced his concerns to either you or me before running to the state athletic association. Had he done so, he would have found out that there is no merit to his complaint. Further, he would not have given the athletic association officials a negative impression of our school district."

"What did the fellow from the athletic association do about Elmer?"

"Nothing really. He explained that there was no violation and even told him that North Richmond's athletic director had asked for a clarification about Jeb playing football for North Richmond. Elmer responded by suggesting that the official might just be covering up the matter."

"So, why don't we just forget about this. Elmer is Elmer. He'll always be a pain in the neck. Why voters keep electing him is beyond me. Sometimes I think they enjoy all the trouble he stirs up."

The superintendent was not willing to let this matter slide. "John, we have to issue some type of reprimand or do something. What he did was unethical. I think you and the entire board should meet with him privately and issue a formal reprimand. Sometimes I think he believes he can get away with this stuff because people are amused by his behavior. Maybe it's time to say enough."

The board president got up to refill the coffee cups. He then returned to his chair. "I don't know. I'm not sure a reprimand will do any good. Elmer's pretty stubborn. We might just give him more publicity, and you know how he loves to get his name in the paper. Matt, how about if you talk to him? You're more experienced in dealing with conflict. Maybe the best way to handle this is to have you give him the reprimand. We should get the support of the other board members, though, and then you can tell him you are speaking for all of us. Don't you think this would be the best way to handle this?"

THE CHALLENGE

Analyze the superintendent's actions in this case. What would you advise him to do at this point?

KEY ISSUES/QUESTIONS

1. The superintendent claims that Mr. Hodson acted unethically in taking his complaint to the state athletic association without informing him or the other board members. Do you agree with the superintendent? What is the basis for your agreement or disagreement?
2. What is the purpose of a reprimand?
3. Instead of reprimanding the board member, what other actions might be taken?
4. In your state, what things are done to ensure that school board members perform their duties ethically?

5. Who should set standards for school board member behavior?
6. Do you believe that the superintendent acted appropriately in taking this problem directly to the board president? Would it have been better to talk to Elmer Hodson first to get his side of the story? Should the issue have been discussed with all board members at the same time?
7. What constitutes a conflict of interest for a school board member? Does your state have laws addressing conflicts of interest for public officials?
8. Does the fact that Mr. Hodson votes against the superintendent's recommendations about 30 percent of the time have any bearing on this case?
9. What are the advantages and disadvantages to the superintendent if he agrees to issue a reprimand to Mr. Hodson on behalf of the school board?
10. What provisions exist in your state for removing school board members from office?
11. Is it possible that the conflict presented in this case can be used to improve conditions in the school district? If so, how?
12. A reprimand could be given to Mr. Hodson publicly or privately. Which would be a better alternative?
13. Does a school board member have any legal authority when acting independently?

SUGGESTED READINGS

Alvey, D., & Underwood, K. (1985). When boards and superintendents clash, it's over the balance of power. *American School Board Journal, 172*(10), 21–25.

Banach, W. (1984). Communications and internal relations are problems for board members. *Journal of Educational Public Relations, 7*(3), 8–9.

Bolman, L., & Deal, T. (1992). Images of leadership. *American School Board Journal, 179*(4), 36–39.

Bryant, M., & Grady, M. (1990). Where boards cross the line. *American School Board Journal, 177*(10), 20–21.

Castallo, R. (1992). Clear signals. *American School Board Journal, 179*(2), 32–34.

Goldman, J. (1990). Who's calling the plays? *School Administrator, 47*(11), 8–16.

Grady, M., & Bryant, M. (1991). School board presidents describe critical incidents with superintendents. *Journal of Research in Rural Education, 7*(3), 51–58.

Hamilton, D. (1987). Healing power: How your board can overcome the heartbreak of disharmony. *American School Board Journal, 174*(9), 36–37.

Hayden, J. (1987). Superintendent-board conflict: Working it out. *Education Digest, 52*(8), 11–13.

Herman, J. (1991). Coping with conflict. *American School Board Journal, 178*(8), 39–41.

Institute for Educational Leadership (1986). *School boards: Strengthening grass roots leadership.* Washington, DC: The Institute for Educational Leadership (see chapters 8, 9).

Irvine, J. (1998). Welcome to the board. *American School Board Journal, 185* (7), 38–40.

Kowalski, T. J. (1999). *The school superintendent: Theory, practice, and cases.* Upper Saddle River, NJ: Merrill, Prentice Hall (see chapter 5).

Kowalski, T., & Reitzug, U. (1993). *Contemporary school administration: An introduction* (pp. 125–128, 368–373). New York: Longman.

Marlowe, J. (1997). Good board, bad board. *American School Board Journal, 184* (6), 22–24.

McDaniel, T. (1986). Learn these rarely written rules of effective board service. *American School Board Journal, 173*(5), 31–32.

Menzies, J. (1986). Power base preferences for resolving conflict: An educational management team consideration. *Journal of Rural and Small Schools, 1*(1), 6–9.

Myer, R. (1983). How to handle a board member who wants to play his own game. *American School Board Journal, 170*(11), 27-29.

Natale, J. (1990). School board ethics: On thin ice? *American School Board Journal, 177*(10), 16-19.

Ondrovich, P. (1997). Hold them, fold them, or walk away: Twelve cardinal rules for dealing with school board conflict. *The School Administrator, 54*(2), 12-15.

Rickabaugh, J. R., & Kremer, M. L. (1997). Six habits to make you a hit with your school board. *The School Administrator, 54*(6), 30-32.

Tallerico, M. (1991). School board member development: Implications for policy and practice. *Planning and Changing, 22*(2), 94-107.

Yukl, G. (1989). *Leadership in organizations* (2nd ed.; pp. 177-180, 191-194). Englewood Cliffs, NJ: Prentice-Hall.

Case **16**

Does the Punishment
Fit the Offense?

BACKGROUND INFORMATION

Highly publicized killings in places like Jonesboro, Arkansas, Paducah, Kentucky, and Jefferson County, Colorado painfully exhibited that schools are not always safe environments. More than half of U.S. public schools reported experiencing at least one crime incident in school year 1996–97, and one in ten schools reported at least one serious violent crime during that school year (National Center for Education Statistics, 1998). Prompted by growing concerns for school-related crimes, many school boards decided to get tough with students who threatened or performed violent acts; by 1997, between 79 to 94 percent of the nation's districts reported adopting a zero-tolerance policy for serious acts of violence (National Center for Education Statistics, 1998).

In this case, a small group of African-American students is expelled for an incident at a football game that school officials labeled a malicious assault. Many in the district's black community called the punishment excessive, arguing that the boys merely were involved in a fistfight. Subsequently when criminal charges are filed against the students, a well-known black political leader gets involved, and conditions get even tenser.

Discipline decisions often generate conflict because individuals and groups in a community do not share a common set of beliefs and values. Even educators often differ markedly in terms of their personal philosophies toward regulating pupil conduct. For example, some administrators and teachers believe that the primary purpose of discipline is to help troubled students; others believe that the primary purpose is to protect the school and community. Tensions between helping and protecting are usually exacerbated when political and racial issues are infused.

Insightful administrators take a two-dimensional approach to conflict. First they address the more obvious management questions associated with resolving the problem. Second, they view conflict as an opportunity for organizational improvement. That is, they ask themselves this question: "How can I use this problem to improve the school district?" As you frame the problems in this case, consider both dimensions.

KEY AREAS FOR REFLECTION

1. Race relations
2. Race and student discipline
3. The appropriateness of zero-tolerance policies
4. Violence in schools
5. Managing political conflict
6. Using conflict to produce positive change

THE CASE

The Community

Centralville is an industrial community with a population of approximately 76,000. The primary industry is a chemical plant owned by a large national corporation. There are two other major employers: a stamping plant that makes truck fenders and a candy company. Approximately 13 percent of the city's residents are African American and approximately 2 percent are Hispanic. In the past two decades, the population of Centralville has declined about 8,000. Much of this decline occurred during the 1980s when auto-related industries cut back production and employment levels. Recent attempts to attract new businesses have only been marginally successful.

The city has a history of segregation in housing patterns. Virtually all of the African-American population resides in two areas just south and west of the center of the city; virtually all Hispanics live in an area just east of the center of the city. A newspaper in the state capital recently described Centralville as a "blue-collar, union town." There have been relatively few new single-family dwellings built in Centralville in the past 25 years, however, new housing starts have occurred in two small towns north of the city.

Recently, efforts have been made to improve community race relations. Several months ago, a local African American leader interviewed on a local radio program said that conditions in Centralville had improved. "Things aren't as bad as they were 25 years ago. Racism was very obvious back then. Now, we are trying to deal with the lingering effects of institutional racism." Just two weeks after his interview, however, a white policeman shot and killed an African American male who had shot at him. The tragedy rekindled pessimism in the African-American neighborhoods.

The School District

The Centralville School District has a total enrollment of approximately 10,000. The peak enrollment, 12,300 students, occurred in 1985. The district operates 12 elementary schools (grades kindergarten to 5), four middle schools (grades 6–8), and two high schools (grades 9–12).

Prior to 1979, the district had only one high school. When the second high school opened, the name of the original school remained Centralville High School. This building is located near the business district of the city. The newer school, Centralville North High School, is located in the city's most affluent residential area.

Although only 13 percent of Centralville's 80,000 residents are black, 44 percent of the district's enrollment is black because many whites send their children to private schools. Data for the two schools are shown below:

Centralville North High School

- Enrollment – 1,850
- African-American enrollment – 18%
- Hispanic enrollment – 1%

Centralville High School

- Enrollment – 2,375
- African-American enrollment – 46%
- Hispanic enrollment – 2%

There are seven members on the district's school board; four are elected from specific areas of the city and three are elected at-large. Currently, two of the board members are African American. The superintendent, Dr. Thomas Yundt, and the principals of both high schools are white males. Dr. Yundt has been in his present position for three years, having moved to Centralville after serving as superintendent in a smaller school district. One of the three assistant superintendents reporting to Dr. Yundt, Dr. Robin Daniels, is African American.

The Incident

Although the two high schools belong to different athletic conferences, they play each other in all sports. The football game between the two schools occurred during the third week of September on a Friday evening. Midway through the second quarter, a brawl broke out in the bleachers causing the game to be stopped. A group of black students appeared to engage in a fistfight and then the turmoil spread indiscriminately through the crowd. School officials, including the principals of both schools, and several law enforcement officers attempted to stop the fight. One of the students involved allegedly grabbed the principal from Centralville High School by the shirt and hit him in the chest with his fist. Although there were no hospital reports of injuries, there were conflicting stories as to whether people had been hurt.

The Centralville School District adopted a zero-tolerance policy with regard to violence at school or school events 18 months prior to the incident at the football game. The two principals identified nine black teenagers who they believed were part of the group initiating the fighting. The principals recommended a two-year expulsion for the seven who were students in the school at the time. The recommendation was based on the board's zero-tolerance policy. In accordance with policies for recommended expulsions, separate hearings were set for the students. Only one student attended his hearing. He and his parents requested that he be allowed to withdraw from school to avoid being expelled—an act that would protect his permanent record. The hearing officer recommended that the expulsion recommendations be upheld for the six students who did not appear at their hearings; he recommended that the other student's request to withdraw from school be honored. Dr. Yundt concurred with these recommendations and presented them to the school board. He pointed out the period of the expulsion, two years, was based on the egregious nature of the offense. However, the students could seek reinstatement after only one year if they produced evidence of positive behavior, such as staying out of trouble, pursuing tutoring and counseling, or performing community service. The board voted six to one to approve the superintendent's recommendation; one of the black board members voted against the recommendation.

The Fall Out

During the weeks that followed the board's approval of the expulsions, police were careful not to label the brawl as "gang-related." Nevertheless, rumors flowed through the community that the fight was the continuation of an altercation that occurred between two groups of teenagers several days earlier. Eventually, criminal charges were filed against the nine black teenagers. Four were charged as adults with felony mob action and one of them, an 18-year-old, was also accused of aggravated battery and resisting a peace officer. The remaining five were charged in juvenile petitions.

Many in the black community believed that the punishment given to the seven students by the school board was excessive. When the criminal charges were filed weeks later, the disapproval changed to anger. At that point, a national civil rights figure, Reverend Arnold James, became involved. He spoke at a rally held in Centralville to protest the treatment of the students and to start a defense fund for the teenagers. Rev. James made the following points in his speech to the angry crowd:

- He condemned the action of the school board and superintendent, arguing that they had rushed to judgment and overreacted.

- He insisted that the key issue in this matter was fairness rather than race. He argued that black students had been disproportionately the subjects of harsh discipline; he cited a statistic indicating that of the six students expelled the previous year, five were black. He also noted that the board had expelled a white student who had committed what he considered to be a much more serious offense (sending a bomb threat note) for only one year.
- He contended that the punishment given to the students was excessive for a fistfight in which no weapons were involved.
- He condemned the filing of criminal charges, insisting that the school board was working in tandem with law enforcement. He noted that by making the students criminals, the board was in essence justifying the unusually long expulsions.

Within days of Rev. James's appearance in Centralville the controversy was covered by media across the country. Both the governor and state school superintendent were drawn into the matter, and even local elected officials started to make public statements about the incident. Unrest in the African-American community was getting progressively worse, and Superintendent Yundt decided to close the schools for three days fearing an outbreak of additional violence.

In the midst of growing national interest, the board president issued a statement in which she noted, "I really resent the fact that we have outsiders coming in telling us how to run our schools." The governor was able to get both sides to attend a daylong meeting that resulted in the school board agreeing to reduce the punishment to an expulsion for the remainder of the school year. In addition, the expelled students would be allowed to attend the district's alternative high school program. Rev. James called the board's concession inadequate, and the governor indicated that he merely tried to bring the two sides together. Both the governor and the state school superintendent maintained the position that the matter should be resolved locally.

Key figures on both sides were inundated with requests for media interviews. Leaders in the local black community met with reporters and restated many of the claims that Rev. James made in his initial speech in Centralville. School officials who previously refused to disclose information about the students now began to make available generic data. For example, Dr. Yundt appearing on a national news show revealed that three of the students were third-year freshman and that collectively the seven students had missed 350 days of school the previous year. In addition, school officials made available an amateur videotape of the incident. The camera captured the last third of the brawl and shows spectators scurrying to get away from a group of teenagers throwing punches and tossing each other down the cement bleacher steps.

In the aftermath of the board's concession and the viewing of the videotape, conservative media commentators and politicians started criticizing Rev. James for misstating the facts and for intensifying the conflict surrounding this situation. They refuted his contention that no one was hurt, and they argued that criminal activity was indeed an issue. They pointed to the video as clear evidence that Rev. James either erred in reporting the facts of this case or purposely misled the public.

Continuing Controversy

Despite the school board's reduction in the penalty, the tension in Centralville did not subside. Rev. James and his supporters filed a 13-page civil rights complaint in U.S. District Court alleging that the school board had violated the students' constitutional rights in the following ways:

- By failing to have an explicit zero-tolerance policy in writing
- By labeling the conduct as "gang-related" without evidence
- By failing to notify the students about alternative education options
- By punishing them too harshly for a fistfight void of weapons

In addition to the lingering anger in the black community, a number of white residents were now criticizing the school board and superintendent for having reduced the penalties for these students.

Rev. James was repeatedly warning community officials and the media the matter still was not resolved. In addition, he was now suggesting that school officials violated privacy laws by disclosing information about the case to the news media. He vowed to continue his activities in Centralville until the teenagers were cleared of criminal charges. He announced that he would lead a march through the city the following week. Clearly, the matter was not resolved, and the superintendent, school board, and other school officials continued to be criticized by leaders in the black community.

THE CHALLENGE

Assume you are the superintendent. What action would you take at this point to deal with the conflict?

KEY ISSUES/QUESTIONS

1. Must a policy be in writing to be considered legally binding as a policy?
2. What is a zero-tolerance policy?
3. What circumstances may have caused so many school districts in the late 1990s to adopt zero-tolerance policies for violent acts?
4. If you were the superintendent, would you have agreed to be interviewed on national television about this case? Why or why not?
5. When the superintendent and school board attorney disclosed that three of the seven students were third-year freshmen, did they violate privacy laws? Did they violate privacy laws when they disclosed that the seven students collectively had missed 350 days of school the previous year?

6. Rev. James cited a case in which a white student had been expelled for just one year for writing a note containing a bomb threat. Do you agree with his contention that this incident was a lesser offense than issuing a bomb threat? Do you agree that the lesser penalty given to the white student was evidence of discriminatory discipline practices?

7. Was Rev. James's claim of unequal treatment of black students nullified when the school board reduced the expulsion period? Why or why not?

8. How do you evaluate the fact that six of the students (or their parents) opted not to attend their expulsion hearing?

9. How do you evaluate the political relevance of the governor and state school superintendent becoming involved in this matter?

10. If you were the superintendent, how would you deal with the African-American board member who voted against the two-year expulsion?

11. What options do the superintendent and school board have with regard to resolving the continuing conflict? Evaluate the potential effectiveness of each option.

12. How can this conflict be used to improve race relations in the community and school district?

13. Identify and evaluate the possible motives of Rev. James becoming involved in this case?

14. Should a student's cumulative record be considered in an expulsion hearing? Why or why not?

15. Should students expelled from school be guaranteed an alternative educational program? Do school officials have a legal responsibility to inform expelled students of alternative forms of education?

16. If you were a principal in this district, would you have supported the board's concession that reduced the period of the expulsions? Why or why not?

SUGGESTED READINGS

Baker, J. A. (1998). Are we missing the forest for the trees? Considering the social context of school violence. *Journal of School Psychology, 36*(1), 29–44.

Bock, S. J., Savner, J. L., & Tapscott, K. E. (1998). Suspension and expulsion: Effective management of students? *Intervention in School and Clinic, 34*(1), 50–52.

Clark, C. (1998). The violence that creates school dropouts. *Multicultural Education, 6*(1), 19–22.

Costenbader, V., & Markson, S. (1998). School suspension: A study with secondary school students. *Journal of School Psychology, 36*(1), 59–82.

Day, D. M., & Golench, C. A. (1997). Promoting schools through policy: Results of a survey of Canadian school boards. *Journal of Educational Administration, 35*(3–4), 332–347.

Edmonson, H. M., & Bullock, L. M. (1998). Youth with aggressive and violent behaviors: Pieces of a puzzle. *Preventing School Failure, 42*(3), 135–141.

Gable, R. A., Quinn, M. M., & Rutherford, R. B. (1998). Addressing problem behaviors in schools: Use of functional assessments and behavior intervention plans. *Preventing School Failure, 42*(3), 106–119.

Gordon, J. A. (1998). Caring through control. *Journal for a Just and Caring Education, 4*(4), 18–40.

Haynes, R. M., & Chalker, D. M. (1999). A nation of violence. *American School Board Journal, 186*(3), 22–25.

Hyman, I. A., & Perone, D. C. (1998). The other side of school violence: Educator policies and practices that may contribute to student misbehavior. *Journal of School Psychology, 36*(1), 7–27.

McEvoy, A., Erickson, E., & Randolph, N. (1997). Why the brutality? *Student Intervention Report, 10*(4).

Morrison, G. M., & D'Incau, B. (1997). The web of zero-tolerance: Characteristics of students who are recommended for expulsion from school. *Education and Treatment of Children, 20*(3), 316-335.

National Center for Education Statistics (1998). *Violence and discipline problems in U.S. public schools: 1996-97.* Washington, DC: Government Printing Office.

Roper, D. A. (1998). Facing anger in our schools. *Educational Forum, 62*(4), 363-368.

Stefkovich, J. A., & Guba, G. J. (1998). School violence, school reform, and the Fourth Amendment in public schools. *International Journal of Educational Reform, 7*(3), 217-225.

St. George, D. M., & Thomas, S. B. (1997). Perceived risk of fighting and actual fighting behavior among middle school students. *Journal of School Health, 67*(5), 178-181.

Thornberry, T. P., & Burch, J. H. (1997). Gang members and delinquent behavior. *Juvenile Justice Bulletin,* June.

Toby, J. (1998). Getting serious about school discipline. *Public Interest,* (133), 68-83.

Walker, H. M., Irvin, L. K., & Sprague, J. R. (1997). Violence prevention and school safety: Issues, problems, approaches, and recommended solutions. *OSSC Bulletin, 41*(1).

Zirkel, P. A., & Gluckman, I. B. (1997). Due process in student suspensions and expulsions. *Principal, 76*(4), 62-63.

Case **17**

Site-Based Conflict

BACKGROUND INFORMATION

Dissatisfaction with the performance of public elementary and secondary schools, coupled with the realization that schools are not likely to improve by simply doing more of what they are already doing, has led to growing interest in school restructuring. The goal of revamping the basic shape of schools has prompted both increased levels of state deregulation and district decentralization. The underlying rationale of school restructuring is that meaningful improvement is most likely if it is pursued at the level closest to students—namely the individual school site. The most popular label used to identify reform activities focused at improving individual schools is *site-based management* (SBM).

In large measure, the current interest in decentralization is sparked by several beliefs:

- Teachers will become more effective if they are treated more like true professionals.
- Decisions about student instruction will be improved if teachers are empowered to truly individualize their work.
- The overall governance of schools will improve if school districts' policies and rules do not restrict the ability of individual schools to address real needs.
- Schools will improve if all those who are part of the school community are allowed to participate in critical decisions.

Clearly, giving individual schools more authority to chart their own courses increases flexibility. But will it produce sufficient accountability and productivity? Critics note, for example, that having more people involved in decisions does not necessarily result in better decisions. Many observers also realize that SBM is dependent on school boards, administrators, and communities being willing to treat teachers as true professionals—a condition that has not existed previously (Kowalski & Reitzug, 1993).

The person usually most affected by decentralization is the school principal (Brown, 1991). This is true for at least three reasons.

- Principals assume greater responsibility for providing leadership (i.e., determining what should be done), while not commonly experiencing a decrease in managerial responsibilities.
- Decision making often becomes more democratic even though the participants may not assume greater responsibility for the consequences of their decisions.
- Participatory decision making typically increases the frequency and severity of conflict, and principals are expected to manage and resolve these tensions.

These conditions tend to magnify the personal philosophies and leadership styles of principals because these attributes have a more visible and direct influence when decisions are school-based.

This case is about an experienced principal who volunteers to participate in a first phase of implementing SBM. In creating a school council, he decides to permit council members to be elected by the groups they represent (teachers, parents, and staff), and although he also is a member of the council, he assumes neither leadership nor an active role. The situation is complicated by the fact that the school council includes representatives of two factions that are constantly vying for power. His laissez-faire attitude angers the council chair, a parent who also is the president of the parent-teacher association.

KEY AREAS FOR REFLECTION

1. Problems associated with decentralized governance of schools
2. Social conflict among individuals and groups in schools
3. Dynamics of group decision making
4. Leadership style and participatory decision making
5. Leadership role in conflict resolution

THE CASE

The Community and School District

Sunland is a prosperous city in a southern state. With a population of approximately 75,000, it has grown nearly 25 percent in the last 20 years. New industries and businesses continue to locate in the area, and it is projected that the population will reach 100,000 by the year 2010. Sunland also is the county seat for LaSalle County.

Serving the entire county, including the city of Sunland, the LaSalle County School District has 3 high schools, 6 middle schools, and 19 elementary schools. Although growth has taken place throughout the county, the greatest and most rapid growth has occurred in Sunland. As a result, a new middle school and 3 new elementary schools have been built there in the past decade.

The Superintendent and Site-Based Management

Three years ago, the school board employed Dr. Ursula Jones as superintendent. The 42-year-old administrator had been associate superintendent for instruction in a large city school system in an adjoining state. Prior to coming to LaSalle County, Dr. Jones had acquired a reputation as a change agent—a characterization that proved to be accurate. During her first year as a superintendent, Dr. Jones developed a plan to decentralize governance in the district. She announced that the adoption of SBM would be done initially on a voluntary basis in elementary schools because principals at this level appeared to be interested and supportive of the concept. In the second year, she interviewed principals who had expressed an interest in becoming involved in the first phase of the project. Three of them were selected to be part of Phase I.

Assistance was provided for the three participating schools. For example, the principals were sent to a two-week SBM seminar during the summer. In addition each school received $20,000 for staff development to be used during the first year. The only restriction placed on these funds was a stipulation that they had to be used to prepare faculty, staff, and selected parents to use SBM. Each participating school also was given budgetary independence in two critical areas: (1) supplies and equipment and (2) travel.

Elm Street Elementary School and the Principal

One of the newest schools in the district is Elm Street Elementary. It opened just four years ago to accommodate expanding populations. Presently, the school has three sections per grade level in grades kindergarten through five, but there are plans to add a fourth section at each grade level. Before the school opened, teachers from across the district applied to transfer there, and about 70 percent of those selected were current school system employees.

Albert Batz was a principal in a smaller elementary school when he was selected to become Elm Street's first administrator. Outgoing and friendly, he is perceived as a "people person." Prior to becoming an administrator he taught fifth grade in the LaSalle County system for 12 years.

Mr. Batz spends virtually all of his time wandering around the school. He loves interacting with students, teachers, and the other employees. It is not uncommon for him to walk into a classroom and join whatever activities are taking place; he always makes two or three trips a day to the teachers' lounge to have coffee and engage in conversation; and one of his favorite midmorning hideaways is the kitchen, where he can get the latest gossip from the cooks and sample the daily dessert.

Some teachers speculate that Albert purposely spends most of his time away from the office in order to avoid management responsibilities. When he came to Elm Street, he brought his secretary, Mrs. Lumans, with him. She is capable of managing many routine matters on her own. She only calls Mr. Batz back to the office when there is a serious problem.

The Implementation of Site-Based Management

When Dr. Jones announced that three elementary schools would be selected for Phase I of SBM implementation, the first volunteer was Albert Batz. He had long been committed to the idea of shared governance, and unlike some of his peers, he was not concerned with maintaining personal power. Before volunteering to be part of Phase I, however, he allowed the school's employees to vote on the matter. Overwhelmingly, they voted to implement SBM.

In addition to being in philosophical agreement with shared governance, decentralization, and teacher empowerment, Albert had another motive for involving Elm Street Elementary School with SBM. Some of the teachers, having come from various parts of the school district, did not get along with each other. In particular, there were two groups that generated continuous conflict. One, consisting of four teachers, came from Harrison Elementary School, an older school in Sunland. The spokesperson for this group was Jenny Bales. The other, consisting of three teachers, came from Weakland Township Elementary School—one of the rural schools in the county district. The designated leader of this group was Leonard Teel. Both groups, however, were unsuccessful in gaining political support from the school's remaining teachers.

Albert believed that Mrs. Bales and Mr. Teel had similar traits and needs. In their previous schools, each had been a dominant teacher—that is, a teacher who had the greatest power to influence others. In watching them fight over every little issue, Albert concluded that they were vying to recapture the stature they had prior to moving to Elm Street School. However, the 15 teachers outside the two factions remained neutral.

When Elm Street was selected for the SBM project, the principal had to establish a governance committee. He created a school council consisting of six teachers, three parents, a representative of the nonprofessional staff, and himself. Rather than appointing the members, he allowed the faculty, the parent-teachers association, and the staff to elect their representatives. Mrs. Bales and the three other teachers in her group, and Mr. Teel and the two other teachers in his group, all became nominees. Two other faculty members were also nominated, creating a situation where nine teachers competed for the six council positions. Twenty-two teachers were eligible to vote, and each could vote for up to six candidates. The final tallies were as follows:

Amy Raddison (not aligned with either faction)	14 votes
Tim Paxton (not aligned with either faction)	14 votes
Jenny Bales	17 votes
Arlene McFadden (aligned with Jenny Bales)	17 votes

Leonard Teel	17 votes
Lucille Isacson (aligned with Leonard Teel)	16 votes
Janice Summers (aligned with Jenny Bales)	15 votes
Tammy James (aligned with Leonard Teel)	14 votes

Bales and Teel, and one ally each, were elected to the council. The other two persons elected, Amy Raddison and Tim Paxton, were relatively young and inexperienced teachers.

Initially, Mr. Batz hoped that service on the school council would bring recognition to both Mrs. Bales and Mr. Teel, and over time, he thought there was a good chance the two would start working together to improve the school. But after meeting with the council for four or five months, he realized that the adversarial relationship between the two teachers was becoming more intense. The council provided a formal arena for political attacks. An incident at an early December meeting exemplified this fact. One of the agenda items was a request to send a team of five teachers, including Mr. Teel and the two teachers loyal to him, to a mid-January conference in California. Mrs. Bales challenged the request.

"Just because we have a substantial budget for staff development doesn't mean that we should send people on vacations."

Leonard Teel shot back immediately, "Vacation! Who said anything about vacation? This is a conference on model SBM programs. Teachers from all over the United States will be there. We can learn a great deal by participating."

"We don't have to go to California to learn about SBM," Mrs. Bales answered. "There are plenty of good programs closer to home. And for that reason, I urge everyone to vote against this request."

Barbara Whitlow, president of the PTA, had been elected as a parent representative to the council and subsequently as the group's chair. The election of a chair took three ballots before anyone received the simple majority that was required, and of course, Mrs. Bales and Mr. Teel were candidates. Although she did not particularly want another time-consuming assignment, Mrs. Whitlow agreed to accept the responsibility.

Now presiding over yet another conflict between Mrs. Bales and Mr. Teel, Mrs. Whitlow turned to Mr. Batz and asked if he would comment on the merits of the travel request. Unlike his demeanor at other times, the principal typically kept a very low profile in council meetings. When put on the spot by Mrs. Whitlow, though, he felt compelled to answer.

"You know that I don't like to take sides. As principal, I need to remain neutral. I have to work closely with all teachers. There is merit to both positions. Is it a good conference? Probably. Are there good conferences and workshops closer to home? Probably. I'm afraid each of us will just have to use good judgment."

The principal's role on the council had been questioned on a number of occasions. Members wanted to know how the council interfaced with Mr. Batz's normal duties as principal. He always answered that he was just another member and wanted to be treated that way. He saw no conflict between the council's responsibilities and his duties as principal. Several members, especially Mrs. Whitlow, initially suggested that he chair the council, but he declined. Mrs. Bales and Mr. Teel, on the other hand, were content to have him play a passive role.

"The purpose of having this council is to avoid one individual having all the power to make decisions," Mr. Teel said. "I agree with Albert that he shouldn't be taking sides."

"Well, so do I," added Mrs. Bales. "So, I move that the request to send five teachers to the conference in California be denied."

"I second that motion," said Arlene McFadden, the teacher on the council loyal to Mrs. Bales.

Mr. Teel immediately requested a secret ballot. This was another trend that deeply disturbed Mrs. Whitlow. The council was increasingly taking secret votes, and she saw this as contrary to building a team spirit. Additionally, all the bickering in the weekly meetings consumed a great deal of energy and little time was left to deal with issues relating more directly to curriculum and instruction.

The next day, Mrs. Whitlow went to see the principal. With the door closed, she demanded to know why he refused to assume any form of leadership on the council.

"I just don't understand how you can sit back and allow Mrs. Bales and Mr. Teel to constantly be at each other's throat. Don't you see how destructive their behavior is to our mission?" she asked.

"Barbara, I still have some hope that those two will come together. Let's give this a little more time. Do you think they are suddenly going to love each other just because I tell them to do so?"

Mrs. Whitlow made it clear that unless he agreed to be more forceful on the council, she would resign. "You know, Albert, I have plenty to do besides spending 10 to 12 hours a week on school council matters. I am willing to put in time—but only if we are making progress. And quite frankly, I don't think that is the case. All I've done is sit and listen to those two argue. From what I have seen, I'm not sure we weren't better off without SBM. I think it is your responsibility to step in and do something to stop this negative behavior."

Mr. Batz pleaded with Mrs. Whitlow not to resign. He said her continued leadership was essential and asked her to be more patient. But he would not make a commitment to change his own behavior. He merely said he would give some thought to becoming more vocal at council meetings.

Two days later, Mrs. Whitlow wrote a letter to Mr. Batz announcing her resignation from the council. In it, she candidly stated her reasons, and copies of the letter were sent to the superintendent, Dr. Jones, and each member of the LaSalle County school board. Her letter also suggested that the whole idea of SBM ought to be examined more closely before being implemented in additional schools. She wrote:

. . . If schools are going to be given all of this leeway and added resources, we need to be certain that proper leadership is maintained.

Simply going to shared decision making does not assure better education for our daughters and sons.

After finishing the letter, Mr. Batz put it in his top desk drawer and walked down
the hall toward the kitchen. A smile came over his face as he got close enough to
smell the freshly baked cookies.

THE CHALLENGE

Analyze the behavior of the principal in this case. Do you agree with Mrs.
Whitlow that he has to take a more active role in the council? Is he exhibiting
leadership?

KEY ISSUES/QUESTIONS

1. Describe the leadership style of Mr. Batz. Have you known principals who
   behave in a similar manner?
2. Is it common for schools to have a dominant teacher (i.e., one who is more
   influential than others)?
3. Should principals be required to chair school councils? Why or why not?
4. Do you agree with the principal's decision to permit council members to be
   elected? What other options could he have used to select council members?
5. Evaluate the structure of the committee. For a school this size, is the committee too large? Too small? Should other groups be represented?
6. Is there a possibility that the competing factions on the council will become
   allies over time? If so, what might cause this to occur?
7. Discuss this case from the perspective of politics and ethics. Is the principal
   behaving ethically?
8. How would you react to this situation if you were the school superintendent?
9. One possible solution to this situation would be to remove the four teachers
   who are members of the competing factions from the council. Would you
   support this action? Why or why not?
10. Why do you think that Mrs. Bales and Mr. Teel are content to have the princi-
    pal play a passive role on the council?
11. Is it better for Mr. Batz to remain neutral than to side with either Mrs. Bales
    or Mr. Teel?
12. Principals involved in shared decision making vary in the degree of control
    they maintain over the process. For instance, some are able to manipulate or
    direct outcomes. How can they do this? Is such behavior ethical?
13. In general, are teachers adequately prepared to be members of school gover-
    nance councils? Why or why not?
14. What is your position regarding SBM? What factors influence your position?
15. In general, do most teachers welcome the opportunity to have more free-
    dom and responsibility in their practice?

SUGGESTED READINGS

Belli, G., & van Lingen, G. (1993). A view from the field after one year of site-based management. *ERS Spectrum, 11*(1), 31–38.

Bergman, A. (1992). Lessons for principals from site-based management. *Educational Leadership, 50*(1), 48–51.

Conway, J. (1984). The myth, mystery, and mastery of participative decision making in education. *Educational Administration Quarterly, 21*(1), 11–40.

Delaney, J. G. (1997). Principal leadership: A primary factor in school-based management and school improvement. *NASSP Bulletin, 81*(586), 107–111.

Epp, J. R., & MacNeil, C. (1997). Perceptions of shared governance in an elementary school. *Canadian Journal of Education, 22*(3), 254–267.

Ferris, J. (1992). School-based decision making: A principal-agent perspective. *Educational Evaluation and Policy Analysis, 14*(4), 333–346.

Fraze, L., & Melton, G. (1992). Manager or participatory leader. *NASSP Bulletin, 76*(540), 17–24.

Golarz, R. (1992). School-based management pitfalls: How to avoid some and deal with others. *School Community Journal, 2*(1), 38–52.

Hoyle, J. (1991). The principal and the pear tree. *Journal of School Leadership, 1*(2), 106–118.

Johnson, P. E., & Evans, J. P. (1997). Power, communicator styles, and conflict management styles: A web of interpersonal constructs for the school principal. *International Journal of Educational Reform, 6*(1), 40–53.

Johnson, P. E., & Short, P. M. (1998). Principal's leader power, teacher empowerment, teacher compliance and conflict. *Educational Management and Administration, 26*(2), 147–159.

Kimbrough, R., & Burkett, C. (1990). *The principalship: Concepts and practices.* Englewood Cliffs, NJ: Prentice-Hall (see chapter 3).

Kohl, P. (1992). Sharing the power: Fact or fallacy? *Action in Teacher Education, 14*(3), 29–36.

Kowalski, T., & Reitzug, U. (1993). *Contemporary school administration: An introduction.* New York: Longman (see chapters 9, 12).

Kowalski, T., Reitzug, U., McDaniel, P., & Otto, D. (1992). Perceptions of desired skills for effective principals. *Journal of School Leadership, 2*(3), 299–309.

Kritek, W., & Schneider, G. (1993-94). Site-based management and decentralization. *National Forum of Educational Administration and Supervision Journal, 11*(1), 3–20.

Lange, J. (1993). Site-based, shared decision making: A resource for restructuring. *NASSP Bulletin, 76*(549), 98–107.

Laud, L. E. (1998). Changing the way we communicate. *Educational Leadership, 55*(7), 23–25.

Leithwood, K., & Menzies, T. (1998). A review of research concerning the implementation of site-based management. *School Effectiveness and School Improvement, 9*(3), 233–285.

Michel, G. (1991). The principal's skills in site-based management. *Illinois Schools Journal, 71*(1), 33–38.

Midgley, C., & Wood, S. (1993). Beyond site-based management: Empowering teachers to reform schools. *Phi Delta Kappan, 75*(3), 245–252.

Miles, W. (1982). The school-site politics of education: A review of the literature. *Planning and Changing, 12*(4), 200–218.

Ogletree, E., & Schmidt, L. (1992). Faculty involvement in administration of schools. *Illinois Schools Journal, 71*(2), 40–46.

Smylie, M. (1992). Teacher participation in school decision making: Assessing willingness to participate. *Educational Evaluation and Policy Analysis, 14*(1), 53–67.

Tyack, D. (1990). Restructuring in historical perspective: Tinkering toward Utopia. *Teachers College Record, 92*(2), 170–191.

Watkins, P. (1990). Agenda, power and text: The formulation of policy in school councils. *Journal of Education Policy, 5*(4), 315–331.

Is This All There Is?

BACKGROUND INFORMATION

Behavior in schools is determined by a combination of personal, professional, and contextual variables. One of the most influential factors is the process of socialization. It begins during professional preparation. At this phase, professors expose students to values and beliefs that constitute the profession's norms. Examples include placing students above all else and making a commitment to lifelong learning. Socialization also occurs when individuals actually begin working in schools. At this point, the intensity and direction of the process are determined by the culture of a specific school.

Adaptations to socialization vary. While some educators find the school's values to be congruous with their own beliefs, others do not. In addition, some might experience conflict between what they learned in professional preparation and what they are asked to do in practice. Within a relatively short period of time, typically one or two years, it becomes clear as to whether an educator has accepted the underlying beliefs of the school's culture. Those who have not may face unpleasant choices. They may be dismissed, resign, or continue to work in an environment where they constantly struggle to reconcile the differences between their own convictions and those of the dominant culture.

This case is about a young female teacher who becomes an assistant principal. During her first year in this position, she faces considerable internal conflict because she and the principals define effective administrative practice differently. As you read this case, consider your own experiences as you started to work in real school settings. Try to remember how you reacted to the socialization process.

KEY AREAS FOR REFLECTION

1. Socialization in organizations
2. Entry into school administration
3. Applications of the professional knowledge base
4. Ethical behavior
5. Determinants of administrative behavior

THE CASE

Amber Jackson sat in her office at Polk Middle School trying to finish paper work that had been assigned to her by the principal. It was nearly 9 o'clock in the evening, and the three night custodians were in the building with her. She was tired and frustrated, making it difficult for her to focus on her work. She kept glancing at the clock, realizing that she was not going to get much sleep that evening.

Amber had started teaching English and physical education at the middle-school level at age 22. Two years later, she started coaching volleyball and enrolled as a part-time student in a master's degree program in English. Although teaching, coaching, and being a graduate student kept her extremely busy, she did not want to give up any of the roles because she enjoyed all three.

Shortly after starting graduate school, Amber thought about the possibility of becoming an administrator later in her career. She examined what she would have to do, educationally and professionally, to pursue that goal. After having completed three courses in English, she transferred to a master's program in educational administration. Dr. Tom Westerbrook, an assistant professor, was assigned as her adviser.

Dr. Westerbrook was nearly 40 years old, and prior to his current job, he had been a principal in a suburban district near San Diego. Amber thought that she had learned a great deal from taking his classes on community relations and the principalship, and she always appreciated an opportunity to have personal conversations with him. Professor Westerbrook eventually became both an adviser and a mentor for Amber. He considered her to be the best student he had encountered in the master's program. As she was nearing completion of her degree, he told her, "Amber, you have a very promising career ahead of you in school administration. You have the intelligence, philosophy, and work ethic to be a highly effective principal. I think you should start looking for a job as an assistant principal now. And after you land a job, you should apply for admission to our doctoral program."

At that time, Amber had been teaching for just five years, and she recently had gotten engaged to an Air Force captain whom she had known in college. Although the prospect of becoming an assistant principal excited her, she had several doubts about heeding the advice she had been given. She wondered if Dr. Westerbrook was really being objective about her readiness to become an administrator. She was not sure whether she wanted to leave the classroom after just five years. And she thought about having to adjust to a new job and to being married at about the same time.

Amber called Dr. Westerbrook and told him that she was going to wait one year before applying for administrative jobs. "I'm getting married in November, and my fiancée is an Air Force pilot. Currently, he is stationed in Texas. His tour of duty with the military will be over in about eight months, and then he plans to work for an airline company. With all this uncertainty about where I might be living in the next few years, I've decided not to apply for other jobs now. But I hope you will still be willing to help me when I look for an assistant principal's job next year."

Over the course of the following school year, Amber got married, and as planned, her husband left the Air Force and took a job with a major airline company. She resigned her teaching position and they moved from southern California to Chicago. Amber applied for both teaching and administrative positions in the Chicago area. By late June, she had two job offers. One was for a teaching position in a rather affluent suburban district and the other was for a middle-school assistant principalship in a much less affluent suburban district. She decided to take the administrative position.

Polk Middle School was constructed in the early 1960s at a time when the population immediately south of Chicago was growing rapidly. Approximately 75 percent of the residents in the community served by the school are of eastern European extraction; the remainder is either African American or Hispanic. The school includes grades 7 and 8, and just over 800 students are enrolled.

Emil Denko has been principal at Polk for nearly 14 years. He is one of the few administrators who resides in the Polk community. The other assistant principal at the school is Ernest Tarver, an African American who has been in his job for nine years. Both Mr. Denko and Mr. Tarver expect to retire within three years.

Amber discovered that Polk was very different from the middle school in which she had worked previously. She had expected more discipline problems at Polk and there were. She expected more academic problems at Polk, and there were. What she did not anticipate was the substantially different attitude about teachers and students. Confrontations between the teachers and administrators at Polk were common, and the conflict was resolved in one of two ways. Either the principal and the teachers negotiated a settlement or grievances were filed under provisions of the teachers' union master contract. Yet, Mr. Denko and Mr. Tarver seemed to have positive personal relationships with individual teachers; it was almost as if the teachers and administrators agreed that their political differences would not become personal.

After having worked at the school for only three months, Amber was becoming dissatisfied with her job. She was distraught about her personal work. She knew that assistant principals had to handle discipline and had to perform management tasks. But she never imagined that her entire job would be consumed by these activities. She even considered resigning in the middle of the school year.

Amber called her former mentor, Dr. Westerbrook and told him about the problems she was having. He told her, "It's difficult for me to give you advice because I don't know your work environment. But before you do anything, I think you should talk to the principal and be candid with him about your concerns. Maybe Polk is just an especially poor work environment and you would be better off in another school. But I don't think you should quit in the middle of the year. That may make it difficult for you to get another administrative job."

Heeding Dr. Westerbrook's advice, Amber met with Mr. Denko and shared her growing dissatisfaction with the job. She outlined two primary concerns.

"I don't understand why teachers have such a low opinion of students at this school. Have they created a self-fulfilling prophecy? Are they giving up on the students who most need their help? We talked about setting student expectations in several of my graduate classes, and I have always been led to believe that setting high expectations is a far better alternative. One of my professors in school administration said that it was especially important for administrators to believe that those around them could succeed."

Mr. Denko was still trying to get past being surprised by Amber's comment that she was becoming dissatisfied with her job.

"How could you be dissatisfied? Here you are, not even 30 years old. You're already an administrator and you're making nearly twice as much as most teachers. And I think you're doing a pretty good job. Are you sure there isn't something outside of work that is bothering you?"

"Yes, I'm sure," Amber replied. "I just feel increasingly uncomfortable about the atmosphere in this school. Everyone seems to be pretty negative about students and their families. Many of the teachers seem to dislike their work, and they don't take much pride in the school. I'm just not used to working in these conditions."

"Well, that may be the problem. You've never really been on the other side of the tracks before. It's easy to be critical and to prescribe solutions when you're looking at a school like Polk from a distance. But being here, working with all these problems every day tends to give a person a different perspective. Did you ever consider the possibility that the teachers are just being honest about their working conditions? Or did you consider that maybe they really are dedicated but they have to let off steam every so often?" he asked rhetorically. "The figures show that about 30 percent of these kids won't graduate from high school—at least not before they become adults. Many of them are from homes where education is not valued. I know. I live here. Sure, we all like to believe that these kids will do well, but the truth is, many of them won't. My professors gave me all these ideals about believing that every student was potentially gifted and that every student could make it in school with help from their teachers. And I heard all of this about 25 years ago. The problem then and now is that many of these professors have no idea what it is like outside of their ivory towers."

At that point, Amber shifted the discussion to another concern. "Emil, I'm also bothered by the fact that I have little or no opportunity to work with teachers on instructional matters. I don't mind handling discipline problems, and I don't mind doing things like supervising students getting on and off of the buses. I expected that I would have these responsibilities—I just didn't expect them to be my entire job. One reason why I wanted to be an administrator was to be able to work closely with teachers on improving their work. When I started teaching, I was fortunate to have an excellent principal who took a great deal of interest in my professional growth. She was a terrific role model for me. And when I was working on my master's degree, my classes focused much more on instructional leadership than they did on supervising the lunch room or writing a discipline report. I just want to know if I will be more involved in other types of administrative duties in the future?"

"Sure, you will," Mr. Denko answered. "For example, we have to do evaluations in March and you'll be involved in that. You'll have about 10 teachers to evaluate and that will require you to do two classroom observations of each them. But you need to understand, most of what we do you're doing now. It takes a lot of work to manage this place. Teachers here do not expect us to be holding their hands. If they want help, they ask for it. And that rarely happens. The union doesn't want them bringing their problems to us."

"Why not?"

"Because, that's the way things are. If teachers believe that we can solve their problems, why would they need a union? The doubts you're having about your work are natural. When teachers move from the classroom to administration, they usually bring grand ideas with them about how they are going to save poor teachers and help troubled students. But you quickly learn that most of these lofty goals are out of your reach. You learn that in the real world of running a school, your job is to keep the place functioning. The taxpayers expect administrators to maintain a safe school environment so students who are serious about their education can learn. That's the way it was when I came to work in this community a long time ago and that's the way it is today. Amber, you're just like other new assistant principals. You're at a point where you miss teaching and being with the students. There's a sense of freedom and power associated with having your own classroom and being able to shut the door to close out the rest of the school. In a couple of months, things will look different. Trust me. You have a real bright future here. In three years, you could be the next principal."

Now approximately five hours after her meeting with the principal, Amber sat at her desk trying to finish a student discipline report. But her thoughts kept drifting back to her concerns and Mr. Denko's responses to them. The discussion with him did nothing to lessen her disappointment about her job. In fact, his suggestion that she might possibly replace him as principal in several years actually heightened her concerns.

At 10:15 P.M., Amber finally finished the report and left her office. She had spent nearly three hours doing paper work, and finishing gave her little satisfaction. As she drove home, she thought about the differences between Polk and the middle school where she previously taught English and coached volleyball. When she got home she called Dr. Westerbrook and told him about her conference with the principal. He still urged her to finish the school year at Polk, but now he advised her to find another position or to enter a doctoral program the following year.

THE CHALLENGE

Assume that Amber is your friend. What would you advise her to do?

KEY ISSUES/QUESTIONS

1. What constitutes a school's culture? How can a culture be identified?
2. Evaluate Amber's perception of the relationship that exists between the administrators and teachers at Polk. Does this relationship reveal anything about Polk's culture?
3. Do you agree with the principal's statement that all assistant principals experience some internal conflict after leaving the classroom?
4. Amber believes principals and assistant principals should spend some of their time working with teachers. While instructional supervision is clearly an ideal role for building-level administrators, is it a real role? What evidence do you have to support your response?
5. Evaluate the advice that Dr. Westerbrook gave to Amber about finishing the school year at Polk.
6. Assume that Amber decides to remain at Polk and seek the principalship when Mr. Denko retires because she believes that she can change the school's culture. Is she being realistic? Why or why not?
7. What elements of this case reflect socialization in graduate school and in the workplace?
8. Assume that Amber remains at Polk but openly criticizes beliefs that many students are doomed to fail. What are the possible consequences?
9. How much teaching experience should administrators have? What is the basis of your answer?
10. The principal in this case indicates that there are considerable differences between the ideals expressed in textbooks and college classrooms and the real conditions in schools. Based on your own experiences, do you agree with him?
11. What are the common sources of job dissatisfaction and job satisfaction among administrators?
12. Amber must make two important decisions: Should she stay at Polk? Should she remain in administration? What factors should be weighed in answering these questions?

SUGGESTED READINGS

Anderman, L. H., & Midgley, C. (1998). *Motivation and middle school students* (ERIC Document Reproduction Service No. ED 421 281)

Anderson, L. W., & Pellicer, L. O. (1998). Toward an understanding of unusually successful programs for economically disadvantaged students. *Journal of Education for Students Placed at Risk, 3*(3), 237–263.

Cantwell, Z. M. (1993). School-based leadership and the professional socialization of the assistant principal. *Urban Education, 28*(1), 49–68.

Giles, R. G. (1998). At-risk students can succeed: A model program that meets special needs. *Schools in the Middle, 7*(3), 18-20.

Glanz, J. (1994). Dilemmas of assistant principals in the supervisory role: Reflections of an assistant principal. *Journal of School Leadership, 4*(5), 577-590.

Golanda, E. L. (1991). Preparing tomorrow's educational leaders: An inquiry regarding the wisdom of utilizing the position of assistant principal as an internship or apprenticeship to prepare future principals. *Journal of School Leadership, 1*(3), 266-283.

Graham, S. (1990). Communicating low ability in the classroom: Bad things good teachers sometimes do. In S. Graham and V. Folkes (Eds.), *Attribution theory: Applications to achievement, mental health, and interpersonal conflict* (pp. 17-36). Hillsdale, NJ: Erlbaum.

Hanna, J. W. (1998). School climate: Changing fear to fun. *Contemporary Education, 69*(2), 83-85.

Hartzell, G. N. (1993). When you're not at the top. *High School Magazine, 1*(2), 16-19.

Koru, J. M. (1993). The assistant principal: Crisis manager, custodian, or visionary? *NASSP Bulletin, 77*(556), 67-71.

Kowalski, T. J., & Reitzug, U. C. (1993). *Contemporary education: An introduction*. New York: Longman (see Chapters 2, 4, 14, and 15).

Marshall, C. (1991). *The assistant principal: Leadership choices and challenges* (ERIC Document Reproduction Service No. ED 342 086)

Michel, G. J. (1996). *Socialization and career orientation of the assistant principal* (ERIC Document Reproduction Service No. ED 395 381)

Rusch, E. A., & Marshall, C. (1995). *Gender filters in the administrative culture* (ERIC Document Reproduction Service No. ED 392 116)

Scoggins, A. J., & Bishop, H. L. (1993). *A review of literature regarding roles and responsibilities of assistant principals* (ERIC Document Reproduction Service No. ED 371 436)

Toth, C., & Siemaszko, E. (1996). Restructing the assistant principalship: A practitioner's guide. *NASSP Bulletin, 80*(578), 87-98.

The Clinic Controversy

BACKGROUND INFORMATION

In many secondary schools, teenage pregnancies and sexually transmitted diseases contribute to escalating drop-out rates. One response has been the establishment of school-based health clinics—especially in urban schools serving large numbers of low-income students. These clinics are intended to provide a range of services from counseling on substance abuse to the distribution of contraceptives. However, because of varying community values, such programs have often generated substantial controversy and conflict.

Within any school community there are pluralistic sets of values. Effective administration involves understanding those values and knowing when conflict among them is likely (Razik & Swanson, 1995). In public education, moral and religious issues are especially volatile. Perhaps the best example is sex education. Some citizens believe that schools are the only reasonable source of information about sex for many students, but other citizens argue that families and churches should address this topic.

This case focuses on the political dimensions of decision making. A superintendent who appoints a committee to examine what can be done to reverse a growing drop-out rate does not receive the direction he was seeking. Although the conclusions in the committee's report appear to be accurate, the recommendations are vague. The superintendent also seeks advice from selected community leaders, but they too fail to offer a specific course of action. Faced with these conditions, he decides to move forward with his own plan, knowing that doing so is a personal risk.

Another focal point of the case is communication. In this vein, the following questions are important: How does the superintendent communicate with his staff? To what degree does the school district interact with the community? Are there established channels of communication that can be used when problems emerge?

Relationships between organizations and their environments are an essential element of organizational theory. These relationships are commonly described on a continuum from "open" to "closed." The former indicates constant interaction between organization and community, while the latter indicates no interaction. The district's climate and the expectations and demands of the community are key variables determining a school district's placement on this continuum. Often intense political disputes in school districts result from decision makers having insufficient or inaccurate information about community values, beliefs, wants, and needs.

KEY AREAS FOR REFLECTION

1. Changing demography and implications for public education
2. Curtailing drop-out problems in high schools
3. Conflict generated by problems having religious and moral implications
4. Communication between public schools and their communities
5. Shared decision making
6. Political dimensions of the superintendency
7. School-based health clinics

THE CASE

The Community

Shelton is a city in the East with just under 100,000 residents. In many ways, it is an exemplar of the American "melting pot"—an industrial city that attracted immigrants of varying races, cultures, and religions. Unlike other cities with economies that are highly dependent on manufacturing, Shelton has retained much of its population. In large measure, this had been attributable to the presence of several truck and recreational vehicle companies. Demand for their products has remained relatively high, and there has been little erosion of jobs to foreign markets.

The primary industries in Shelton include the following:

- Truck trailer factory, 950 employees
- Two recreational vehicle companies, 840 employees
- Automobile ignition plant, 560 employees
- Lawnmower assembly plant, 400 employees

Official census data indicate that the population in Shelton actually increased during the 1990s by about 8 percent.

Although the nature of the community has changed over the past two decades, a number of ethnic neighborhoods still are evident. For example, there are two relatively large Italian-American neighborhoods. Residents of German and Polish ancestry also remained clustered in separate parts of the city. Since the mid-1960s, the fastest-growing population groups have been African Americans and Hispanics. The most recent census provided the following demographic data:

> White – 59 percent
> African American – 31 percent
> Hispanic – 8 percent
> Native American – 1 percent
> Other – 1 percent

The city has its own hospital and a relatively new shopping center. The downtown area, however, is slowly dying. Most stores have relocated or have gone out of business. Several strip malls have been built on the fringes of the city, and many residents now shop at a large mall built in an adjoining county. Railroad tracks seem to be everywhere in Shelton. Being stopped by freight trains is a common occurrence as you drive through the city.

The School District

The Shelton City School District is one of four school systems in Parma County. Statistics for the district are as follows:

> High schools:– 4
> Middle schools:– 9
> Elementary schools:– 26
> Current enrollment:– 24,900

The superintendent is Dr. Fredrick Ochman, a veteran administrator in his sixth year as the district's chief executive. Prior to coming to Shelton, he served as superintendent in two smaller districts. He is perceived by his staff to be a "hands-on" leader who likes to get involved personally with key issues.

The central office staff includes 14 professional employees, three of whom are assistant superintendents reporting directly to Dr. Ochman:

> James Effrin, assistant superintendent for business
> Lucy Natali, assistant superintendent for pupil personnel services
> Jeremy King, assistant superintendent for instruction

A seven-member board governs the school district. Just three years ago, voters passed a referendum altering the method for selecting board members. Members had been appointed by the mayor to three-year terms. Now they were chosen in nonpartisan elections. As a result of this change, the school board has become more diverse with regard to race and socioeconomic status. Only two members who were in office when Dr. Ochman was appointed superintendent remain on the school board.

Dr. Ochman's Major Accomplishments

Perhaps Dr. Ochman's most visible accomplishments in Shelton have been balancing enrollments among the district's four high schools and building community support for schools. For at least 20 years, the attendance boundaries for these schools had not changed, and loyalties to the schools remained intense. Changing demographics, however, had presented two problems. The enrollments among the four schools were starting to vary considerably; the largest enrolled about 1,500 students, while the smallest enrolled only about 800 students. The more serious problem was racial balance. Minority student enrollments varied among the four schools from a low of 8 percent to a high of 68 percent.

Dr. Ochman's realized that the most direct approach to both problems would be to redraw the attendance boundaries—an act that almost certainly would generate intense conflict. So instead of pursuing this solution, he established an ad hoc committee to help him develop a plan for creating a magnet school-within-a-school concept at each high school. Four areas were selected as magnet school themes: mathematics-science, social studies, fine arts, technology. The concept essentially created an open enrollment at the high school level for students who opted to enter a magnet program. Preferences were given to transfer requests that improved racial balances. The program succeeded. Minority enrollments at the four schools now ranged from a low of 17 percent to a high of 54 percent; total enrollments now ranged from 900 to 1,400.

The second accomplishment for which Dr. Ochman has received high praise is building and maintaining community support for schools. He did this through two initiatives. The first was a policy that required each school to have an advisory council composed of teachers and parents; the intent was to ensure ongoing communication between the school and community. The second was the development of a comprehensive community education program. Adult education classes and recreational programs brought literally hundreds of taxpayers into the schools.

The New Challenge

As part of the district's strategic planning process, student and financial data are analyzed annually by central office administrators. The data revealed that the high school graduation rate in the district was steadily declining; figures for the previous year indicated that approximately 25 percent of the district's students did not complete the twelfth grade. Two factors appeared to be responsible for the declining graduation rate. First, the drop-out rate had increased markedly among female students. Whereas 10 years ago boys were twice as likely not to complete high school as girls, the current figures indicated virtually no difference in graduation rates. Second, the drop-out rate was increasing most rapidly among those students who came from lower socioeconomic families (as identified by free-lunch data).

When Dr. Ochman saw the drop-out data, he immediately acted to address the issue. His first move was to establish an ad hoc committee consisting of three administrators, six teachers, four parents, and four students. Dr. Natali was appointed as the committee's chair. The superintendent charged the group with two tasks: verify the causes for the increasing drop-out rate; recommend positive actions to ameliorate the situation. The committee was given a budget of $8,000.

After six months, the committee presented the superintendent with a written report. Included were the following conclusions:

1. The relatively stable drop-out rate for male students is largely explained by the continued existence of low-skill jobs in the community and surrounding areas. Such employment opportunities tempt male students who are not performing well academically to leave school prematurely.
2. The socioeconomic status of the family seems to influence student decisions about staying in school. Students from low-income families often are given little encouragement to do well academically. In some instances, they may even be encouraged to quit school so that they can get a job and supplement family incomes. In many low-income families, there is only one parent, and not infrequently, this parent has not finished high school.
3. One fact stands out with respect to the accelerating drop-out rate among female students. Many who left school without graduating were pregnant. Students involved in a pregnancy are five times more likely to drop out than those who are not. If the pregnant student is from a low-income family, she is four times more likely never to graduate from high school.
4. The overall rate of pregnancies among high school students has increased 45 percent in the last 10 years. Nearly 65 percent of the students who became pregnant qualified for free lunches.
5. Most students involved in a pregnancy have had virtually no consultation, sex education, or health care. Again, this was especially true of students from low-income families.

Although the committee members reached consensus on the report's conclusions, they had strong differences of opinion regarding the recommendations. Consequently, only three suggested actions were listed in the report:

1. The school district should implement a sex awareness program.
2. Consideration should be given to establishing an alternative school for students who cannot function in the regular high schools. Such an option may encourage more students to stay in school.
3. The school district should work with the council of churches in the community to address the moral nature of this problem.

The report was distributed to administrative staff and the school board. Dr. Ochman asked the secondary school principals to make it available to teachers and other employees. Six weeks later, Dr. Ochman met with the administrative staff to discuss reactions to the report. The administrators challenged neither the data nor the conclusions, but some did not support the recommendations. A few expressed uneasiness about the school becoming more involved in sex education; others stated concerns that an alternative school would encourage an even higher percentage of students to withdraw from regular high school programs.

Dr. Ochman subsequently invited nine community leaders to meet with him to review the problem and the report. They included the mayor, the administrator of the hospital, the director of the mental health clinic, a priest, a minister, a rabbi, a physician, the director of the local family planning agency, and the president of the school board, David Potter. Like the district's administrators, these individuals agreed that the conclusions were accurate but they disagreed over appropriate courses of action.

Three months after the report was written, Superintendent Ochman concluded that the differences of opinion expressed by district administrators and community leaders reflected the sentiments of the entire community. Thus, he believed that implementing the committee's three recommendations would produce conflict.

A Course of Action

Assuming that any proposed action to the drop-out problem would have its critics, Dr. Ochman looked beyond the report for solutions. One program that captured his attention was the student health clinic. Such clinics had been established in other districts, especially in urban school systems. Although the clinics were controversial, they were gaining support among educators and social service providers as a realistic alternative for dealing with controversial issues such as premarital sex, birth control, and abortion. The establishment of the clinics also was attributable to an increasing rate of sexually transmitted diseases among teenagers. In addition to dealing with matters of sexual behavior, these clinics provided counseling in areas such as substance abuse, prenatal care, and child care.

In an effort to learn more about student health clinics, Dr. Ochman and Dr. Natali visited two high schools in separate districts that had such programs. Both were located in urban settings and primarily served students from low-income families. Both principals they visited made positive comments claiming that students had benefited from the clinics. Dr. Ochman, however, was more interested in determining how faculty and the community had reacted. When questioned about this, the principals provided little information. However, both said that they were not aware of any organized opposition to the program.

On returning to Shelton, Dr. Ochman arranged another meeting with the group of nine community leaders who had previously reviewed the report. He told them about student health clinics, outlined their possible objectives, and shared information he had gathered during his visits to the two high schools.

Two of the clergy immediately expressed concern. The others had little to say. But when asked if they would publicly support the creation of student health clinics in Shelton's high schools, only the school board president said that he would. Several of the others said that they would need more information before responding. Although not committing their support, the agency directors offered to cooperate with the school district if the clinics were established.

If the health clinics were to be created the following school year, the superintendent realized that a decision had to be made quickly. Although he understood the risk associated with this alternative, he presented the concept to the school board in the executive session prior to the regularly scheduled May meeting. The board president, Mr. Potter, said that he supported the initiative. There were no questions from the other board members nor did any of them indicate how they would vote if the clinics were actually proposed. Dr. Ochman told them that he would probably submit a recommendation to establish health clinics at the June board meeting.

The day after the May board meeting, the superintendent met with the four high school principals and two of the assistant superintendents, Dr. King and Dr. Natali. He told them that he would recommend the clinics at the next board meeting. He added that the clinics would probably operate under agreements with the county mental health agency, the city hospital, and the welfare department. These agencies would provide support services when necessary.

Two of the principals reacted negatively. They warned that there would be substantial community opposition. One principal said he supported the program and the fourth principal said he was undecided.

The mixed reactions from the four persons most responsible for implementation did not dissuade Dr. Ochman. He drafted the following recommendation for the June board meeting:

Superintendent's Recommendation: That a student health clinic be established to provide assistance for students with a variety of health and emotional problems at each of the four high schools. Such problems will include drug and alcohol abuse and teenage pregnancies. A full-time director is to be employed for each of the clinics. A total of $257,000 is to be budgeted for this program in the next fiscal year.

Dr. Ochman purposefully avoided terms such as "birth control" and "sex education." He also prepared background information for the school board that outlined the proposed linkages with community agencies.

After receiving the recommendation five days prior to the June meeting, three board members called the superintendent and told him that they would vote against it. Board member Tony Companni was the most adamant.

"I don't have a problem helping kids who get mixed up with drugs. But no way am I going to sanction our schools getting in the business of running birth control clinics or dictating sexual standards. Your recommendation doesn't tell me what is actually going to take place in these clinics. How do I know that we're not going to be giving out free condoms to kids? So, I'm voting against the recommendation and I plan to speak against it at the meeting."

Velma Jackson, a board member who had decided to support the recommendation, called Dr. Ochman and suggested that he withdraw the recommendation so that the board could have more time to study the issue. She believed that the recommendation would be defeated if a vote were taken at the June meeting. Dr. Ochman told her that delaying the matter, even one month, would mean that the clinics could not be implemented for another year. He added that he had already told the principals he would present the recommendation in June.

When Dr. Ochman presented the recommendation publicly at the June meeting, Mrs. Jackson immediately moved to table it. She argued that more time was needed to answer questions about the proposal. The three board members who already had told the superintendent that they would vote against his recommendation were also opposed to Mrs. Jackson's motion. Most of the audience appeared to support them; each was applauded after declaring opposition to the clinics and to the effort to table the matter. The motion to table passed, however, by a vote of four to three.

The next morning the local newspaper, the *Shelton Daily Examiner,* carried an editorial urging the school board to defeat the superintendent's recommendation for student health clinics if it were brought before them again. The editorial was followed by other expressions of community opposition, such as letters to the editor and letters to board members.

During the three weeks after the June board meeting, Dr. Ochman also was inundated with letters opposing the clinics. A fourth board member had indicated publicly that he probably would not support the recommendation. The newspaper also reported that a confidential source had revealed that at least two high school principals were opposed to the clinics.

Two of the three board members who had initially committed to vote against the superintendent's recommendation pleaded with him to drop the matter. They said that they did not want to see him destroyed by this political issue. The three assistant superintendents also urged him to retreat.

In the weeks following the June board meeting, Dr. Ochman received little support for his idea. Only a handful of taxpayers and staff offered encouragement. Even Mr. Potter, the board president who previously said he supported the ideas, was now quiet. As the July board meeting drew near, Dr. Ochman had lunch with him. Mr. Potter, an attorney who handled a number of cases involving juveniles, said that he still supported the recommendation. But he warned the superintendent, "It has little chance of being approved. There may be as many as five votes against it. Listen, everyone will understand if you pull back. It may be the prudent thing to do."

THE CHALLENGE

Place yourself in Dr. Ochman's position. What would you do with the recommendation for the health clinics?

KEY ISSUES/QUESTIONS

1. What information presented in the case about the community is relevant to the decision the superintendent must make?
2. Why are moral and religious issues so controversial in public elementary and secondary education?
3. Evaluate the superintendent's behavior with respect to formulating a recommendation in this matter. What would you have done differently if you were the superintendent?
4. To what extent might an administrator's personal values and beliefs affect decisions in controversial areas such as health clinics?
5. When an administrator's personal beliefs conflict with the professional knowledge base, which should direct behavior?
6. What are the policies in your local high schools relating to pregnant students? Do you support these policies? Why or why not?
7. To what extent should the superintendent have relied on information gathered from the two urban high schools he visited?
8. Is it legal and ethical for school board members to state publicly how they will vote on a superintendent's recommendation prior to the board meeting at which the matter will be addressed?
9. Assume that the superintendent decides to withdraw the recommendation. What are the political and ethical ramifications?
10. Interpret the behavior of the agency directors who did not commit to support the clinics but did commit to cooperate with the schools if they were established.
11. Are the superintendent's successes with magnet programs and community involvement relevant to this case? Why or why not?
12. Evaluate the behavior of the high school principals. Did they act appropriately?
13. Can you identify any alternative actions that may have produced more public support for the superintendent's recommendation?
14. Do you think the clinics would have been more acceptable to the public if they were called something else? Would they have been more acceptable if there had been assurances that they would not deal with contraception and abortion counseling?

SUGGESTED READINGS

Albert, K. (1989). *School-based adolescent health programs: The Oregon approach* (ERIC Document Reproduction Service No. ED 323 272)

Berger, M. (1982). The public schools can't do it all. *Contemporary Education, 54*(1), 6–8.

Bonjean, L., & Rittenmeyer, D. (1987). *Teenage parenthood: The school's response.* Bloomington, IN: Phi Delta Kappa Foundation (Fastback No. 264).

Buie, J. (1987a). Schools must act on teen pregnancy. *The School Administrator, 44*(8), 12–15.

Buie, J. (1987b). Teen pregnancy: It's time for schools to tackle the problem. *Phi Delta Kappan, 68*(10), 737–739.

Cook, L. (1987). This proposed health clinic triggered a rhetorical meltdown. *American School Board Journal, 174*(5), 27–28.

Cuban, L. (1988). A fundamental puzzle of school reform. *Phi Delta Kappan, 70*(5), 341–344.

Dryfoos, J. (1998). School-based health centers in the context of education reform. *Journal of School Health, 68*(10), 404–408.

Dryfoos, J. (1991). School-based social and health services for at-risk students. *Urban Education, 26*(1), 118–137.

Edwards, L., & Brent, N. (1987). Grapple with those tough issues before giving that clinic the go-ahead. *American School Board Journal, 174*(5), 25–27.

Ennis, T. (1987). Prevention of pregnancy among adolescents. Part I. The school's role. *School Law Bulletin, 18*(2), 1–15.

Evans, R., & Evans, H. (1988-89). The African-American adolescent male and school-based health clinics: A preventive perspective. *Urban League Review, 12*(1-2), 111–117 (see entire issue related to alleviating teenage pregnancies).

Forste, R., & Tienda, M. (1992). Race and ethnic variation in the schooling consequences of female adolescent sexual activity. *Social Science Quarterly, 73*(1), 12–30.

Frymier, J., & Gansneder, B. (1989). The Phi Delta Kappa study of students at risk. *Phi Delta Kappan, 71*(2), 142–146.

Hahn, A. (1987). Reaching out to America's dropouts: What to do? *Phi Delta Kappan, 69*(4), 256–263.

Harold, R., & Harold, N. (1993). School-based clinics: A response to the physical and mental health needs of adolescents. *Health and Social Work, 18*(1), 65–75.

Harrington-Lueker, D. (1991). Kids and condoms. *American School Board Journal, 178*(5), 18–22.

Kasen, S., Cohen, P., & Brook, J. (1998). Adolescent school experiences and dropout, adolescent pregnancy, and young deviant behavior. *Journal of Adolescent Research, 13*(1), 48–72.

Kirby, D., & Lovick, S. (1987). School-based health clinics. *Educational Horizons, 65*(3), 139–143.

Kowalski, T., & Reitzug, U. (1993). *Contemporary school administration: An introduction.* New York: Longman (see chapters 11, 12).

Nelsen, F. (1988). What evangelical parents expect from public school administrators. *Educational Leadership, 45*(8), 40–43.

Norris, B. (1985). High school pregnancy clinic survives storm. *Times Educational Supplement, 3617* (October 25), 17.

Nudel, M. (1992). Health for hire. *American School Board Journal, 179*(10), 36–38.

Patterson, H. (1993). Don't exclude the stakeholders. *School Administrator, 50*(2), 13–14.

Razik, T. A., & Swanson, A. D. (1995). *Fundamental concepts of educational leadership and management.* Upper Saddle River, NJ: Merrill, Prentice Hall (see chapter 4).

Rienzo, B., & Button, J. (1993). The politics of school-based clinics: A community-level analysis. *Journal of School Health, 63*(6), 266–273.

Scott-Jones, D. (1993). Adolescent childbearing: Whose problem? What can we do? *Phi Delta Kappan, 75*(3), K1–K12.

Timczyk, K. (1995). Building a better safety net. *American School Board Journal, 182*(8), 41–42.

Will, S., & Brown, L. (1988). School-based health clinics: What role? *American Teacher, 72*(3), 4.

Case **20**

Substance Abuse and Student Discipline

BACKGROUND INFORMATION

Substance abuse policies and rules remain a source of controversy for school administrators. This is because members of the school community often disagree about the causes of these problems and how they should be handled. As an example, some principals believe that illegal drug use is a criminal matter, and they are more inclined to advocate harsh penalties and zero-tolerance policies. Others believe that substance abuse is a disability and keeping a student in school should be the first priority when administering discipline. All administrators, however, recognize that illegal drugs and alcohol in schools are disruptive and dangerous.

The principal who is the central character in this case establishes an in-school suspension program as a means of reducing expulsions and drop outs. Some parents object to this program, saying that students caught using drugs should not be permitted to remain in school. These criticisms become more intense when two students in the in-school suspension program are arrested for selling cocaine in the school's parking lot. The conflict causes the principal to not only question the program but also her future as a principal.

KEY AREAS FOR REFLECTION

1. Career decisions
2. Readiness for the principalship
3. Job satisfaction
4. Control of pupil conduct

5. Job-related stress
6. Principal and staff relationships
7. Political dimensions of controversial decisions

THE CASE

"Are you crazy?" Lowell Tatum asked his wife as the two were having dinner at their favorite restaurant in San Francisco. "Now let me get this straight. You want to leave your nice job as coordinator of English Education to become a high school principal? You ought to think about this. You know what high school students are like."

Patricia Tatum has met challenges successfully all of her life. Born in Los Angeles in a low-income family, she is the oldest of six children. Neither of her parents graduated from high school, but they set high expectations for their children with respect to education.

All through school, Patricia was a good student and a leader. Her interests were diversified. She was an athlete, a cheerleader, and president of the student council. When she graduated from high school, she ranked sixth in a class of 389. She received an academic scholarship to attend a private university, which was only 20 miles from her home. Even though she maintained two part-time jobs, she finished her degree in four years and graduated cum laude.

One of Pat's part-time jobs during college was as a teacher's aide in a parochial elementary school. It was there that she first thought about becoming a teacher. She found working with students to be tremendously satisfying. However, she was majoring in English and had no plans to obtain a teacher's license. In addition, she had not given up on her original career goal—to become a lawyer. Two law schools recently had accepted her for admission. But as the last semester of her senior year started, she became increasingly undecided about her future. Six weeks before graduating, she made her choice.

Foregoing law school, Pat accepted a position as a copy editor with a small publishing firm and enrolled in a master's program that would qualify her to be licensed as a high school English teacher. While in graduate school, Pat met Lowell Tatum. He too was a graduate student, completing a master's in business administration. Lowell was a stockbroker in Los Angeles. Shortly after they finished graduate school, they got married. Now possessing his M.B.A. degree, Lowell received a promotion that required him to transfer to the firm's San Francisco office. Pat applied for teaching positions in that area, and a suburban district hired her to teach English at the high school level.

Four years later Pat and Lowell had their first child. Lowell convinced her to take a one-year leave of absence so she could spend time with their child. Rather than returning, Pat decided to resign from her teaching position. She gave birth to a second child two years later. During the six years she was away from teaching, Pat took several classes at a local university. Encouraged by several of her professors, she subsequently enrolled in a doctoral program in educational administration.

Just before Pat turned 35, she completed her Ed.D. program and wanted to renew her career in education.

She applied for several assistant principal jobs. There were two such vacancies in the district where she was employed previously. Several weeks after filing applications, the personnel director contacted her via telephone. But instead of discussing the assistant principalships, he inquired if she would be interested in interviewing for the coordinator of English position. Pat had not considered working in a central office, largely because she had no previous administrative experience. Subject area coordinators were staff administrators who essentially worked on curriculum and instruction projects. She decided to pursue the opportunity and ended up getting hired.

Initially Dr. Tatum enjoyed her job. Each time she visited a school, however, she was reminded of how much she missed working with students. Toward the end of her first year as a coordinator, she talked about her professional future during her evaluation conference with Dr. Ernesto Javier, the associate superintendent for instruction and her supervisor. The two had developed a positive relationship, and she was comfortable being candid with him.

"I don't want you to think I'm unhappy, because I'm not," she told him. "It's just that I miss being with students. I can't explain it."

Dr. Javier was an experienced administrator, having been a principal for 14 years prior to accepting his present position.

"What are you trying to tell me? Do you want to return to teaching?"

"I think what I would really like is to work as a building-level administrator," she answered. "That's what I intended to do when I finished my doctorate, but when this opportunity came along, I thought I should try it."

Dr. Javier understood that some administrators prefer to be in schools. He looked at Dr. Tatum and said, "I don't think we will have any assistant principal positions open for next year. As you know, we just hired two new people last year. I will help you find a job in another district if that is what you really want. Personally, I hope you stay here. You're doing really well in this job, and I have had many positive comments from teachers and principals about your work."

Dr. Tatum left the meeting feeling good about Dr. Javier's evaluation of her performance. She had not told her husband about her thoughts of changing jobs, and she decided to wait until school was out in about three weeks before deciding whether to look for a new position.

About two weeks after their meeting, Dr. Javier called Dr. Tatum and asked if she could meet with him so that they could continue to discuss her future. They met that afternoon.

"Pat, Mr. Malovidge at Western Valley High School just submitted his resignation. He is moving to Seattle," Dr. Javier told her. "I talked to the superintendent this morning, and we have decided to name an interim principal. It's pretty late in the year to be conducting a search. You expressed interest in working at the building level. I shared that information with the superintendent. To get right to the point, we would like you be principal at Western Valley this fall."

Dr. Tatum was caught off guard. She struggled to respond.

"Why me?" she finally asked. "Don't the assistant principals want the job?"

"That's the problem. Two of them do. I think picking one over the other would be a mistake. It would cause a great deal of conflict. And besides, I think the school needs fresh ideas."

Dr. Tatum requested that she be given two or three days to think about the job offer. Dr. Javier said he needed an answer in 48 hours.

"Before I leave, would you explain the implications of this being an interim position," she requested.

"Certainly. If you do well and want to remain in the job, you would have an excellent chance of being named the permanent principal. We will conduct a search around December or January, and at that time, you will have to decide if you want to be an applicant. At least you will find out if you like working at the building level more than you like working in the central office. If you decide not to apply, you can return to your present job."

After leaving Dr. Javier's office, Dr. Tatum called her husband and suggested that they have dinner at their favorite restaurant. She told him to be prepared for a surprise.

The prospect of his wife becoming a high school principal was disconcerting to Lowell. Although he supported her career, he worried that being a high school principal would be too demanding and stressful. When he questioned whether this was the best decision for her, she told him she had already decided to take the job.

Western Valley High School has about 2,300 students in grades 9 through 12. The school's student population is diverse, both economically and racially. Most students come from middle-class homes and about 55 percent of the graduates enroll in four-year institutions of higher education.

As the district's English coordinator, Dr. Tatum had been to Western Valley High School about a dozen times in the previous year. She knew the members of the English department and the administrators.

Two of the school's three assistant principals, Joe Howard and Bill Fine, were upset that Dr. Tatum had been named interim principal. They had substantially more experience than she, and they felt that they had not been given a fair chance to be named principal. The third assistant principal, Sally Farmer, was approximately Dr. Tatum's age, and she had just finished her first year as an administrator. Ms. Farmer had only met Dr. Tatum's once, but she was relieved that Dr. Tatum was named interim principal instead of either of the other two assistants.

In her first meetings with the assistant principals after starting her new job at Western Valley, Dr. Tatum outlined aspirations and expectations for the next year. She stressed that she wanted the four of them to work as a team and asked for their input as to how the administrative assignments should be divided. Collectively, they decided that Dr. Tatum and Ms. Farmer would have primary responsibility for the instructional programs. Mr. Howard would be responsible for most management functions, such as food services, scheduling, budgets, and the like. Mr. Fine agreed to supervise extracurricular programs, including athletics. Student discipline, the assignment none of them wanted, was divided among the four of them.

After school started, Dr. Tatum realized that she would not be able to spend most of her time working with instructional programs as she had planned. No matter how meticulously she scheduled her time, unforeseen problems interfered. And although the four administrators were sharing discipline responsibilities, almost all of the more serious cases ended up in her office. This was especially true of students who had gotten caught using illegal drugs or alcohol.

The former principal had taken a hard line toward substance abuse, and as a result, Western Valley had the highest expulsion rate among the district's four high schools. The assistant principals generally supported the harsh rules because they diminished the need for them to make decisions related to problems in this category. Dr. Tatum, however, was less inclined to exclude students from school, particularly for a first offense. She tried to persuade the assistant principals to accept her philosophy but was unsuccessful. In an effort to bypass this barrier, she appointed a committee to review the school's disciplinary rules and regulations. Two parents, one a social worker and the other a psychologist, Mr. Fine, and four teachers were appointed to the committee.

The committee studied policy and rules in other districts and high schools. They also received testimony from several experts and representatives of law enforcement. After several months, the committee recommended the establishment of an in-school suspension program for first-time offenders. The vote to support the recommendation was four to three, with the assistant principal and two teachers voting against it. Mr. Fine wrote a minority opinion warning that Dr. Tatum would be making a big mistake if she moved away from the present zero-tolerance rule.

Although Dr. Tatum agreed with the committee's recommendation, she wanted to discuss the matter with Dr. Javier before acting. She especially wanted to determine if the district's policy on drugs would permit an in-school suspension. Dr. Javier explained that the district's policy allowed schools to establish their own penalties for first time offenders; individuals caught using or selling drugs and alcohol a second time had to be expelled. Thus, she could change the school's zero-tolerance rule for first time offenders, provided that the change was approved by the superintendent and school board.

Dr. Javier then asked, "You know we just advertised the vacancy for your job two weeks ago. The superintendent and I think you are doing fine. Given that you probably have the inside track to get the job, do you really want to stick your neck out by changing the substance abuse rules? Especially at this time?" She did not respond.

Dr. Tatum spent much of the following week weighing the positives and negatives relative to creating an in-school suspension program. She decided to accept the committee's recommendation. Within two weeks, the superintendent and school board approved her request to change the rule for first-time offenders.

The in-school suspension program was started on March 1. At first, there was little overt opposition. Three weeks later, Dr. Tatum learned that she had been selected as the school's regular principal. Through the remainder of that school year, there were few problems with the in-school suspension program. Even Bill Fine was beginning to think that it might work.

As the next school year got under way, the administrators had to deal with many drug-related discipline cases. By late October, the in-school suspension program was bulging at the seams. For the first time since starting the program, Dr. Tatum was receiving complaints about it. One parent wrote the following letter:

Dear Dr. Tatum:

It has come to my attention that students who are caught using drugs are being allowed to stay in school. As a parent, I think this sends the wrong message. My wife and I tell our children that using illegal drugs is a serious offense. I'm not sure that your approach to dealing with the problem reinforces what we tell them. I urge you to discontinue the in-school suspension program.

Critics of the in-school suspension program argued that the in-school suspension program had actually encouraged students to use illegal drugs. Bill Fine, who just a few months ago was saying that the new program might work, was now telling everyone that he opposed the idea from the start. Joe Howard and Sally Farmer did everything they could to distance themselves from the program. Dr. Tatum, however, continued to believe that the change was in the best interests of the students and the school. The expulsion rate during the last semester of the previous school year was the lowest in the last five years. So despite the mounting criticism, Dr. Tatum continued the in-school suspension program.

Just two days after the second semester began in early January, two students who were already in the in-school suspension program were arrested for selling cocaine to undercover police in the school's parking lot. The students had been put in the suspension program in early December after being caught smoking marijuana in a restroom.

The arrests made the evening news, and for the next few days, the media covered the story extensively. A television reporter interviewed several parents who said that this would have never happened had the principal not changed the school's zero-tolerance rule. Most of the media reports tied the in-school suspension program to this incident.

One of the local television stations did a ten-minute report on drugs at Western Valley High School. The report started with the reporter making the following comments:

In-school suspension at Western Valley. A solution or a part of the problem? Parents and teachers at Western Valley are up in arms over an in-school suspension program for first-time drug and alcohol offenders. Parents and faculty who favored a zero-tolerance policy for all offenders have heavily criticized the program, started last year by the school's principal. Concerns about in-school suspension were heightened by the recent arrests of two students who were already in this program. They were caught selling cocaine to undercover police in the school's parking lot. School district officials said they are conducting their own investigation and they would be making a decision about letting the in-school suspension program continue.

Two days after the arrests, Dr. Tatum met with the district's superintendent, Dr. Nicolas Constantine, at his request. He asked Dr. Tatum if the students who were placed in the in-school suspension program received any special assistance. She said that they were required to see their school counselors at least one hour each week; the counselor could recommend that a student complete a drug education program as a condition for being readmitted to the school's regular program. Neither of the students who had been arrested had been referred for such a program. Dr. Constantine reminded Dr. Tatum that the district operated an alternative high school, and students who were expelled could continue their education there.

"Why do you think in-school suspension is better than having these students at an alternative school?" he asked.

"Many expelled students don't enroll at the alternative school. Our records clearly show that. This issue was examined in detail by the committee that recommended the in-school suspension program," Dr. Tatum explained.

As the meeting ended, Dr. Constantine said that the in-school suspension program could continue, but closer supervision over the students had to be provided. In addition, he wanted assurances that every student assigned to the program would have to complete a substance abuse program.

Dr. Javier took a more pragmatic position. "Listen Pat, these things happen. This isn't the first time students got busted for selling drugs in the parking lot, and it certainly won't be the last. But I have to tell you, I don't think you ought to continue the suspension program. You're taking too much heat over this." Two days later, Dr. Tatum received an anonymous letter that was more stinging than any of the previous complaints. The person who wrote it called Dr. Tatum incompetent and charged that the superintendent was protecting her simply because she is an African-American female. The letter was written on Western Valley High School stationery.

For the first time in her brief career as a principal, Dr. Tatum doubted whether she had what it took to survive in this difficult job. She knew that schools in other districts had been able to operate in-school suspension programs successfully. She wondered if her detractors could be correct. Maybe she was incompetent.

Dr. Tatum called Dr. Javier. She shared her self-doubts and requested his counsel. Dr. Javier carefully weighed his response.

"Pat, I probably am to blame for getting you into this job. If you are unhappy, maybe you should get out. But if you're considering leaving just because of the in-school suspension issue, you're making a mistake. If it's not drug problems, it will be something else. That's the life of a high school principal. If you decide you want out of Western Valley, I'll find you a job back here in our division—but only if you really want out of the principal's job. Don't let go of all your dreams and your goals just because of one problem."

THE CHALLENGE

Place yourself in Dr. Tatum's position. What would you do?

KEY ISSUES/QUESTIONS

1. Do you think Dr. Tatum was adequately prepared to become principal of a large high school? Why or why not?
2. Given the attitudes of the assistant principals, was it a good idea for Dr. Tatum to appoint a committee to study substance abuse?
3. Was it a good idea to move forward with the in-school suspension program given the divided opinions on the committee?
4. What is your impression of the behavior of the three assistant principals in this case? Were they behaving appropriately?
5. The four administrators at the high school shared discipline responsibilities. Was this a good idea? Why or why not?
6. What are the advantages and disadvantages of in-school suspension programs? To what extent do they involve risk?
7. What are the arguments for and against zero-tolerance policies?
8. Does your state have laws stipulating what must be done to students in public schools if they are caught using or selling illegal drugs? If so, what are these laws?
9. What alternatives could Dr. Tatum have pursued for first-time offenders?
10. Do you think that women face special problems in the secondary principalship?
11. Do you think that the criticism being directed at Dr. Tatum is fair?
12. Do you agree with the superintendent's directive that every student who receives in-school suspension must complete a substance abuse program? Why or why not?
13. Should districts allow individual schools to determine if they have zero-tolerance rules? Why or why not?

SUGGESTED READINGS

Buscemi, M. (1985). What schools are doing to prevent alcohol and drug abuse. *The School Administrator, 4*(9), 11–14.

Daria, R. (1987). Remedy for drug abuse: Honesty, discipline, help for troubled students. *American School Board Journal, 174*(8), 37, 54.

Donnermeyer, J. F., & Davis, R. R. (1998). Cumulative effects of prevention education on substance use among 11th grade students in Ohio. *Journal of School Health, 68*(4), 51–58.

Erickson, H. (1985). Conflict and the female principal. *Phi Delta Kappan, 67*(4), 288–291.

Fertman, C., & Toca, O. (1989). A drug and alcohol aftercare service: Linking adolescents, families, and schools. *Journal of Alcohol and Drug Education, 34*(2), 46–53.

Hughes, W. (1998). *Substance abuse policies in Ohio schools* (ERIC Document Reproduction Service No. ED 424 558)

Johnston, J. (1989). High school completion of in-school suspension students. *NASSP Bulletin, 73* (521), 89–95.

Knopf, C. (1991). Middle school/junior high in-school suspension programs: Do we have what we need? *NCA Quarterly, 65*(3), 457–459.

Kowalski, T., & Reitzug, U. (1993). *Contemporary school administration: An introduction* (pp. 88–94). New York: Longman (see chapters 11, 14).

Lohrmann, D., & Fors, S. (1988). Can school-based educational programs really be expected to solve the adolescent drug abuse problem? *Journal of Drug Education, 16*(4), 327–339.

Rosiak, J. (1987). Effective learning demands drug-free schools. *NASSP Bulletin, 71*(497), 128-133.

Schreiner, M. E. (1996). Bold steps build safe havens. *School Business Management, 62*(11), 44-46.

Sheets, J. (1996). Designing an effective in-school suspension program to change student behavior. *NASSP Bulletin, 80*(579), 86-90.

Sheppard, M. (1984). Drug abuse prevention education: What is realistic for schools? *Journal of Drug Education, 14*(4), 323-329.

Sullivan, J. (1989). Elements of a successful in-school suspension program. *NASSP Bulletin, 73*(516), 32-38.

Sullivan, P. (1998). When kids get hooked. *Our Children, 23*(8), 6-10.

Watson, D., & Bright, A. (1988). So you caught them using drugs: Now what? *Thrust, 17*(3), 34-36.

Whitfield, D., & Bulach, C. (1996). A study of the effectiveness of in-school suspension (ERIC Document Reproduction Service No. ED 396 372)

Zirkel, P. A. (1996). Discipline and the law. *Executive Educator, 18*(7), 21-23.

Zorn, R. (1988). New alternatives to student suspensions for substance abuse. *American Secondary Education, 17*(2), 30-32.

21

Let's Not Rap

BACKGROUND INFORMATION

As America became a more diverse society, new challenges were created for public school districts. These new responsibilities were most apparent in urban districts; however, administrators in virtually all types of geographical settings now face them. Increased diversity can be both an asset and a source of conflict. On one hand, it helps to better prepare students to be functional adults in a multicultural society and global economy. On the other hand, it creates a social environment in which political strife among groups holding different values and beliefs becomes likely.

This case describes a situation in which two cultural groups are at odds over a school convocation. A "rap" group's offer to present a program encouraging students not to use illegal drugs has been accepted by the school's administration. When the convocation's program is announced publicly, Jewish families in the school-community immediately demand that it be cancelled. Their objections relate to information that several members of the group have been labeled by the media as anti-Semites. Members of the school's African American community respond by demanding that the program take place.

As you read this case, pay particular attention to how both economic and ethnic diversity often become intertwined. If decisions made by public officials were always determined by majority opinions, administration would largely entail taking votes or opinion polls. In truth, administrative decisions are an intricate mixture of professional knowledge, personal convictions, politics, economics, and legal considerations.

KEY AREAS FOR REFLECTION

1. Multicultural school environments
2. School and community relationships
3. Factors influencing administrative decisions
4. Resolving conflict
5. Free speech and public schools

THE CASE

The Principal

Barb Doran is principal of Roosevelt High School, a well-known secondary school located in a suburb of a major city in a mid-Atlantic state. She has been in this position for less than two years, but she has already established a reputation as an effective administrator.

After teaching English for 12 years, Ms. Doran has had three progressively challenging administrative positions. The first was as assistant principal of a 350-student middle school, the second was as principal of a 500-student rural high school, the third was principal of Roosevelt—a school that is over five times as large as the one in which she previously worked.

The Bad News

Barb Doran had just returned from a conference in Orlando, Florida. She was driving from the airport to her office at approximately 7:30 in the evening. The car's radio was tuned to a station that aired a local talk show. After listening for just a few minutes, Barb realized that the focus of the show's discussion that evening was Roosevelt High School. She increased the volume so she could hear every word.

"I think the principal should have the courage to cancel this program. What good does it do to expose our children to anti-drug messages if the people who are delivering the messages also preach hate toward some groups in our society? There are more acceptable ways to tell high school students not to use drugs. That's my opinion."

The next caller took an opposite position, "We all know there have been racial tensions at Roosevelt High. People in the African-American community know that African-American students don't get treated equally or fairly. Someone told me that a white kid got caught smoking in the restroom, and he had to go to detention for only one hour. The very next day a black kid got caught smoking, and he got a three-day suspension. Now if that's true, you have to admit that the administrators are not treating everyone the same way. So, I think this principal is going to cancel the convocation. When it comes down to picking between the Jewish community and the African-American community, there is no doubt in my mind what the principal is going to do."

Without responding to the caller, the show's host prepared for a commercial break, "For those of you who just tuned in, tonight's topic deals with yet another controversy at Roosevelt High. Should the school allow a "rap" group to deliver an anti-drug program? Some parents accuse the group's members of being anti-Semites; they say, cancel the program. Others disagree. They argue that canceling the program will be another slap in the face to the African-American community. What do you think? Here is your chance to join the debate. Give us a call at 555-1500. I'll be back in a moment to take more calls."

Barb Doran stared at the road ahead as she continued toward her office. She knew that the convocation had been scheduled, but she was not aware that it has sparked a firestorm. She whispered to herself, "Why me, Lord?"

The School

Roosevelt enrolls about 2,750 pupils. Most come from middle-class families; however, students from families at all levels of the economic continuum are represented. The student population is also mixed racially, ethnically, and religiously. Nearly 40 percent of the student body is classified as minorities (31 percent African American, 4 percent Asian, 3 percent Hispanic). About 10 percent of the students identify their religion as Judaism, and another 5 percent indicate that they are Muslims.

Over the years, the school has won numerous athletic and academic awards. It is considered to be one of the finest schools in the state, and political and educational leaders have frequently cited it as a model multicultural environment. About 60 percent of the graduates enroll in four-year institutions of higher education.

PARA

Recently during an interview with a newspaper reporter, Ms. Doran said that her greatest concern about Roosevelt High was the criticism that African-American students were not being treated fairly. A group of about 25 parents formed an organization last year called PARA (Parents Advocating Racial Awareness). At a press conference announcing the formation of the group, leaders said that their purpose was to ensure fair and equal treatment of Roosevelt students. They argued that the following problems existed at the school:

1. The curriculum did not offer African-American students ample opportunity to study their own cultural heritage.
2. Teachers and administrators treated African-American students more harshly than others when they disciplined them.
3. School officials had done little to ensure that the African-American community would have a representative voice in critical decisions affecting the school and its students.

Sensitive to these criticisms, the principal attended PARA meetings whenever she could. She also appointed a member of PARA to the principal's advisory council; a group of six teachers, six parents, and six students (one-third of whom were now African American).

The Nature of the Problem

Several weeks before the conflict about the convocation became public, Reggie Colter, a senior student, had an appointment with the principal to suggest a possible convocation program. Reggie, the only African-American member on Roosevelt's Student Council, often was the spokesperson for black students. His father, an attorney, is a member of PARA.

During their meeting, Reggie told the principal, "I have a great opportunity for our school, and I wanted to see how you felt about it. My cousin is a sound technician for a music group called The Inner City. They're on a concert tour and scheduled to appear in this city in the near future. One of the things they do while on tour is to present several free shows at high schools. They do this as a public service to discourage students from using drugs. My cousin said he could probably get them to do a show here when they are in town. Is it possible we could arrange this?"

"Well, I don't know, Reggie. I've never heard of this group. What type of show do they do?" Ms. Doran asked.

"They are a 'rap' group. During these school programs, they do some of their popular songs and talk about how drugs can really mess up students. The group's members grew up living with these problems, and they have the ability to reach students. My cousin said that there won't be any foul language or dirty dancing."

Reggie then showed her a promotional brochure put out by the group.

"And the best thing, Ms. Doran, is that they do this without charging the school. If you go see them in concert, you'd probably have to pay $30 or more for a ticket. My cousin said he would need to know if we are interested as soon as possible."

Ms. Doran showed interest in the idea. She thought that the PARA and other elements of the African-American community would respond positively if such a program were held at the school. She told Reggie to see Wallace Slater, one of the assistant principals, about making arrangements for the convocation. Mr. Slater was in charge of extracurricular activities and the only African-American administrator at the school.

Mr. Slater asked Reggie to provide him with a list of schools where this convocation had been held. About week later, he produced a list identifying 13 high schools. The assistant principal contacted administrators at two of them. Because they were located in different states, the principal did not realize that the two he selected enrolled predominately African-American students. The feedback about the rap group was positive, and officials at both schools said they highly recommended the program. Feeling comfortable about the proposal, Mr. Slater told Reggie to have a representative of the group call him so they could confirm a date and time.

The assistant principal then wrote the following note to Ms. Doran.

Barb,

I talked to Reggie this morning about the proposed convocation. I checked this group out with two principals who had the program presented in their schools. They didn't have any problems. They said students reacted positively. Unless I hear otherwise, I will move forward to schedule the group. As soon as a date is set, I'll let you know.

Wallace

About two weeks later, the principal received another note indicating that a date and time for the convocation had been determined.

Shortly after Ms. Doran left to attend the conference in Orlando, concerns about the impending appearance of The Inner City at Roosevelt High started to surface. The convocation was announced in the student paper, and some Jewish parents recognized the name of the group. About three months prior to the announcement, a national tabloid carried a story suggesting that The Inner City was guilty of anti-Semitism. The charges were made after the group recorded a record containing lyrics that blamed Jews for oppressing inner-city blacks. The tabloid story contained several derogatory quotes from the group's members on this topic.

After the convocation was announced in the student paper, copies of the tabloid article were distributed among members of the Jewish community. Almost overnight, a major controversy erupted. In response to demands that the program be canceled, PARA said that it would wage a major protest if that were done.

Wallace Slater and the other assistant principals decided to wait until Barb Doran returned from the conference to make a final decision on the convocation. They thought that the conflict might dissipate, and even if it did not, they concluded that waiting a few days to make a decision would not matter.

Reaching a Decision

As Ms. Doran reached the high school, she was still listening to callers voice opposing views on the impending convocation. When she walked into her office, she immediately saw a stack of mail sitting on her desk. At the top was a folder containing information about the "rap" group controversy. A copy of an article from yesterday's newspaper was one of the items in it.

Another Controversy Erupts at Roosevelt High

Some parents of Roosevelt High School students are objecting to a convocation that is to be presented by a music group called "The Inner City." The parents contend that at least two members of the group have made anti-Semitic statements to the press and that lyrics in some of their songs are distasteful and not in the best interests of racial harmony. Principal Barb Doran has not been available for comment. Assistant principal Wallace Slater said the group would deliver an anti-drug message. He said their appearance had nothing to do with either politics or race, and he went on to note that appearances at other high schools had not resulted in problems. He said school officials are examining the matter and will make a decision about the convocation shortly. Superintendent Paul Tolliver said he would talk to Principal Doran when she returns to her office tomorrow.

Also in the folder were over two dozen phone messages pertaining to the convocation. Ms. Doran telephoned Dr. Tolliver at his home.

"Barb, I'm glad you're back," he told the principal after answering the phone. "I suppose by now you know what is going on. What do you know about this 'rap' group?"

"I did not know about the anti-Semitism charges until tonight. I learned about it listening to the radio on my way to my office from the airport. Before I left for Florida, Wallace Slater checked out the group, and all of the feedback he got was positive. We didn't see any reason not to schedule the event. If we had said no, PARA would have been all over us about denying an African-American group the opportunity to perform before our students."

"I tried to reach you in Orlando this afternoon, but you had already checked out of the hotel. Listen, we have to make a decision on this and the sooner, the better. The Jewish community is up in arms, demanding that we cancel the program. This PARA group is getting a lot of attention from the media, and they are making all kinds of threats about boycotts and protests if the program is canceled. You have to wonder how we end up with these seemingly no-win situations."

"Dr. Tolliver, I accept responsibility for this. I gave Wallace approval to move forward. I have been trying to work with PARA, and maybe I was too anxious to score positive points with them. It appears that I should have been more cautious. I will meet with my administrative staff first thing tomorrow morning, and I'll have a recommendation to you by 10 A.M. You can be assured of that."

"Barb, let's say this situation were reversed. Let's say it was a Jewish group that had been accused of putting out an anti–African-American message. Would we bring them into the school—even if they were delivering an anti-drug message?"

"Are you saying, Dr. Tolliver," asked Ms. Doran, "that I should cancel the program?"

"No, I'm not necessarily saying that. I'm just trying to point out that there are good arguments on both sides of this issue. You know I don't like to interfere in the way you operate the school. I have confidence that you and your staff will do whatever is best."

Ms. Doran sat at her desk and thought about possible options to resolve the controversy. She tried to imagine how she would react as an African-American parent or student if the convocation were canceled. She also considered how she might react as a Jewish parent or student if the convocation were held. Personally, she believed that schools should provide a forum for the exchange of ideas, provided that those ideas did not violate community standards. But where were the parameters for those standards? With all of these thoughts running through her mind, she called the three assistant principals and asked them to meet with her at 6:30 the next morning.

During that meeting, Ms. Doran outlined the problem and indicated that a decision had to be made that morning. Mr. Slater, who had more involvement with the issue than any of the others, suggested that the convocation be held as scheduled. However, he recommended that it be followed by a discussion between the group's members and leaders of the Jewish community.

"If this controversy exists, why not discuss it? Shouldn't students hear both sides? Of course, we don't know if the parties would agree to those terms," he told the other administrators.

The other two assistant principals offered different options. One suggested that the convocation be canceled. "The best way to resolve this is just to back away from it. Within two weeks, everyone will have forgotten about it."

The other assistant principal proposed having two simultaneous convocations—one presented by the "rap" group and the other presented by a panel of community leaders and students on the topic of multiculturism. "We would allow students to select which one they would attend."

Getting three different proposals from her assistants was not what the principal wanted. As the discussion continued, she judged that they would not reach consensus. The meeting was concluded because the students were starting to arrive. Ms. Doran looked at the clock on the office wall. In less than two hours, she had to call Dr. Tolliver. Should she reconvene the meeting with her assistants? Should she move forward and make the decision alone? If so, what decision should she make?

THE CHALLENGE

Assume you are the principal. What would you do?

KEY ISSUES/QUESTIONS

1. Develop a list of possible decisions and evaluate the merits of each.
2. Does the school district in which you work or reside have policies and rules that would have provided direction for the principal in this matter? If so, what are they?
3. What weight should be given to input obtained by the assistant principal from officials at two schools where the group had previously performed?
4. Should the assistant principals have contacted the principal immediately when the controversy over the convocation erupted? What, if any, difference would it have made if they had done so?
5. To what extent should high schools provide a forum for controversial ideas?
6. Assume that the principal cancels the convocation. Is there a potential legal problem? If so, what is it?
7. The superintendent in this case allows the principal to make the decision. If you were the principal, would you prefer to have had a superintendent who would have told you what to do? Why or why not?
8. Organizational theorists point out that conflict can be a catalyst to change. In this situation, what positive changes might occur as a result of this conflict?

9. What are some common sources of conflict among ethnic and racial groups in a multicultural setting?
10. Do you believe that the high school administrators acted appropriately in considering and subsequently scheduling the convocation? Why or why not?
11. When the principal met with the three assistants, she allowed them to present alternative solutions. The outcome was three different proposals. If you were the principal, would you have conducted this meeting differently? If so, how?
12. Are there ways that community leaders could be involved in making a decision about the convocation? If so, how? What are the advantages and disadvantages of involving them?
13. Assume that the convocation is canceled. Are you concerned about a precedent being set? If so, what is the nature of your concerns?

SUGGESTED READINGS

Banister, J., & Maher, M. (1998). Recentering multiculturalism: Moving toward community. *Urban Education, 33*(2), 182-217.

Harrington-Lueker, D. (1993). Practicing tolerance. *Executive Educator, 15*(5), 14-19.

Hollen, G. (1984). School assemblies as supplements to classroom learning. *NASSP Bulletin, 68,* 134-135.

Kowalski, T., & Reitzug, U. (1993). *Contemporary school administration: An introduction.* New York: Longman (see chapters 8, 9).

Margolis, H., & Tewel, K. (1988). Resolving conflict with parents: A guide for administrators. *NASSP Bulletin, 72*(506), 26-28.

Martinson, D. L. (1998). Vulgar, indecent, and offensive student speech: How should public school administrators respond. *Clearing House, 71*(6), 345-349.

McLeer, J. (1983). Understanding anti-Semitism. *Curriculum Review, 22,* 99.

Noguera, P. A. (1999). Confronting the challenge of diversity. *School Administrator, 56*(5), 16-19.

Pate, G. (1988). Research on reducing prejudice. *Social Education, 52,* 287-289.

Sheets, R. (1998). A theoretical and pedagogical multicultural match, or unbridled serendipity? *Multicultural Education, 6*(1), 35-38.

Sherman, R. (1990). Intergroup conflict on high school campuses. *Journal of Multicultural Counseling and Development, 18*(1), 11-18.

Stover, D. (1991). Racism redux. *Executive Educator, 13*(12), 35-36.

Stover, D. (1990). The new racism. *American School Board Journal, 177*(6), 14-18.

Valverde, L. (1988a). Principals creating better schools in minority communities. *Education and Urban Society, 2*(4), 319-326.

Valverde, L. (1988b). Principals embracing cultural reality. *Teacher Education & Practice, 4*(1), 47-51.

Zirkel, P. (1998). Boring or bunkum? *Phi Delta Kappan, 79*(10), 791-792.

Zirkel, P., & Gluckman, I. (1983). Stop, don't raise that curtain. *Principal, 62,* 45-46.

Case **22**

We Don't Want the Devil Teaching Spelling

BACKGROUND INFORMATION

Teacher empowerment (professionalism) and increased liberty (greater community control) have been widely accepted as state, local district, and individual school reform initiatives. Yet, these two objectives have some basic incongruities, making them difficult to implement simultaneously. For example, empowerment gives educators greater autonomy—a condition that is supposed to result in higher levels of individualized instruction. Increased liberty is supposed to foster political and economic support and ensure that schools are responding to community as well as individual students needs. But how does a principal balance citizen participation in governance with teachers' rights to control their practice? For example, should the school council or the faculty make the final decision about which reading or science textbook to adopt?

Administering a school democratically is difficult. Principals are expected to maintain control while involving teachers, parents, and students in decision making. Tensions between control and participation have always existed in public education. Corwin and Borman (1988) wrote:

> ... district administrators are held accountable for things they cannot always control. This condition is a product of decentralization processes within formally centralized school districts. School districts are organized officially as hierarchies. Implementing educational policy is legally and politically the responsibility of high-level district administrators.

> However, in practice only certain decisions are centralized. Many others
> have been decentralized, and administrators can never fully control
> such responsibilities. (p. 212)

Modern reforms, such as site-based management, are accentuating the difficulties
inherent in pursuing professionalism and participation at the same time.

Administrators who allow teachers to control decisions about instructional
materials do not escape accountability for the outcomes. This is true of the elementary school principals in this case. They allowed a group of teachers, participating in the district's gifted and talented program, to send instructional materials requisitions to an assistant superintendent without their approval. The
arrangement emerges as a pivotal issue when some parents condemn software
programs as being inappropriate for young children.

KEY AREAS FOR REFLECTION

1. Parental objections to instructional materials
2. The parameters of professionalism and teacher empowerment
3. Delegating authority and accountability
4. Censorship in public schools
5. Relationship between district and school administration

THE CASE

"I really like this software program. It fits nicely with what we are trying to accomplish in gifted eduction. And besides, the students will like the content."

The evaluation came from Sandy Oberfeld, a second-grade teacher who was
demonstrating the product. She was talking to 17 colleagues in a meeting at
Samuels Elementary School. The teachers were reviewing instructional materials
for use in the district's gifted and talented program.

"I agree," said Beatrice Sachs. "My children like something different. They
have so many toys and gadgets at home, it's hard to motivate them. I think Sorcerer is a novel way to get them to work independently on their spelling. We are
dealing with a generation of students who have learned to think and process information by watching television and playing video games. Computer games typically capture their attention."

The elementary school gifted and talented program in the Maple Creek
School District is clustered in three of the system's 10 elementary schools. Serving two affluent suburban communities in the Midwest, the district ranks in the
top 2 percent in the state in per-pupil expenditures for instruction.

The teachers who participate in the gifted and talented program meet once
every two months after school. They get together to discuss materials, share
ideas, and coordinate curriculum. Sandy Oberfeld, who was demonstrating the

product, was the group's coordinator. She had learned about Sorcerer while attending a teachers' conference.

The teachers reacted positively to Mrs. Oberfeld's demonstration. However, one of them, Lucy McNeil, suggested that some parents might object to this product.

"You know in this day and age," she said, "one is never sure what standards parents will use in evaluating instructional materials. Fundamentalist groups, as an example, have criticized computer games similar to this one. They think anything related to magic or witchcraft is evil and somehow linked to the devil."

There were no reactions to Mrs. McNeil's comments. Mrs. Oberfeld asked for further input, and three or four teachers said they wanted to purchase the software. After hearing no objections, the decision was made to prepare a requisition to purchase 60 copies of the product—20 for each of the three participating schools.

For at least the last 15 years, teachers in the school district had considerable autonomy to select supplemental instructional materials for use in their classrooms. This independence extended to the elementary school gifted and talented program, but because this program was not housed in every school, it had its own budget. Until four years ago, the principals in the three participating elementary schools attended the bimonthly gifted and talented staff meetings. They stopped going because they felt their participation was no longer necessary.

The requisition to purchase 60 copies of Sorcerer was sent from Mrs. Oberfeld to the assistant superintendent for instruction, Dr. Wilbur Youngman. He had the responsibility of overseeing the program's budget. When he received the requisition, he did not question it nor did he contact any of the principals. He merely verified that sufficient funds were available to transact the purchase and sent it to the business office with his approval.

After the copies of Sorcerer were delivered, all 18 teachers involved with the program made them available to their students. They could be used in school or students could take them home for a period of one week. Sorcerer is constructed around a system of rewards and punishments given to students based on their spelling performance. As expected, most of the students liked the software.

About one month after Sorcerer was made available to students, the first parental complaint about the product was registered. Elizabeth Baker, the mother of a second-grade student at Lakeside Elementary School, called Nancy Tannin, the school's principal.

"Miss Tannin, I'm calling you about a computer game one of the teachers gave to my daughter, Sally. She is in the gifted and talented program, and as you know, students who are involved regularly bring home books and other supplementary materials. I became inquisitive about this game because Sally just couldn't leave it alone. And she was so intense when she was playing it. She told me the game was called Sorcerer. I had never heard of it. Do you know what I'm talking about?"

The principal had never heard of Sorcerer, and she admitted that fact to Mrs. Baker. She then told her that the teachers purchased materials.

"Well, don't you have to approve the purchase?" the mother asked.

"Normally, yes. But the gifted and talented program is a district initiative. So the assistant superintendent for instruction is in charge of approving purchases. I'm not certain what the problem is. Do you think your daughter is spending too much time with it? Or do you think that the product is not very good?"

"My concern is about the nature of the product. The theme deals with witchcraft and black magic. Now I realize that its purpose is to improve spelling skills, but why is it necessary to use controversial material? You may think I am overreacting—and maybe I am. But in this day and age, parents have to be especially sensitive about their children being exposed to undesirable values and beliefs."

Miss Tannin suggested that she would have to look into the matter before she could respond to the concern. Although she said this, the principal had already assumed that Mrs. Baker was either overreacting or misinformed. Two days later, Miss Tannin discussed Mrs. Baker's concern with one of the teachers who participated in the gifted and talented program. The teacher told the principal that Sorcerer was very popular with the students and indicated that all of teachers approved of the product's purchase.

Miss Tannin then telephoned Mrs. Baker and told her that she had investigated the matter. She told the mother about the conversation she had with one of the teachers.

Mrs. Baker asked, "Did you look at it? Did you actually sit at a computer and examine the game?"

"Well, no. I didn't think that was necessary," Miss Tannin answered. "Our teachers are competent professionals. I trust them to make good decisions about instructional materials."

Mrs. Baker became angry. "Maybe the teachers are wrong this time. How long would it have taken you to view the product? I think it is reasonable to hold a principal accountable for the types of materials that are used in a public school. I'm not going to drop this matter. So be prepared."

After the conversation with Mrs. Baker, Miss Tannin telephoned the other two principals in the schools participating in the gifted and talented programs, Deloris Gragolis and Mitch Sancheck. She asked them if they had received complaints about Sorcerer. Both affirmed that they had each received a call in the past two days. Like Miss Tannin, they also had talked to teachers about the product and received assurances that it was not offensive. Collectively, they arrived at the following strategy:

- They would send a memorandum to Dr. Youngman alerting him to the situation.
- They would send copies of the memorandum to all 18 teachers participating in the program.

- They would write letters to the complaining parents indicating that they would not restrict use of the program. Rather, they urged the parents to instruct their children not to use the product if they found it to be offensive.

Two weeks after Mrs. Baker first complained to Miss Tannin, a letter to the editor, signed by 16 individuals, appeared in the local newspaper condemning the use of Sorcerer.

We are parents of elementary school children who participate in the gifted and talented program in the Maple Creek School District. Recently, our children have been exposed to a distasteful and evil set of materials called Sorcerer. These materials are supposed to assist our children with their spelling skills, but in reality, they expose them to witchcraft and other evil concepts.

The adoption of Sorcerer is yet another example of how our public schools have become a pawn for those who wish to drag society into the mud. Parents who support our public schools with hard-earned tax dollars should not have to be concerned that positive values taught at home are being eroded by activities in school.

Perhaps the most discouraging element of our complaint is that the school administration appears unwilling to do anything about this situation. Our calls to principals have either been ignored or we have been told that teachers have the authority to select these materials. As taxpayers and parents, we urge others to join our protest. Let's keep our schools free of materials that promote witchcraft, devil worship, and other evil ideas. Call your school board member now and voice your objection!

The district's superintendent, Philip Montgomery, learned about the situation when he read the letter. He called Dr. Youngman the next morning anticipating that there would be inquiries about the letter from school board members. Dr. Youngman told him that the principals had discussed the matter with the teachers and neither the teachers nor the principals felt that the parents' objections were valid. The superintendent told Dr. Youngman that he wanted to meet with him, the principals involved, and Mrs. Oberfeld to discuss the matter in greater detail.

The next day, the six educators met in the superintendent's conference room. Dr. Montgomery indicated that he already had received telephone calls from four of the school board members about the letter that appeared in the paper. He asked those present three questions: What are the parents' specific objections? Why are these materials still being used if they are objectionable to some families? Who made the decision to buy the materials in the first place?

"Sorcerer is similar to a popular video game that got some negative publicity recently," explained Mrs. Oberfeld. "At the time we decided to purchase it, we did not anticipate that some parents would object. And even if we knew that some might complain, I'm not sure we would have made a different decision. If we let right-wing religious groups dictate what we use in our schools, we'd be in big trouble. Now that they no longer think that communists are hiding under every desk, they think the devil is running the public schools. The fact of the matter is that this program motivates children to work on their spelling. Students are not required to use it. If some parents find it objectionable, all they have to do is tell their children not to use it. Why should other students be deprived just because a group of fundamentalist parents find the software objectionable?"

Dr. Montgomery asked the principals if they had any comments. Miss Tannin spoke first.

"We have a great deal of confidence in Mrs. Oberfeld and the other teachers who work in this program. They all agreed to purchase these materials. When I received a complaint, I asked a teacher in my building to explain why it was purchased. When I told her about the concern, she said that students were not required to use Sorcerer. She also said that she disagreed with the parent's judgment about the product."

"But did any of you look at the material?" the superintendent asked.

The three principals and Dr. Youngman said that they had not done so.

"Who authorized this purchase?" the superintendent asked.

Miss Tannin answered, "The teachers recommended buying Sorcerer, and the requisition was sent to Dr. Youngman."

"Well technically, I approved the purchase," Dr. Youngman said. "But I can't be looking over teachers' shoulders. My job, quite frankly, is simply to see that there is money in the budget and that the requisition has been processed properly. I don't think any of you want me to be deciding what you are going to use for instructional programs in your schools."

Mrs. Oberfeld was disturbed by what she was hearing. "Before we start blaming each other, we ought to step back and think about what is at issue here. Are we going to allow a group of parents, a small group at that, to dictate what we use in our schools? I think these individuals would like to control every decision. If they get their way on this, their behavior will be reinforced and they'll be back with some other ridiculous demand. These people believe in censorship. They want to control what we read and how we think."

Miss Tannin spoke next. "Assume that any administrator would have blocked the purchase of this software. Wouldn't that have created a major problem? How would the teachers respond if we told them that we will not approve requisitions because someone might complain about the material being purchased? I think we have to face up to what is at stake here. This is censorship."

Mitch Sancheck then added to her comments, "We have a great deal of faith in our teachers. Quite frankly, I feel very comfortable having them rather than these parents decide what materials are best for students."

Dr. Montgomery indicated that he did not want to unduly restrict instructional decisions made by teachers. He pointed out, however, that he was uncomfortable with the fact that principals were bypassed in the acquisition process. "When I was a principal, I had to sign every requisition that originated in my building," he told the others. "But I had no choice. We had a policy that required my approval. Our policy here is different. It stipulates that one administrator with supervisory responsibility for the program in question and the business manager must sign each requisition. This problem clearly demonstrates that we can bypass principals and still be in compliance with the policy. We have two decisions to make. First, what do we do to resolve the current problem? Second, what should be done to prevent this problem from recurring?"

Miss Tannin answered, "You may be in a better position to answer those questions. Maybe we should revise our policy so that principals cannot be bypassed."

Dr. Montgomery got up from his chair and said, "That certainly is one possibility; but before we move in that direction, we should weigh all possible consequences. For instance, what would occur in the gifted and talented program if one principal refused to sign a requisition? I want you to continue meeting until you have answers to my questions. I have to go to a luncheon but I'll be back in about two hours. When I return, I hope you will have a recommendation regarding how we respond to these parents."

THE CHALLENGE

Assume you are one of the principals in the meeting. What is your preferred recommendation for resolving the current problem? What is your recommendation for preventing this problem in the future?

KEY ISSUES/QUESTIONS

1. Evaluate the process that was used to purchase materials for the gifted and talented program. Was the conflict with the parents caused by the process or by negligence?
2. Do you think that the three elementary school principals behaved responsibly in this case? Evaluate their behavior from the following perspectives: (a) professional responsibility, (b) moral and ethical leadership, and (c) effective management.
3. Should teachers have the freedom to select the instructional materials they will use? Why or why not?
4. Assess the argument that the materials should not be removed because their usage is voluntary. Put yourself in the position of a parent. Is this an acceptable response from the school district's officials? Why or why not?
5. Why is it possible for the teachers and parents to have such different views of the software in this case?

6. While some school districts have literally hundreds of policy statements, others have relatively few. As a principal, which type of district would you prefer? Provide a rationale for your response.

7. Evaluate the decision of the principals to quit attending the bimonthly meetings for the teachers involved in the gifted and talented program.

8. What are the tensions between liberty and professionalism that contribute to the problem in this case?

9. Does your local school district have a policy for purchasing supplementary instructional materials? If so, what is the policy?

10. Assume that Sorcerer is removed from the schools as demanded by the group of parents. How do you think the teachers would respond?

11. The concept of local school districts is based on the value of liberty in American society. Does the configuration of local school boards encourage or discourage the formation of pressure groups that try to influence educational policy? Defend your response.

12. Evaluate the manner in which the three elementary principals handled this matter. If you were one of them, what would you have done differently?

13. The case provides some information about the meeting at which the teachers decided to purchase the software. Based on this information, what is your evaluation of the decision-making process that was used?

SUGGESTED READINGS

Bailey, G. (1988). Guidelines for improving the textbook/material selection process. *NASSP Bulletin, 72*(515), 87–92.

Blacker, D. (1998). Fanaticism and schooling in the democratic state. *American Journal of Education, 106*(2), 241–272.

Browder, L. H. (1998). The Religious Right, the Secular Left, and their shared dilemma: The public school. *International Journal of Educational Reform, 7*(4), 309–318.

Donelson, K. (1987a). Censorship: Heading off the attack. *Educational Horizons, 65*(4), 167–170.

Donelson, K. (1987b). Six statements/questions from the censors. *Phi Delta Kappan, 69*(3) 208–214.

Fege, A. F. (1993). The tug of war over tolerance. *Educational Leadership, 51*(4), 22–24.

Georgiady, N., & Romano, L. (1987). Censorship—Back to the front burner. *Middle School Journal, 18,* 12–13.

Jones, J. L. (1993). Targets of the right. *American School Board Journal, 180*(4), 22–29.

Kowalski, T. J., & Reitzug, U. C. (1993). *Contemporary school administration: An introduction.* New York: Longman (see chapter 10).

McCarthy, M. (1988). Curriculum censorship: Values in conflict. *Educational Horizons, 67*(1), 26–34.

McCarthy, M. (1985). Curriculum controversies and the law. *Educational Horizons, 64*(3), 53–55.

Meadows, B. J. (1990). The rewards and risks of shared leadership. *Phi Delta Kappan, 71*(7), 545–548.

Molnar, A. (1993). Fundamental differences? *Educational Leadership, 51*(4), 4–5.

Napier, M. (1992). *Teachers making decisions when we know the censors are watching* (ERIC Document Reproduction Service No. ED 355 540)

Pajak, E. (1989). *The central office supervisor of curriculum and instruction.* Boston: Allyn & Bacon (see chapter 11).

Pajak, E., & McAfee, L. (1992). The principal as school leader, curriculum leader. *NASSP Bulletin, 76*(547), 21–30.

Pierard, R. (1987). The new religious right and censorship. *Contemporary Education, 58*(3), 131-137.

Rowell, C. (1986). Allowing parents to screen textbooks would lead to anarchy in the schools. *Chronicle of Higher Education, 33*(26), 34.

Smith, S. (1998). School by school. *American School Board Journal,* 185(6), 22-25.

Sullivan, P. (1998). Parent involvement. *Our Children, 24*(1), 23.

Traw, R. (1996). Beware! Here there be beasties: Responding to Fundamentalist censors. *New Advocate, 9*(1), 35-36.

Weil, J. (1988). Dealing with censorship: Policy and procedures. *Education Digest, 53*(5), 23-25.

Zirkel, P., & Gluckman, I. (1986). Objections to curricular material on religious grounds. *NASSP Bulletin, 70*(488), 99-100.

Case **23**

Does Decentralization
Lead to Inequities?

BACKGROUND INFORMATION

For much of the twentieth century, centralized control was the norm in public education. Some critics have concluded that this condition was produced by administrator self-interests—that is, it was attributable to power-hungry superintendents who wanted to achieve total control over their districts. In truth, several other conditions were much more responsible for centralization. The emulation of business practices, especially the application of scientific management principles, was one of them. Another was the relationship between states and local districts that required compliance with uniform curricula and standards (Kowalski, 1999). And yet another was a compliance mentality that evolved from legislation that made schools even more susceptible to litigation (e.g., civil rights legislation, special education legislation) (Tyack, 1990). One purpose of centralized control is to ensure uniform compliance with laws, policies, and regulations.

Centralization, however, inevitably produces some organizational problems. For example, highly centralized school systems tend to be insensitive to individual student needs. Further they do not readily adjust to changing conditions, such as new community needs or changing economic conditions. Partly for these reasons, ideas skewed toward state deregulation (reducing state mandates) and district decentralization (ideas such as site-based management) have become popular school reform initiatives. Such actions are presumed to allow schools to individualize instruction and to create democratic governance systems involving teachers and parents. However, several scholars who have studied change in schools (e.g., Fullan & Stiegelbauer, 1991) caution that centralization errs in the direction of over-control and decentralization errs in the direction of chaos. Accordingly, they do not see the challenge for administrators as one of choosing between centralization and decentralization but rather one of creating an appropriate balance between the two organizational conditions.

In this case, a superintendent decentralizes budgets and requires schools to establish governance councils. In less than two years, some parents charge that the policy has resulted in resource and program disparities across the district's elementary schools. A parent, who is an attorney, questions the legality of the policy on the grounds that his children do not have access to educational opportunities equal to those provided in the district's other elementary schools. The conflict focuses largely on the tension between liberty (allowing individual schools to chart their own course) and equality (the responsibility of the school district to provide equal educational opportunities).

KEY AREAS FOR REFLECTION

1. Centralized and decentralized governance
2. Conflict between liberty and equality
3. Relationship between district and school administration under site-based management
4. Managing change in school districts
5. The role and responsibilities of school councils
6. The decentralization of budgets and effects on school spending and programs

THE CASE

The Community

Haver Ridge is the seat of government for Marvin County in central Illinois. With a population of approximately 19,000, the community has grown about 15 percent since the mid-1950s. Virtually all of the population increase occurred as a result of a new industrial park that was constructed on the edge of town in the early 1970s. The four new businesses that located in Haver Ridge resulted in nearly 400 new jobs.

Marvin County is predominately rural, with grain farms consuming about 80 percent of all the acreage. Haver Ridge and Fellington are the only two cities in the county, the latter having a population of approximately 10,000. Several small towns are scattered around the county, but each consists of little more than a grain elevator and a few stores. About 15 years ago, a new hospital and a municipal airport were built midway between Haver Ridge and Fellington.

River Valley Community College and the East Marvin Community School District are two of the largest employers in Haver Ridge. Collectively, they have about 850 employees. The college's primary service area is Marvin and two other counties.

THE SCHOOL DISTRICT

A number of years ago, the elementary and secondary public schools in Marvin County were reorganized into two districts. Their boundaries were established by drawing a line down the center of the county from north to south; and as a result, both districts are large geographically. The East Marvin County School District, the larger of the two in terms of enrollment, has its district offices in Haver Ridge. Also located in Haver Ridge are this district's high school, middle school, and three of its five elementary schools.

The three elementary schools in Haver Ridge are Adams, Clark, and Lincoln. Among them, Clark is clearly the most unique. It is housed in an old building in the downtown area. The site is very small and the sizes of the instructional spaces are below modern standards. By comparison, Adams and Lincoln are located in residential areas on much larger sites, and the two buildings are less than 20 years old. The average age of the teaching staff at Clark Elementary School is 51, about 10 years more than the averages at the other two elementary schools in Haver Ridge.

The School Board

Twenty years ago, farmers dominated the school board in the East Marvin County School District. That condition has changed considerably. A list of the board members, their occupations, and years of service on the school board is given below:

Board Member	Occupation	Years on the Board
Delbert Daniels	Bank loan officer	3
Sheila Edell	Housemaker (married to a farmer)	10
George Grogan	Dean of instruction at Marvin County Community College	3
Bill Lucas	Owner of the local restaurant	7
Victoria Price	English instructor at Marvin County Community College	1
Ned Sustanit	Plant manager, truck trailer factory	5
Joe Wildman	High school counselor in another school district	1

Mr. Lucas is president of the school board.

Occasionally, votes cast by the board members are not unanimous, but such outcomes are issue-related. Members respect and like each other. In general, the school board has had a positive relationship with the local teachers' union; the union endorsed several members when they were school board candidates.

The Administration

When a long-term superintendent retired three years ago, the board employed Dr. Burton Packard to replace him. Dr. Packard had been working as an assistant superintendent for instruction in a district located in a suburb of Chicago. He is a mid-career administrator with a reputation as a strong instructional leader. During his interview for the superintendency, he told the board that he believed in democratic schools and teacher empowerment. When asked to explain these beliefs, he told the board members, "I think teachers and parents should be our partners, and that includes collaborating with us when we make important decisions about our schools." His philosophy appealed to most of the board members.

Ryan Fulton is the district's assistant superintendent for instruction. He moved to his present position six years ago after having served as principal of Haver Ridge High School for eight years. Jane Westman, the assistant for business, moved to her present position four years ago after having served as principal at Lincoln Elementary for 13 years.

Two of the district's seven principals have been employed while Dr. Packard has been superintendent. They are Dr. Elaine Byers at the middle school and Mrs. Norene Vidduci at Adams Elementary School. Both had been employed by other school districts. Only two of the district's five elementary schools, Adams and Lincoln, have assistant principals.

Implementation of Site-Based Management

Shortly after arriving in Haver Ridge, Dr. Packard announced that he would be moving the district's administration toward decentralization. He said that the changes would begin in the elementary schools the following school year. He cited three objectives for his proposed changes:

- The schools would have greater freedom to determine instructional priorities.
- School-based councils composed of administrators, teachers, and parents would make decisions about instructional priorities.
- The district's budgeting and fiscal management practices would be changed so schools could plan and control their own fiscal resources.

He explained that over-regulating curriculum and instructional practices on a district-wide basis reduced school effectiveness.

Although the school board members cheered the superintendent's ideas, several elementary school principals were less enthusiastic. The two rural schools, Milltown and Wild Creek, had long-standing traditions of parental involvement; each already had an active parent-teacher association. The principals at these schools did not think that school councils would affect them very much. They were, however, troubled by the prospect of having to manage a school budget. The principal at Clark, Mrs. Simpson, was the most apprehensive. Both she and most of her staff did not think a school council would work well at Clark. In addition, they feared that allocations for school budgets would be done on a per pupil basis, an action that would place them at a disadvantage because they had a higher percentage of special needs students than did the other elementary schools. The remaining two elementary school principals at Adams and Lincoln were highly supportive of Dr. Packard's objectives.

The elementary principals were given five months to develop a decentralization plan. These plans had to include the following information:

- The composition of the school's council
- Methods for selecting council members
- Details about budget planning and management

After reviewing the plans, Dr. Packard met with the principals individually. He pointed out facets of the plans that bothered him, but since none of these concerns was deemed critical, he did not require changes.

The First Two Years of the Program

After the first two years of decentralization, there were noticeable differences among the schools. For example, cooperative learning was being used at Adams Elementary School, and a considerable portion of that school's resources had been used for teacher-staff development, the purchase of microcomputers, and the purchase of materials used to implement the concept. At Lincoln Elementary School, technology was a top priority. Following is a summary of the conditions at the five elementary schools after the second year of decentralization.

School	Council Membership	Primary Foci
Adams	6 teachers, 6 parents, principal	Cooperative learning; investment in computers, staff development, and instructional materials
Clark	6 teachers, 4 parents, principal	Traditional programming; remedial programs; investment in materials and supplemental texts
Lincoln	4 teachers, 8 parents, principal	High technology environment; emphasis on increasing time on task and high levels of individualized instruction; investment largely in technology and remodeling the media center
Milltown	4 teachers, 4 parents, principal	Traditional programming; investment in computers and instructional materials
Wild Creek	4 teachers, 4 parents, principal	Mastery learning; investment in computers, staff development, and consultants

The school councils functioned differently in the five schools. At Adams and Lincoln, teachers and parents frequently suggested agenda items. This was also true, but to a lesser degree, at Milltown and Wild Creek. At Clark, teachers and parents never asked to put items on the agenda, and they were largely passive during council meetings. The council meetings at Clark, which were held once each month, were highly predictable. Mrs. Simpson would construct the agenda, do most of the talking, and the members would vote to support whatever she recommended. Often only one or two of the four parent members would attend a meeting. The teachers on the Clark council basically viewed the meetings as a waste of time.

The Problem

Each year, students in grades 2, 4, and 6 are required to take standardized achievement tests. Students receive individual results and schools receive an average score for each grade level. For at least the last seven years, Lincoln has had the highest average test scores in the district—Clark has had the lowest. Listed below are the results for sixth-grade students for the past three years. Years two and three are years under the decentralization plan.

School	Average Test Scores			Rank in District		
	Yr 1	Yr 2	Yr 3	Yr 1	Yr 2	Yr 3
Adams	57.3	58.2	58.3	2	2	2
Clark	48.7	48.3	48.1	5	5	5
Lincoln	59.2	60.1	61.2	1	1	1
Milltown	55.2	55.3	55.3	3	4	4
Wild Creek	54.6	55.4	55.7	4	3	3

In past years, the local newspaper paid little attention to these scores, but that changed because of Dr. Packard's decentralization program. The editor assigned a reporter to write a series of articles trying to connect test scores with the superintendent's decentralization plan. The articles suggested that increases in test scores at Lincoln might be the result of the school's investment in technology and hinted that the poor performance of Clark's students might be tied to the school's emphasis on remedial work. In essence, the stories gave the impressions that the decisions made by the school councils affected student performance on the tests.

Dr. Packard reacted to the articles in an interview with the reporter who had written them. He told her that it was premature to make the connections suggested by her articles. He also expressed confidence that Principal Simpson and the Clark school council were making appropriate decisions for the students at that school. He told the reporter that many factors were responsible for student performance on standardized tests, including some that were beyond the school's control. He cited the social and economic conditions of a student's home life as examples. The reporter also interviewed several school board members, and discovered that Dr. Packard had made these same comments about the test scores to them. The board members did not express any disagreement with the superintendent's views. The board president, Mr. Lucas, did say that he expected that the test scores would improve even more after the decentralization initiatives had their full effect.

Several parents of Clark students were unhappy about the test results, and they were inclined to believe that the reporter was correct in tying test performance to budgetary decisions. The most vocal of these parents was Anthony Bacon, an attorney and director of employee relations at the community college. He objected to the idea of allowing schools to have their own budgets and to determine their instructional priorities. After reading the newspaper articles, he attended a school board meeting and voiced his misgivings to the board and superintendent publicly.

Mr. Bacon knew only two of the school board members, Dr. Grogan and Mrs. Price. He knew them because they were both employees of the community college. He had never met Dr. Packard prior to the board meeting. After being recognized by the board president, Mr. Bacon read a prepared statement:

Ladies and gentlemen, Dr. Packard, and members of the school staff, I appear here today as a concerned parent. I have two children who attend Clark Elementary School. When we moved to this community four years ago, my wife and I bought an older home in the downtown area. One of our hobbies is restoring older homes. We were concerned initially about having our children attend Clark Elementary School, largely because the other elementary schools in Haver Ridge are newer and people told us they were better schools. Before we made a final decision about purchasing the house, I called the former superintendent and he assured me that programmatically, all the elementary schools offered the same opportunities to students. Based on that assurance, we made the decision to buy the house.

It appears that conditions in the school district started changing two years ago after Dr. Packard initiated his decentralization plan. And that is essentially why I am here today. I realize that decentralizing governance is a popular idea, but letting schools go in different directions also creates problems. I have not objected to decentralization previously, because I did not realize that the elementary schools in this district would become so different. The recent series of newspaper articles opened my eyes.

This evening I am here to share several specific concerns. First, it is obvious to me that the school councils do not operate the same way in the five elementary schools. A parent on the Clark council told me that her role essentially involved rubber stamping decisions already made by the principal. But at Lincoln, the parents and teachers appear to have a much broader role—one that permits them to introduce agenda items and speak freely about their concerns. For example, Mary Burgess, the director of instructional technology at our college, is a member of the Lincoln Elementary School council. She played a pivotal role in getting the school to invest in technology.

Second and more importantly, I believe that decentralization will not only fail to narrow gaps in resources and student performance, it will actually widen them. Each school received the same amount of money per student. But the needs of students at Clark are generally greater than at the other elementary schools. And this fact apparently was ignored. The principal at Clark, Mrs. Simpson, told me that she devoted more resources to remedial activities because so many students at the school needed the extra help. As a result, Mrs. Simpson had far less money to purchase technology.

I believe the school district should share its resources equally with all schools—and this includes human resources. Mrs. Burgess could have shared her technology expertise with all principals. Why should Lincoln be the only school that benefits just because her children attend that school? At what point do board members and the superintendent intervene when resources being provided to schools are clearly unequal? Imagine where we would be today if the federal government took a "hands off" approach to dealing with racial segregation decades ago. In essence, school board members and Dr. Packard are the federal government. You ensure equal opportunity for all students. I respectfully request that you reexamine your decentralization plan and take immediate actions to restore uniform programs and resources across our district's schools.

Mr. Bacon then distributed copies of his statement. The board president thanked him for his comments and turned to look at Dr. Packard. He asked the superintendent if he wanted to respond to Mr. Bacon's comments. The superintendent indicated that he would look into the matter and issue a reply in the next two weeks.

Mr. Bacon's statement caused several of the board members to have second thoughts about supporting decentralization. Two of them telephoned Dr. Packard in the days following the meeting and suggested that he not take this matter lightly and suggested that he be especially thorough in responding.

One week after the April board meeting, the board president called for a special executive session and asked Dr. Packard and the school district's attorney to be present. The purpose was to have Dr. Packard share his reply to Mr. Bacon before it was issued. At the meeting, the superintendent outlined the following points:

1. Mr. Bacon's contention about the operations of the councils was partially correct. However, differences in procedures and roles were not by design. Mrs. Simpson, the principal at Clark, had tried repeatedly to get stronger parental involvement in her school's council. The parents and teachers are not prevented from placing items on the agenda nor are they discouraged from speaking openly. They simply have done neither.

2. When the council was first formed at Clark, Mr. Bacon was issued an invitation to be a member, but he declined.
3. It was true that investments in computers and other technology at Clark were far below what they were at other schools. It was also true that each school had received budget allocations based on the same per-pupil amount.
4. The decision to invest heavily in remedial materials at Clark was recommended by Mrs. Simpson but approved by the school's council and supported by the school's faculty.
5. The number of students from low-income families enrolled at Clark is indeed increasing. For example, the number of free and reduced lunches increased by approximately 7 percent over the past two years. This factor, more than any other, may be responsible for slight declines in test scores. And even if this is not the reason, it is most unlikely that decisions related to decentralization are responsible.
6. All students in the school district are receiving the same basic education prescribed by the state department of education. If Mr. Bacon's arguments were taken at face value, virtually every school district with more than one elementary school would have some inequities.

In conclusion, Dr. Packard recommended that the board not alter its policies on decentralization, including its policy on budgetary allocations. He did say, however, that Mrs. Simpson would be directed to allocate at least 25 percent of next year's equipment and supply funds to purchase additional computers and/or software for her school. The board's attorney indicated that, in his opinion, Dr. Packard's response was appropriate. After discussing the matter, the board directed Dr. Packard to send his response to Mr. Bacon.

After receiving the official response from the superintendent, Mr. Bacon called Dr. Grogan, one of the board members. He said,

"I don't think the superintendent's perception of equal opportunity is correct. Seeing that all schools provide the minimum curriculum prescribed by the state is a matter of adequacy, not equality. If students at Lincoln spend eight hours a week working with computers, and students at Clark spend only two, is that equality? Just for a moment, George, forget about the legal dimensions of this issue. Answer the question as a professional. You are an educator and administrator. Is it ethical or moral to provide these opportunities to some students while denying them to others?"

Dr. Grogan responded, "Our attorney looked at Dr. Packard's response, and he feels the superintendent is correct about the equity issue. Schools across this country are moving toward decentralization. If there were serious legal problems, do you think this would be still be moving in that direction?"

Dr. Grogan urged Mr. Bacon to recommend ways that his concerns might be addressed without the district retreating from its commitment to decentralize. The following day, Mr. Bacon met with Dr. Packard, but instead of offering suggestions, he again argued that the superintendent's perception of equal treatment was unsatisfactory.

Dr. Packard responded, "The differences among our schools are not that great. For example, the number of computers at Milltown is essentially the same as it is at Clark. There are many ways to educate children. Computers are not the only answer, nor are they the only measure of educational opportunity. If schools did not have an opportunity to make decisions based on specific school needs, Clark may not have been appropriately responsive to the need for more remedial work. Schools can never be totally equal—nor should they be. I believe schools are most effective when they are responsive to the real needs of their clients."

The conversation went on for about an hour, but it did little to diminish the differences between the two men. Over the course of the next few weeks, Mr. Bacon enlisted the support of five other families in the Clark community to support his position. In mid-May, this group retained the services of a law firm in the state capital, and they prepared to challenge the school district's decentralization plan in court. An attorney representing the group wrote a letter to Dr. Packard and the school board president threatening that a suit would be filed unless actions were taken before the next school year to reverse the inequities created by decentralization.

Several board members were now very concerned about the decentralization plan, but they were not prepared to withdraw their support. The day after receiving the attorney's letter, the board president, Mr. Lucas, again summoned the board, Dr. Packard, and the school attorney to an executive session. The attorney was asked to comment about the potential lawsuit.

He said, "As I told you before, I think that Dr. Packard's response is reasonable. I cannot assure you that we would win the lawsuit. But if you are asking me if we can mount a reasonable defense, my answer is yes. As you know, however, litigation is expensive, time consuming, and there is no guarantee that we will win."

The board members were now divided. Two said that they would not continue to support the superintendent's decentralization program unless Mr. Bacon's concerns were resolved. Three others expressed a commitment to continue the program even if a lawsuit were filed. The remaining two indicated they were undecided. The board president asked Dr. Packard to comment. He said, "In light of the differences of opinion, I would like to think about this. Let's meet again in one week, and I'll be prepared to give you a recommendation regarding the future of decentralization in this district."

THE CHALLENGE

Assume you are the superintendent. What would you recommend to the board at this point?

KEY ISSUES/QUESTIONS

1. What are the advantages and disadvantages of Dr. Packard deciding to stand firm and not alter the decentralization program?

2. Evaluate the superintendent's decision to require Clark Elementary to allocate at least 25 percent of next year's equipment and supply budget to purchasing technology. Was this a good decision? Why or why not?
3. In your opinion, what is the primary problem presented by this case? Is it a legal, ethical, political, economic, or an educational problem?
4. Based on what you read, do you think the administrative staff was adequately prepared to implement the changes required by the superintendent? Why or why not?
5. Do you agree with the superintendent's statement that achievement test scores over the past two years probably were not influenced by any actions related to decentralization?
6. Can decentralization really lead to inequities? If so, how?
7. At Clark Elementary School, the principal played a much more dominant role on the school council than did other principals on their school councils. Is this a problem? Why or why not?
8. Both parents and teachers on the Clark Elementary School council were passive or indifferent. Based on evidence in the case, what may have caused them to be this way?
9. Was it a good idea to decentralize budgeting and fiscal management? Why or why not?
10. One of the purposes of decentralization is to allow schools the flexibility to address the specific needs of the students being served. In this vein, do you believe differences in how the elementary schools used their resources were a problem?
11. What could the superintendent do to retain the concept of decentralization and address the grievances articulated by Mr. Bacon?
12. The superintendent suggested that some inequities exist across all public schools. Do you agree?
13. What should the superintendent have done differently in trying to move the district toward decentralization?
14. What does "balancing centralization and decentralization" mean?
15. Mr. Bacon was invited to serve on the Clark council but declined. Does this fact have any bearing on his challenge?

SUGGESTED READINGS

Bauer, S. C. (1998). Designing site-based systems: Deriving a theory of practice. *International Journal of Educational Reform, 7*(2), 108–121.

Bray, M. (1991). Centralization versus decentralization in educational administration: Regional issues. *Educational Policy, 5*(4), 371–385.

Brick, B. H. (1993). Changing concepts of equal educational opportunity: A comparison of the views of Thomas Jefferson, Horace Mann, and John Dewey. *Thresholds in Education, 19*(1–2), 2–8.

Candoli, I. C. (1995). *Site-based management in education: How to make it work in your school.* Lancaster, PA: Technomic (see chapter 3).

DiBella, C. M., & Krysiak, B. H. (1997). The art and science of letting go. *School Business Affairs, 63*(11), 22–26.

Florestal, K., & Cooper, R. (1997). *Decentralization of education: Legal issues* (ERIC Document Reproduction Service No. ED 412 616).

Fullan, M., & Stiegelbauer, S. (1991). *The new meaning of change* (2nd ed.). New York: Teachers College Press.

Hughes, L. W. (1993). School-based management, decentralization, and citizen control—A perspective. *Journal of School Leadership, 3*(1), 40-44.

Kowalski, T. J., & Reitzug, U. C. (1993). *Contemporary school administration: An introduction.* New York: Longman (see chapters 12, 13, 16).

Leithwood, K., Jantzi, D., & Steinbach, R. (1998). *Do school councils matter?* (ERIC Document Reproduction Service No. ED 424 644)

Lifton, F. B. (1992). The legal tangle of shared governance. *School Administrator, 49*(1), 16-19.

Mitchell, J. K., & Poston, W. K. (1992). The equity audit in school reform: Three case studies of educational disparity and incongruity. *International Journal of Educational Reform, 1*(3), 242-247.

Myers, J. A. (1997). Schools make the decisions: The impact of site-based management. *School Business Affairs, 63*(10), 3-9.

Patterson, J. (1998). Harsh realities about decentralized decision making. *School Administrator, 55*(3), 6-8, 10, 12.

Peternick, L., & Sherman, J. (1998). Site-based budgeting in Fort Worth, Texas. *Journal of Education Finance, 23*(4), 532-556.

Polansky, H. B. (1998). Equity and SBM: It can be done. *School Business Affairs, 64*(4), 36-37.

Reyes, A. H. (1994). The legal implication of site-based budgeting (ERIC Document Reproduction Service No. ED 379 753)

Tyack, D. (1990). Restructuring in historical perspective: Tinkering towards utopia. *Teachers College Record, 92*(2), 170-191.

24

The Principal's Vision

BACKGROUND INFORMATION

If you asked school board members and superintendents if principals should be visionaries, the vast majority would respond affirmatively. But if you were to ask them to define a visionary, you would receive a range of responses. In part, this is because school officials do not share a common perspective of how institutional change should occur. Some favor top-down approaches; they characterize visionaries as leaders who have a specific reform agenda and the skills to get others to accept it. Some favor democratic approaches; they characterize visionaries as leaders who use their considerable knowledge about process and programs to facilitate community consensus.

The idea that one administrator can reconstruct a school by using his or her vision of the future is nested in the myth of administrator as savior. This is the notion that executives can single-handedly transform failing organizations in relatively short periods of time (Murphy, 1991). In truth, public schools are terribly complex, and meaningful and lasting change almost always requires widespread community support. Accordingly, vision statements ought to reflect these characteristics:

- They should be based on more than one person's dreams and biases.
- They should identify where a school wants to be at some point in the future.
- They should be shaped by accurate data and reliable forecasts about society and education (Kowalski, 1999).

- They ought to be developed collectively by representatives of the broad school community (Fullan, 1993).

Based on these criteria, a visionary principal is not an all-knowing dictator, but rather a leader to who uses knowledge and skills to facilitate a democratic process of setting future goals.

This case demonstrates how different perceptions of visionary leadership can generate problems. As you read it, consider the expectations placed on principals in your community. Are the principals expected to impose change, to facilitate change, or to remain passive? And to what extent do the prevailing role expectations contribute to or hinder meaningful school improvement?

KEY AREAS FOR REFLECTION

1. Visioning
2. School culture
3. Principal leadership style
4. Professionalism versus democracy
5. Role expectations

THE CASE

The Community and School District

The Lightville Community School District includes two predominately rural townships in south central Missouri. The town of Lightville is a typical small farming community. It has two grain elevators and several small businesses. Most residents of the school districts live on farms.

The school district operates three schools with a total enrollment of about 1,100 students. All of the schools are relatively new and located on a single rural campus about two miles from Lightville. The elementary school, opened 12 years ago, was the first building erected on the 93-acre site. Last year, construction was completed on the new middle school and new high school. Previously, secondary level students attended Lightville Junior/Senior High School, a building that was more than 60 years old.

The seven members of the school board are elected to four-year terms. Three of them have been in office for more than 12 years, and three others have been in office for more than eight years. The superintendent, Stan Rawlings, has spent his entire career working in the district, and he has been superintendent for the past 17 years.

The Middle School and the New Principal

At the urging of Superintendent Rawlings, the board decided to build a separate middle school to serve grades 6 to 8. The school, with an enrollment of less than

270 pupils, was designed to accommodate teacher teams and block scheduling—two popular concepts in middle schools. Edgar Findley, who had been principal of the former junior/senior high school was appointed principal of the new high school. Prior to the new secondary schools becoming operational, his assistant principal retired, thus, the superintendent and school board had to search for a middle school principal.

Susan Potter, an experienced teacher who had been working in suburban St. Louis, was selected to be Lightville Middle School's first principal. She had 17 years of experience working in the middle grades, two of them as an assistant principal and the remainder as a science and mathematics teacher. Susan viewed the position in Lightville as a great opportunity. The school was small, the faculty was highly experienced, and the community was very supportive of public education.

Superintendent Rawlings had convinced the school board that a new principal should be employed at least one semester before the new school would open. Ms. Potter started working in the school district on February 1, approximately six and one-half months prior to the following school year. Her two major responsibilities over the first several months were to make programming and staffing decisions.

No instructional planning had occurred prior to designing the new middle school. The superintendent merely had instructed the architects to create an environment that could accommodate teaming and block scheduling. Working with the superintendent and high school principal, Mrs. Potter was able to identify most of the teachers who would be assigned to the middle school. Subsequently, she put together a visioning and planning committee to assist her in making decisions about the organization of the school and its programs.

The Committee

With input from Superintendent Rawlings and the school board members, Susan appointed four teachers and four parents to the visioning and planning committee. Five of the members were females, and the four teachers represented different areas of the school's curriculum.

At the committee's first meeting, Principal Potter outlined her philosophy and objectives regarding the committee's responsibilities:

- The committee should operate democratically.
- Consensus should be the preferred method for making decisions.
- The principal should be a voting member of the committee but not the committee chair.
- The committee's first task should be to develop a vision statement that would provide directions for the planning phases.
- The vision statement should reflect the collective values and beliefs of the committee members.

- The broader community, including the middle school's faculty, should have an opportunity to react to the proposed vision statement before it is adopted.

While no one disagreed with these guidelines, several committee members indicated that they had expected the principal to chair the committee.

Helen Burke, an English and social studies teacher, was chosen to be the committee's chair. She was chairperson of the English Department at the junior/senior high school, and married one of the school board members. Her husband also is a farmer and a respected community leader. Helen surprised many of her colleagues when she opted to be assigned to the new middle school rather than the new high school. She had been an advocate for building two separate secondary schools rather than retaining the junior/senior high school concept.

The Conflict

Helen and Susan quickly became friends. They were about the same age, and Helen was delighted that the school district had employed its first female principal. Two days after the initial committee meeting, the two women met to discuss the agenda for the committee's next meeting.

Helen began the conversation by saying, "Susan, I want you to know that I will do anything I can to help you develop a quality school. We are looking to you to provide the leadership we need. So don't ever hesitate to call upon me to help you get things done. We have an excellent committee, and I am certain that the members will support your ideas to the fullest."

"I appreciate that, Helen, and I am grateful that you have agreed to serve as the committee's chair. Obviously, the others see you as a natural leader," Susan responded. "We have a great deal of work to do in the next few months, and virtually everything depends on the committee's ability to finish its work on time."

Susan then reiterated that the committee's first task was to fashion a vision statement. She explained that the statement would provide a framework for making important decisions about how the school would be organized and how instruction would be delivered.

Helen then told her, "After you interviewed with the school board, my husband told me that you were a visionary leader—just the type of person we need to give direction to our new school. I think we should spend most of next meeting having you share your philosophy of middle school education. People here respect administrators, and they look to our superintendent and principals for guidance about important educational decisions. The committee will support your goals."

Susan was surprised by Helen's comments. She sensed an expectation that the principal would present a vision statement and the committee would routinely approve it.

"Helen, I really appreciate your kind word, however, I don't think we should start by having me dictate the directions for the new school. As I noted in our first committee meeting, a vision statement should reflect the collective thinking of the school-community. Every committee member should have an opportunity to reflect on what they believe the new middle school should become in the next decade. I'm new to this community. I don't really feel comfortable making assumptions about the local culture."

"But Susan," Helen said, "you're the expert. You are the person we hired to lead us in developing our new school. I really think the committee members expect you to outline the mission and goals for the new school."

"I don't have a problem providing the committee members with literature about the middle school philosophy. And I don't have a problem offering my opinion when asked. But if we start by having me outline what the school should be like, I'm afraid members of the committee will be intimidated or fall victim to groupthink," Susan commented.

"What is groupthink?"

"It is basically a process that causes individuals to agree to positions that appear to be supported by key individuals or a majority of the group—even when the individuals do not personally agree with the positions. More simply, it's going along to get along," Susan explained.

Helen thought for a moment and then said, "I don't think we need to worry about groupthink with this committee. If a committee member doesn't agree with something, he or she will let you know. They are not bashful. But on the other hand, I'm not sure how much the committee members know about the middle school philosophy—and that includes the teachers on the committee. If we start our work by having members state their views and biases, we may not have a vision statement by the time school opens in August. You said that time was limited, and that is another reason why I think you need to articulate your vision to us."

Sensing that they would be unable to agree on this key point, Susan suggested that the issue be discussed with the entire committee. She asked Helen to permit her to state her views on a process for developing a vision statement.

Helen answered, "If that is what you prefer, fine. But I think you'll find that the other committee members feel pretty much as I do."

At the next meeting, Helen explained that she and Susan had met to discuss how the committee would proceed with developing the vision statement. She added that the two had different opinions about this matter.

"First, let's listen to Susan. She feels strongly about this matter, and I think we need to consider her feelings," Helen told the members. "After she is finished, we will determine which process we want to use."

Susan explained that vision statements should reflect the collective thoughts of those who belonged to a school's broader community. "Sure, I can give you a boilerplate vision statement that reflects common elements of the middle school philosophy. But some of those elements may not be appropriate for the Lightville

School District. Let me give you an example. Not all middle schools treat social activities in the same way. Should sixth grade students be allowed to attend dances? Should the sixth grade be fully integrated academically with other grades? Often community values and beliefs influence the answers to such questions. I would like to hear your views on these matters. I want to hear what you value and believe about education. That doesn't mean we will agree. But it ensures that each committee member will have an opportunity to share his or her dreams and aspirations for the school."

Dan Kelby, a physical education teacher, was the first committee member to respond. "I have several thoughts about the new school, especially related to athletic programs. But if we start sharing our biases, we may be here forever. I think things would proceed more quickly if you provided your vision and we could react to it. Chances are we are going to agree with most of your thoughts."

Several other committee members said that they agreed with Dan.

Susan then commented, "Several days ago when I met with Helen, I told her why I was apprehensive about proceeding in the manner suggested. If I provide a vision, it places you in the position of reacting to my thoughts rather than feeling free to present your own ideas. You know this community much better than I. I can provide general ideas, but I don't know the culture of your community."

Helen then asked Susan, "What process do you prefer for developing a vision statement?"

"Each member of the committee should share his or her basic values and beliefs. Then we should try to reach consensus about a vision statement. I will participate, but my views should not be treated any differently than any other member's views."

"Susan, we all appreciate your sensitivity to our community values," Helen said. "And I know that you are trying to be democratic. However, you are a professional leader and we are expecting you to provide leadership. Your knowledge and experience with middle school education should not be devalued. Just because we begin with 'your' vision doesn't mean that we will not end with 'our' vision."

After about 10 minutes of additional discussion, a motion was made to have the principal craft a vision statement as a starting point for the committee's work. Seven members of the committee voted to support the motion, one abstained, and Susan voted against the motion. Helen met with Susan after the others left.

"I hope you don't take this the wrong way, Susan. You said you didn't know our culture. Well, part of our culture is that we believe that administrators should lead. We are accustomed to having principals present ideas, not reacting to them. I hope you will trust us on this matter. When we finish, we will have a vision statement that we and the entire community will support."

Helen's words did not make Susan feel better. She concluded that Helen had probably discussed this issue with most if not all of the other committee members prior to the meeting; and it was apparent that Helen could influence them. Susan was convinced that the committee would automatically accept whatever she presented. If that happened, the new school would open without her really knowing the true feelings of the community and faculty. Even worse, the committee members might treat the vision statement as being "her agenda."

The next committee meeting was scheduled for the following week. Susan tried to identify and evaluate her options.

THE CHALLENGE

Put yourself in Susan's position. What would you do?

KEY ISSUES/QUESTIONS

1. Evaluate Susan's position on developing a vision statement. Is her position congruous with the professional literature?
2. What is your definition of a visionary leader? What is the basis of your definition?
3. What is the relationship between a vision statement and long-range planning?
4. Evaluate the general environment in the case. Is the rural nature of the community relevant? Why or why not?
5. In the professional literature, what values and beliefs are commonly associated with a middle school philosophy?
6. In the case, Susan alludes to a community culture. What does this mean?
7. Should the community culture and school district culture play pivotal roles in developing a vision statement? Why or why not?
8. A majority of the committee members voted to have Susan present a vision statement to them so that they could critique it. Identify the advantages and disadvantages of Susan complying with this decision.
9. The concept of professionalism suggests that teachers and administrators should have autonomy and greater authority over their practice. Yet, public schools are supposed to be democratic institutions. What is the nature of the potential conflict between professionalism and democracy? How might Susan deal with this conflict in trying to get the committee to draft a vision statement?
10. Evaluate the fact that Helen's husband is on the school board. If you were the principal in this case, would this information be relevant to your decision about a process for drafting the vision statement? Why or why not?
11. What is groupthink? Did Susan provide an adequate definition of this concept?
12. Do you agree with Susan's fears that committee members will be either intimated or victims of groupthink?

SUGGESTED READINGS

Blendiger, J., & Jones, L. T. (1989). Start with culture to improve your schools. *School Administrator, 46*(5), 22-25.

Brouillette, L. (1997). Who defines "democratic leadership?": Three high school principals respond to site-based reforms. *Journal of School Leadership, 7*(6), 569-591.

Cline, R. J. (1990). Detecting groupthink: Methods for observing the illusion of unanimity. *Communication Quarterly, 38*(2), 112-126.

Fullan, M. (1993). *Change forces: Probing the depth of educational reform.* New York: Falmer Press.

Fullan, M., & Hargreaves, A. (1997). 'Tis the season. *Learning, 26*(1), 27-29.

Giba, M. A. (1999). Forging partnerships between parents and teachers. *Principal, 78*(3), 33-35.

Hallinger, P., & Heck, R. H. (1998). Exploring the principal's contribution to school effectiveness: 1980-1995. *School Effectiveness and School Improvement, 9*(2), 157-191.

Hipp, K. A. (1996). Teacher efficacy: Influence of principal leadership behavior (ERIC Document Reproduction Service No. ED396 409)

Hord, S. M. (1998). Creating a professional learning community: Cottonwood Creek School. *Issues about Change, 6*(2).

Keedy, J. L., & Finch, A. M. (1994). Examining teacher-principal empowerment: An analysis of power. *Journal of Research and Development in Education, 27*(3), 162-175.

Kowalski, T. J. (1999). *The school superintendent: Theory, practice, and cases.* New York: Longman (see Chapter 8).

Krajewski, B., & Matkin, M. (1996). Community empowerment: Building a shared vision. *Principal, 76*(2), 5-6, 8.

Lashway, L. (1998). Teacher leadership. *Research Roundup, 14* (3).

Lounsbury, J. H. (1996). *Key characteristics of middle level schools* (ERIC Document Reproduction Service No. ED401 050)

Murphy, J. T. (1991). Superintendents as saviors: From terminator to Pogo. *Phi Delta Kappan, 72*(7), 507-513.

Saunders, L. (1998). Learning together. *Thrust for Educational Leadership, 28* (1), 18-21.

Schwann, C., & Spady, W. (1998). Why change doesn't happen and how to make sure it does. *Educational Leadership, 55*(7), 45-47.

Smith, S. C., & Stolp, S. (1995). Transforming a school's culture through shared vision. *OSSC Report, 35*(3), 1-6.

Starratt, R. J. (1995). *Leaders with vision: The quest for school renewal.* Thousand Oaks, CA: Corwin.

Wilkes, D. (1992). *Schools for the 21st Century: New roles for teachers and principals* (see chapter 2) (ERIC Document Reproduction Service No. ED345 345)

Subject Index

This index is designed to assist you in locating subject areas in the cases. The subjects listed here include both major and minor topics included in the cases.